STANDARDS OF AMERICAN LEGISLATION

STANDARDS OF AMERICAN LEGISLATION

Ernst Freund

WITH A PREFACE BY
FRANCIS A. ALLEN

PHOENIX BOOKS

THE UNIVERSITY OF CHICAGO PRESS
CHICAGO & LONDON

This book is also available in a clothbound edition from
THE UNIVERSITY OF CHICAGO PRESS

THE UNIVERSITY OF CHICAGO PRESS, CHICAGO & LONDON
The University of Toronto Press, Toronto 5, Canada

© *1917, 1965 by The University of Chicago. All rights reserved. First published 1917. Second Edition 1965. First Phoenix Edition 1965. Composed and printed by* THE UNIVERSITY OF CHICAGO PRESS, *Chicago, Illinois, U.S.A.*

PREFACE TO THE 1917 EDITION

This book gives in somewhat expanded form the substance of a series of lectures delivered at Johns Hopkins University in March, 1915. The origin of the book explains its character: it is an essay of constructive criticism, and not a systematic treatise. Its purpose is to suggest the possibility of supplementing the established doctrine of constitutional law which enforces legislative norms through *ex post facto* review and negation by a system of positive principles that should guide and control the making of statutes, and give a more definite meaning and content to the concept of due process of law. It is hoped that the book may be found to be a sight contribution to the rapidly growing movement for the improvement of our statute law.

PREFACE TO THE 1965 EDITION

ERNST FREUND AND THE NEW AGE
OF LEGISLATION

Ernst Freund is one of the great and distinctive figures
in the history of American legal scholarship. The high regard of his contemporaries is perhaps sufficiently suggested
by Mr. Justice Frankfurter's tribute: "I don't think I ever
met anybody in the academic world who more justly
merited the characterization of a scholar and a gentleman
than did Ernst Freund."[1] A more particular recognition
of Freund's unique contribution was expressed by an
English legal periodical at the time of his death: "All [of
Freund's] treatises have a very peculiar quality of their
own, unlike anything else in the whole range of English
and American legal literature. The author's Teutonic education produced an inexhaustible industry, a remarkable
capacity for inventive classification, and a power of subtle
and penetrating analysis. . . . He stands out pre-eminently
as 'a pioneer in scholarship,' to quote the phrase used in
the dedication to him of [a] recently published volume.
. . ."[2]

Perhaps the most persuasive demonstration of Freund's
quality may be found in the facts that, although his major

[1] Frankfurter, Some Observations on Supreme Court Litigation and Legal
Education 1 (The Ernst Freund Lecture, The Law School, University of Chicago, February 11, 1953).

[2] Note, 49 Law Quarterly Review 177 (April, 1933).

preoccupations were in the most fluid and volatile of legal subject matters—constitutional law, administrative law, and legislation—and although his first major work appeared sixty years ago,[3] his writing still possesses the power to stimulate thought and to illuminate contemporary issues. Undoubtedly there are many reasons for the continuing relevance of his work. One of the most important of these was Freund's willingness to relate his writing to a broad base of social theory which was, in turn, the product of his remarkable erudition and the wide range of his interests and sympathies. Unlike many of the great legal scholars of his era, he did not devote his life to the elaboration and rationalization of particular areas of common-law adjudication. This is not to say, of course, that Freund was indifferent to legal issues possessing immediate utilitarian importance. A glance at his bibliography reveals clearly enough that Freund was interested in much that is of direct concern to the practicing attorney. But it is significant that, with one possible exception, none of Freund's major treatises can be described as a practical guide to litigation or counseling. His important study of *The Police Power* might be so characterized. Freund himself is said to have modestly intended the work as a "practitioner's handbook,"[4] but no modern reader is likely to accept this as an adequate description. Freund's theoretical concerns are revealed in his earliest published writ-

---

[3] Freund, The Police Power: Public Policy and Constitutional Rights (1904). Hereinafter cited as "Pol. P."

[4] Van Hecke, "Ernst Freund as a Teacher of Legislation," 1. U. Chi. L. Rev. 92 (1933).

ings. In the preface to his first volume, *The Legal Nature of Corporations*, he wrote: "The subject of the following essay belongs to a field of study and investigation that has been comparatively little cultivated in this country: the analysis and nature of legal conceptions without immediate or exclusive reference to practical questions."[5] If Freund's influence with the bench and bar was less striking than that of certain other legal scholars of his generation, it was largely because of his refusal to devote his principal attention to matters of immediate professional concern. But the very depth and breadth of his interests contributed to the survival of his work and go far to explain its present importance.

LIFE AND CAREER

Ernst Freund was born in New York on January 30, 1864, while his German parents were paying a brief visit to the United States. His early education was almost wholly German. He was a student at the Kreuzschule in Dresden and the Gymnasium at Frankfort am Main, and later attended the University of Berlin and the University of Heidelberg. He received the degree of J.U.D. from the last-named institution in 1884. Shortly thereafter Freund migrated to the United States, and practiced law in New York City from 1886 until 1894. He began his teaching

---

[5] Freund, The Legal Nature of Corporations 5 (1897). Freund was not unaware that theoretical writing in the law was confronted by its own particular perils, for he adds: "Such analysis is apt to lose itself in metaphysical speculations and refined distinctions of little substantial value: it has therefore fallen into some measure of disrepute even in Germany, where legal science and abstract jurisprudence were for a long time almost convertible terms."

career at Columbia College in 1892, when he joined the faculty as acting professor of administrative law. He was granted a Ph.D. in political science from Columbia in 1897. In 1931, the year before his death, he received an honorary LL.D. from the University of Michigan.

In 1894, Freund began his thirty-eight years of association with the University of Chicago when he accepted an appointment to the political science faculty of the new university as instructor of Roman law and jurisprudence. He quickly gained an enviable reputation as a teacher and a scholar; and when, in 1902, the Law School of the University of Chicago was established, Freund was appointed to the original faculty as professor of law. Within two years Freund had published *The Police Power*, and in the three decades that followed he produced a steady stream of articles, books, teaching materials, and reports, including his best known writing: *Cases on Administrative Law* (1911, 2d ed., 1928), *Standards of American Legislation* (1917), *Administrative Powers over Persons and Property* (1928), and *Legislative Regulation* (1932). In 1929, he was appointed to first John P. Wilson Professor of Law. In 1916, he married Harriet Walton. She and two adopted daughters survived his sudden death on October 20, 1932.

Ernst Freund is remembered as more than a legal scholar. For all his devotion to intellectual pursuits, his life reveals an admirable amalgam of the active and the contemplative. Being a practical legislative draftsman of unusual skill, he was inevitably drawn into vigorous campaigns for legislative law reform. He played a principal role in the drafting of the new charter for the City of Chicago.[6] In 1908, he was appointed by the governor of Illinois to the National Conference of Commissioners on Uniform State Laws, a position he was to occupy until his death almost a quarter of a century later.[7] From 1915 to 1927, he was a member of the conference's Committee on Scope and Program, and contributed importantly to decisions concerning the subjects to be undertaken for uniform legislation. The Report of 1922, dealing exhaustively with the policy and future program of the organization, was largely his.[8] In addition, Freund formulated many of the standards governing the drafting of uniform legislation and personally prepared a substantial number of the uniform acts. This drafting activity encompassed an impressive range of subjects: marriage and divorce, guardianship, child labor, narcotics, and many more. But Freund was not content to play merely a draftsman's role; he actively participated in the promotion of legislative reform. His correspondence reveals many instances of his involvement in law-reform efforts throughout the country. He was especially prominent in obtaining legislative acceptance of uniform legislation in Illinois. At the time of his death, Illinois had adopted fourteen of the uniform

[6] See Freund, "Some Legal Aspects of the Chicago Charter Act of 1907," 2 Ill. L. Rev. 427 (1908).

[7] The fullest account of Freund's activities in the National Conference of Commissioners on Uniform State Laws is to be found in Kent, "The Work of Ernst Freund in the Field of Legislation," 1 U. Chi. L. Rev. 94 (1933). See also Kent, "Ernst Freund (1864–1932)—Jurist and Social Scientist," 41 J. Pol. Econ. 145 (1933).

[8] Handbook and Proceedings, Nat. Conf. Comm. U. L. 180 (1912).

acts, all but one of which were enacted while he was a member of the conference. In anticipation of the convention which drafted the proposed Illinois constitution of 1920, Freund was retained as counsel by the City of Chicago. After a period of research, drafting, and consultation, Freund formulated provisions dealing with local government based on the principle that Chicago should "possess for all municipal purposes full and complete power of local self-government and corporate action." The reaction to these proposals and Freund's skill in promoting them have been described by a contemporary observer: "Instantly he became the target of attacks. Men, spurred by sectional feeling or political aims, assailed him as an impractical visionary, derided him as a fanciful professor. Against these attacks he arrayed fundamentals of government, constitutional principles. He restated his views with courteous deference but with learned authority. Toward changes in phraseology he interposed no pedantic pride; but, against any change that might be an impediment in the path of progress, he was adamant. The force of his intellect, the integrity of his character, and the charm of his personality triumphed. The majority rallied to him. His provisions, granting home rule to Chicago, were adopted as proposed!"[9]

One of the prominent aspects of Freund's character and personality was what writers of the past generation sometimes described as a social conscience. He was moved

[9] Wormser, "Legal Learning Dedicated to the Progress of Society," 19 The University Record 45, 47 (January, 1933).

by the human problems of an industrial civilization, and
responded to movements for the amelioration of suffering
and distress. To some extent these interests were reflected
in his scholarly production, as in his study of illegitimacy
laws commissioned by the Children's Bureau of the United
States Department of Labor.[10] He maintained close contacts with persons engaged in Chicago's welfare and social-
work programs. He took an active role in founding the
School of Social Service Administration at the University
of Chicago in 1920. He was a member of the first board of
the Immigrant's Protective League and continued his
affiliation with the organization for some twenty-five
years, serving for a time as its president. He drafted the
act which established the Illinois State Immigrants' Commission.[11] In her memorial tribute to him, Jane Addams
said: "He never once failed to be sensitive to injustice
and preventable suffering."[12] Harriet Vittum, another
prominent social worker of the period, described him as
one of the most useful men in Chicago.[13]

Teaching was undoubtedly one of the central concerns
of Freund's life. He had strong views on the legal education of his time, and (as will be discussed more fully in
later paragraphs) he sought to achieve certain reforms in
the methods and substance of American law teaching. His
former students recall Freund with affection and respect,

[10] Illegitimacy Laws of the United States (1919).
[11] See Addams, "The Friend and Guide of Social Workers," 19 The University Record 43, 44 (1933); Woodward, "Ernst Freund," 19 The University
Record 39, 41 (1933).
[12] Addams, *op. cit. supra* note 11, at 44.
[13] Van Hecke, *op. cit. supra* note 4, at 92.

and many remember him as the great teacher in their days at the University. A graphic picture of Freund's methods in the classroom was sketched by one of his students:

Yet his passionate eagerness and dynamic enthusiasm for his subject made these classes, particularly the one in Statutes, the intellectual climax of each student's day. Not, however, that we claimed at that time that we understood him fully. Or that he made us content. On the contrary, we emerged from the class in Statutes uncomfortable, confused and bewildered. Most of us had spent more than two years in the orderly process of tracing the intricate designs of the mosaic of judge-made law, carefully laid down in the historical-approach casebooks of the period. But Mr. Freund swept us from the German Civil Code to the English Acts of Parliament, to the Statutes at Large of the Congress and into the myriad session laws and statute books of the several states, where could be found for our guidance no rationalizations, in written opinion or treatise. Worse still, we were placed in the position of legislators or draftsmen facing prospectively a problem. Policies had to be determined, the appropriate devices discovered with which these policies could be best expressed and their administration and enforcement facilitated. It was our first contact with the distressing uncertainties involved in the constructive formulation of the law, our first attempt to cope with anticipated difficulties.[14]

The picture of Ernst Freund at leisure and in his social contacts emerges with unusual clarity from the comments of those who knew him. He was modest and unassuming in manner, and managed his human relations with unfailing courtesy and consideration. The range of his private interests was exceptional. Mr. Justice Frankfurter recalls his "exquisite appreciation for the pursuit of music and painting and the arts generally."[15] Another interest is

[14] *Id.* at 93.   [15] Frankfurter, *op. cit. supra* note 1, at 2.

rather unexpectedly revealed in *Standards of American Legislation*. Discussing the then recent legislative assaults on horse racing in the state of New York, Freund observed: "It is understood that this drastic legislation has effectually done away with the previous system of legalized gambling, but that it has also been prejudicial if not fatal to the raising of thoroughbred horses in the United States."[16] Freund proved to be a poor prophet, but one welcomes this evidence of his appreciation of good horse flesh. "The wide range of his reading and his interest in human beings made him a delightful member of any company. His unique talents made him a leader in his profession and in the intellectual life of the University. The integrity of his character and the constancy of his affections made and kept for him a host of friends."[17]

THE INTELLECTUAL WORLD OF ERNST FREUND

The life of Ernst Freund spans the years between the Civil War and the New Deal. In this period "the great transformation" in American life occurred. "As if the forces of change had been pent up for a century, a torrent of events [came] pouring down on mankind."[18] Throughout the Western world, the forces of change produced a new age of legislation. In the United States, the Interstate Commerce Act of 1890 and its subsequent amendments inaugurated an era of federal regulation and estab-

---

[16] Freund, Standards of American Legislation 88 (1917). Hereinafter cited as "S.A.L."

[17] Woodward, *op. cit. supra* note 11, at 42.

[18] Polanyi, The Great Transformation 4 (Beacon ed. 1957).

lished many of the characteristic features of American administrative law. The Sherman Act was only the most conspicuous of the numerous legislative enactments directed against the trusts. In the decade between 1889 and 1899, for example, some seventy antitrust statutes were adopted in twenty-seven state and federal jurisdictions.[19] In the second decade of the twentieth century, the Clayton Act and the Federal Trade Commission began their careers. Factory legislation, laws regulating the hours of labor and other aspects of the labor contract, workman's compensation, public utility regulation, and agitation for schemes of social insurance—all became prominent features of American life at or near the turn of the century. This remarkable outburst of legislative innovation brought with it judicial reaction and restraint. Cases like *Lochner* v. *New York*[20] and *Ives* v. *So. Buffalo R. Co.*[21] were among the most widely discussed public events of the day.

Throughout his professional life, Freund viewed these occurrences with interest and concern. He brought to his analysis an unmatched knowledge of comparable legislative developments in the industralized societies of Western Europe. He was one of the first American scholars to give detailed attention to the problems of achieving efficient and effective government while preserving individual rights and volition in an age of widespread legislative regulation. Freund was no uncritical admirer of all that had been done in the name of legislative reform. His under-

---

[19] Pol. P. at 331.

[20] 198 U.S. 45 (1905).   [21] 201 N.Y. 271, 94 N.E. 431 (1911).

lying attitudes were expressed in a public lecture delivered to the Bar Association of St. Louis in 1923. "It is a different matter," he said, "when we consider a deliberate course of legislation, which seems to represent a national and world wide tendency. Not that we therefore need to consider it as wise or perfect; but the presumption is that it responds to some demand of the time, and that it is inevitable, and temporarily at least legitimate."[22] And again: "Most of those who are beyond middle life have been educated to regard neutrality with reference to business as the orthodox and desirable attitude of the state. The theory which that attitude reflects was probably well suited to a period of profound economic transformation which could have been directed by law neither successfully nor intelligently. Now the lines of that transformation have become tolerably clear, and since one of the outstanding features of the new organization of business is the service of large numbers of persons by particular concerns, standardization of methods is almost inevitable, and it is perhaps equally inevitable that this standardization should in the course of time express itself in law. The tendency in other words seems to be toward legislative regulation of economic activity."[23] But if the main tendencies of modern legislation may be regarded in some sense as inevitable, Freund did not doubt that the form and impact of legislative regulation could be significantly controlled and conditioned by deliberate and intelligent effort.

[22] Freund, "Historical Survey" in Growth of American Administrative Law 40 (1923).
[23] *Id.* at 20.

Nor did he doubt that failure to take appropriate pre-
cautionary measures may result in the most serious consequences to vital social and individual interests.

All Freund's major volumes are concerned with the
new problems created by legislative law making. Indeed,
they may be viewed collectively as a single work, since
each of the volumes deals with particular aspects of the
larger theme. *The Police Power*, published by Freund
early in his career as a law professor, seeks to define the
constitutional scope and limits of legislative powers of
regulation. The first paragraph of his Preface exposes the
fundamental tension between freedom and restraint inherent in all regulative endeavors. The "police power,"
he says, should be defined as the "power of promoting the public welfare by restraining and regulating the
use of liberty and property."[24] In *Standards of American Legislation* and *Legislative Regulation*, the latter published in the final year of his life, he turned directly to the
problems of law making by legislatures and undertook to
identify the basic principles of sound legislation and the
distinctive techniques of statutory law. But an age of
legislation is almost inevitably an age of administration,
and Freund's pioneering works on American administrative law are a natural expression of his general concerns.
Cases on Administrative Law, which for more than two
decades dominated American law school instruction in the
field,[25] and *Administrative Powers over Persons and Prop-*

[24] Pol. P. at iii.

[25] See the perceptive Comment, "Ernst Freund—Pioneer of Administrative
Law," 29 U. Chi. L. Rev. 755 (1962).

erty, perhaps Freund's best known work, complete the list of his major productions.

Freund brought to his work a high intelligence and an erudition that have rarely been matched in the history of American legal scholarship. It was an erudition of many dimensions. First, it should be noted that Freund possessed unusual command of the various divisions of Anglo-American law and that his knowledge encompassed the law in its historical as well as in its modern manifestations. Freund's interests were by no means confined to the public-law subjects. He wrote and taught in the law of real property (including wills and future interests). His articles range over such diverse areas as domestic relations, corporations, torts, municipal corporations, criminal law, jurisprudence, and international law. Second, because of his German education and subsequent studies, Freund possessed a thorough grasp of the Continental legal systems. It is accurate to regard Freund as one of the first and most important American comparative-law scholars. His *Administrative Powers over Persons and Property* bears the subtitle *A Comparative Survey;* and readers of *Standards of American Legislation* will be impressed by his skillful use of German, French, and English legislative materials. Freund at no time made a fetish of the comparative technique, but employed it as a natural and necessary device for the comprehensive consideration of the subjects he treated. Finally, Freund's erudition encompassed more than law.

He earned a doctorate in political science, taught for a

decade in the political science departments of two universities, and in 1915 served as president of the American Political Science Association. He read extensively in the literature of sociology and economics, and possessed a detailed knowledge of commercial practice. His interest in legislation very early directed his attention to the relations of law and social science; and, although he distrusted the enthusiastic movements for "integrating" law and the social sciences that burgeoned in the later years of his life, his comments on the contributions of the social sciences to law making and legal scholarship are still entitled to respectful consideration.[26]

Standards of American Legislation provides an admirable introduction to Freund's work and thought. Written originally as a series of lectures for delivery at Johns Hopkins University in 1915, it is the most graceful and engaging of Freund's books. It should be read not as a systematic treatise but as a collection of related essays. Freund professed no great regard for the work, and characteristically described it as a series of impressionistic notes.[27] It in fact represents the reflections of a mature scholar of great learning on a vital subject, and it contains insights which retain their freshness and a relevance even after the passage of half a century. The quality of the *Standards* was widely recognized when it first appeared, and the book was awarded the James Barr Ames Medal

---

[26] See Kent, "Ernst Freund (1864–1932)—Jurist and Social Scientist," 41 J. Pol. Econ. 145 (1933).

[27] Van Hecke, *op. cit. supra* note 4, at 92.

by the Harvard Law School.   The present volume presents
the text of the work as it appeared in the 1931 printing.
The index has been considerably expanded, and a "Summary of Contents" that accompanied earlier printings has
been omitted.

It is perhaps just to say that the *Standards* deals with
matters of "technical" interest, for it is concerned with
problems of social technique.   But the matters are not
technical in any narrow or trivial sense of the term.
Freund is concerned with the new problems of law making
confronting the industrialized democracies of the Western
world. These are the problems of effective implementation
of legislative policy within a framework of values that
accord high priority to individual rights and individual
freedom.   He is primarily concerned with the legislative
product, and directs attention to the organization and
procedures of legislatures only when such matters bear
directly on the form and substance of statutory law.   For
the same reason he does not concern himself with such
problems as apportionment and legislative representation,
lobbying, or corruption.   In this volume, he speaks primarily of principles and standards and accordingly gives
comparatively little detailed attention to the intricacies
of statutory drafting or interpretation.   The latter subjects were of concern to him, and one interested in a fuller
treatment of these matters may turn to his treatise on
Legislative Regulation.[28]   Needless to say, the *Standards*
does not attempt a comprehensive history of the develop-

[28] Freund, Legislative Regulation (1932).

ment of social policy in the manner of Dicey's classic work.[29]

No serious examination of American legislation can avoid discussion of the relations of legislative and judicial power. This was even more clearly true in Freund's day than it is in ours. It is significant that the opening paragraph of the *Standards* adverts to these problems. He does not hide his conviction that many of the then recent decisions invalidating legislative acts on constitutional grounds were mistaken. Thus, *Lochner* v. *New York*,[30] in which the Supreme Court of the United States struck down a state law limiting the working hours of bakers, is succinctly branded a "judicial blunder."[31] Referring to *Ives* v. *So. Buffalo R. Co.*,[32] which invalidated the New York workman's compensation act, Freund says: "It is perhaps easier to criticise the decision of the Court of Appeals of New York than to explain how the highest court of the greatest state of the Union could have possibly reached the conclusion it did by a unanimous vote."[33] It is clear, also, that Freund believed that the judicial doctrines of "liberty of contract," which achieved sudden prominence at the turn of the century, announced no defensible or intelligible principle of constitutional law. As early as 1904, he had written: "It is the merest commonplace that some restraint of liberty of contract and business, some discrimination, is not merely valid, but

[29] Dicey, Law and Public Opinion in England (1905).
[30] 198 U.S. 45 (1905).
[31] S.A.L. at 98.
[32] 201 N.Y. 271, 94 N.E. 431 (1911).   [33] S.A.L. at 110.

essential to the interests of society. Can the fundamental law be satisfied with the proclamation of rights of absolutely indeterminate content, directly contrary to other recognized principles, or is not limitation and definition of some sort absolutely essential to an intelligible rule of law?"[34] He sounds a similar note in the *Standards:* "But then, from a legal standpoint, the essential thing is not the right, but its qualification, and an undefined claim to freedom of contract presents in reality no justiciable issue."[35] Speaking more generally, he also remarks that "the theory of constitutional law as found in the opinions interpreting due process of law is perhaps the least satisfactory department of American jurisprudence."[36]

If Freund's position is not to be misapprehended, however, it should be clearly understood that although he believed that many judicial applications of constitutional standards were mistaken and much constitutional doctrine ill-conceived, he never challenged the legitimacy of judicial review or doubted its necessity in the American system. He does not call for the abandonment of the doctrines of substantive due process in the areas of economic regulation; and there is reason to believe that he would have been disconcerted by the developments that approach this result in the modern law of the Fourteenth Amendment.[37]

[34] Freund, "Jurisprudence and Legislation" 9 (Vol. VII, Congress of Arts and Sciences, Universal Exposition, St. Louis, 1904).

[35] S.A.L. at 3–4.
[36] *Id.* at 220.
[37] See, *e.g.*, Nebbia v. New York, 291 U.S. 502 (1934); West Coast Hotel Co. v. Parrish, 300 U.S. 379 (1937); Lincoln Federal Labor Union v. Northwestern Iron and Metal Co., 335 U.S. 525 (1949).

Although he believed that "liberty" does not provide a proper criterion for constitutional adjudication, he asserted the importance of judicial protection against arbitrary legislative invasion of vested rights. At several points in the *Standards* he protests the failure of the courts to assume a more active role. "Indeed, there is rather reason to fear that the courts will exercise the guardianship committed to them with less confidence and boldness than is desirable."[38] For Freund, certain kinds of legislative intervention were clearly iniquitous and indefensible. He unreservedly condemns many of the state licensing laws which he saw as creating wholly unjustifiable barriers to the entry of persons into productive occupations.[39] Freund's quarrels with the performance of the courts of his day did not extend to the "underlying philosophical concept" of the due process clause: "[I]t stands for the idea that it is not the mere enactment of a statute in constitutional form that produces law, but the conformity of that enactment to those essentials of order and justice which in our minds are indispensable to the nature of law."[40] He adds, however: "Viewed in the light of history, these essentials are few. . . ."[41]

But Freund went further. He saw in the "liberty of contract" cases, which he freely criticized, evidence of legislative as well as judicial failure. "It would be untrue to say," he wrote in 1904, "that all of the legislation that has been declared unconstitutional has been vicious or

---

[38] S.A.L. at 212.
[39] *Id*. at 99–103.
[40] *Id*. at 207.
[41] *Ibid*.

oppressive, and none of it has been absolutely arbitrary or unreasonable; but most of it has been of doubtful wisdom or expediency, and probably all of it has inflicted or threatened to inflict serious injury on legitimate interests. And it is probably true that, in a great majority of cases, those interests received their first hearings under forms giving some assurance of impartial and adequate consideration in the courts of justice."[42] The same point is elaborated in the *Standards:* "A statute enacted at the request of labor interests generally seeks to redress some injustice or grievance, but very often the practice which employers are forbidden to continue has some element of justification in the shortcomings of labor; and a mere one-sided prohibition without corresponding readjustments leaves the relations defective, with the balance of inconvenience merely shifted from one side to the other. Under such circumstances the courts are much inclined to assent to the claim that there has been an arbitrary interference with liberty or a violation of due process, and there is a sufficient falling short of sound principles of legislation to make adverse judicial decisions intelligible."[43]

Freund's comments on the relations of legislative and judicial power lead naturally to the primary theme of the *Standards:* the search for adequate principles to guide modern legislative law making. As has been observed, he regarded the judicial function as vital and could assert that "our main reliance for the perpetuation of ideals of

[42] Freund, *op. cit. supra* note 34, at 9–10.
[43] S.A.L. at 240–241.

individual liberty must be in the continued exercise of the judicial prerogative."[44]   But equally important is Freund's strongly expressed conviction that constitutional law is incapable of serving as an adequate source of legislative principles.   This theme recurs throughout Freund's major works.   It seems not too much to say that one of his principal scholarly objectives was the freeing of American public law from what he conceived to be the crippling dominance of constitutional law.[45]   Freund identifies a number of considerations which, in his view, render constitutional law an insufficient guide for modern legislation. In one of his articles, he argues that the adversary process in constitutional litigation is incapable of unearthing the range of facts required for sound judgments on the wisdom of legislative measures.[46]   At other times, he emphasizes the inevitable vagueness of constitutional standards.   Even when the legislation under attack suffers from serious deficiencies, judicial condemnations expressed in the language of due process or liberty of contract rarely expose the vice with necessary precision.[47]   Of perhaps particular relevance to the modern reader is his argument that because constitutional adjudication is primarily concerned with the limits of power, it provides poor guidance for the

[44] *Id.* at 212–213.

[45] One manifestation of this position was Freund's insistence that the study of administrative law requires a focus on the administrative process rather than on such constitutional problems as delegation and separation of powers.   See Comment, "Ernst Freund—Pioneer of Administrative Law," 29 U. Chi. L. Rev. 755 (1962).

[46] Freund, *op. cit. supra* note 34, at 11–12.

[47] S.A.L. at 211–212, 220.

wise uses of conceded power. Reliance on constitutional standards may therefore result in lesser rather than greater protections of individual rights. "[T]he extreme of power tends to become the norm of legislation. For unfortunately the only utterances upon the constitutional justice of legislation that carry any authority are those from the courts; from this lawyers are likely to conclude that there are no non-judicial principles applicable to constitutional rights; and legislators (many of whom are lawyers) seem to believe that the principles enforced by the courts are the true and only principles of legislation."[48] On another occasion, he wrote: "[W]e have become so accustomed to rely upon written constitutions for legislative restraint, that we have lost to a considerable degree the habit of voluntary restraint which is politically so much more valuable."[49] We are in danger of "confusing what is sustainable with what is right."[50] These points have been made frequently since Freund wrote, and undoubtedly, had been expressed before; but they have rarely been made as effectively.

Freund's search for standards of legislation leads him, naturally enough, to a consideration of the common law and the processes of common-law adjudication. He recognizes that the common law is a system of principle and, as

[48] *Id.* at 284–285.

[49] Freund, "The Problem of Intelligent Legislation," 4 Proceedings of the American Political Science Association 69, 77–78 (1907).

[50] *Id.* at 78.

such, gains allegiance and acquires legitimacy.[51]   Clearly,
however, the system of judge-made law is insufficient to
satisfy the requirements of the modern era.   Most of the
reasons adduced by Freund to support this conclusion are
familiar and need not be canvassed here.   His final point
is arresting, however, and deserves attention.   "[T]he
spirit of the common law," he writes, "was too neutral for
an effective offensive against practices injurious to the
weaker elements of society."[52]   In an earlier paragraph he
had developed the same point with perhaps unconscious
irony: "When interests are litigated in particular cases,
they not only appear as scattered and isolated interests,
but their social incidence is obscured by the adventitious
personal factor which colors every controversy.   If policy
means the conscious favoring of social above particular
interests, the common law must be charged with having
too much justice and too little policy.   It has fallen to the
task of modern legislation to redress the balance."[53]
Freund's general point is a valid and important one: the
kind of law that is made depends significantly on the kind
of law-making agency that is employed.   The courts are
well adapted to weigh the competing claims of individual
litigants; but they are poorly equipped to resolve broad
issues of policy involving, for example, the reallocation of
resources among large social groups or classes.   Judicial

---

[51] "Permanence and uniformity are in themselves elements of strength and
authority; and with all its defects the common law has never failed to command that respect which belongs to a settled and consistent rule."   S.A.L.
at 261.

[52] *Id*. at 71.   [53] *Id*. at 48.

law making in the latter areas is confronted by a dual peril: it may ignore considerations relevant to intelligent policy formulation, or, in taking them into account, it may inspire doubts about the integrity of the judicial process. Freund, writing half a century ago, saw the first as the primary danger. Recent developments in our public law illustrate that today the latter may also be a source of concern.

Ultimately, Freund concludes that valid principles of legislation can be discovered only by a study of legislation itself; and he visualizes a science of jurisprudence which would make the statutory law the object of intensive analysis and historical investigation. "It is indeed from the combined legislative, administrative, and judicial experiences that we gather the problems of legislation and their solution, but the solution does not proceed from or rest upon judicial authority, but must be worked out upon the basis of a discipline hardly recognized either in England or in this country—an independent science of jurisprudence."[54] For Freund, principle in legislative law making is essential not only to its effectiveness but its very legitimacy. "So long as legislation claims to produce law it must also strive to realize in its product that conformity to principle from which law derives its main sanction and authority."[55] But what precisely is meant by "principle" in legislation? Freund concedes the difficulties of meaningful and comprehensive definition. In an earlier essay, he wrote: "By principle I understand the permanent and

[54] *Id.* at 214.   [55] *Id.* at 215.

non-partisan policy of justice in legislation, the observance of the limits of the attainable, the due proportion of means to ends, and moderation in the exercise of powers which by long experience has been shown to be wise and prudent, though it may be temporarily inconvenient or disappointing in the production of immediate results."[56] In the *Standards* he says: "[I]n any event it is something that in the long run will tend to enforce itself by reason of its inherent fitness, or, if ignored, will produce irritation, disturbance, and failure of policy. It cannot, in other words, be violated with impunity, which does not mean that it cannot be or never is violated in fact."[57] Finally, he confesses: "We can hardly say more to begin with than that it means a settled point of view, and any closer analysis requires careful differentiation."[58]

Freund, unlike many enthusiasts for legislative reform both in his day and in our own, was acutely conscious of the "limits of the attainable" in legislative law making. He recognized that there are certain regularities in human behavior, certain conditioning factors in the traditions, habits, and values of a people, which can be ignored by the law maker only at his peril. Freund was never tempted to believe that water can be induced to run uphill by an act of Congress. "That the fight is won in the courts settles nothing if the principle is unsound. The court tells us that valuable interests may be sacrificed to conjectural apprehensions, but the practical needs of the community

---

[56] Freund, *op. cit. supra* note 49 at 77.
[57] S.A.L. at 218.   [58] *Id.* at 216.

reject and finally overthrow the conclusions."[59]   So also,
a criminal statute that does not adequately define the
scope of liability "is not only unjust to the defendant, but
disadvantageous to the prosecuting government, not only
because it will make convictions difficult, but because it
will diminish the vigor and confidence of official enforcement."[60]   Certainly, the beginning of wisdom in legislative
law making is to acquire an adequate factual basis for
action. "[T]he determining factor in justifying legislation
is that both defect and remedy have some basis of evidence
and have ceased to be a matter of mere surmise and allegation."[61]   He thought it possible that "[t]he time may come
when courts will be justified in demanding that the
legislature shall act only upon some evidence somewhere
placed on record."   But, he adds, "that time has hardly
yet arrived."[62]   Indeed, the absence of appropriate concern for the facts is one of the characteristic and deplorable
aspects of legislative practice.   "The student of the history
of legislation has constant occasion to wonder, not merely
at the absence of impartial and authoritative statements
of facts and conclusions, but at the entire failure on the
part of those demanding legislative interference to make
an impressive or plausible, or, for that matter, any kind

---

[59] *Id.* at 94–95. See also Freund, Illegitimacy Laws of the United States 56
(1919): "The practicability of such legitimation of the child by the fiat of the
law should be carefully scrutinized. The normal legal relation between parent
and child involves the social foundation of a lawful or de facto marriage; without
this, it is in fact a different relation—a fact which no dictate of legislation can
alter."

[60] S.A.L. at 225.

[61] *Id.* at 128.   [62] *Id.* at 99.

of a presentation of their case."[63]   Even with the most conscientious effort, legislation, like all other forms of social action, runs the risks of unanticipated consequences. "It is also necessary to have a proper appreciation of the unintended reactions of the proposed legislation resulting either from its normal operation . . . or from the conditions of enforcement . . . or from attempts at lawful evasion . . . or from illegal evasion. . . ."[64]   On the whole, Freund was profoundly skeptical of the capacity of legislation to effect sudden and significant alterations in the structure of society.   "[G]enerally speaking, the function of legislation [is] to remedy grievances and correct abuses, and not to reconstruct society *de novo* or to force standards for which the community is not prepared."[65]

The foregoing discussion, whatever its general interest, leaves Freund the task of identifying and analyzing particular principles of legislation.   No attempt is made in the *Standards* to present a comprehensive canvass of such principles.   Instead, Freund is content to offer illustrations of the kinds of considerations that might be made the objects of more systematic elaboration in the science of jurisprudence he visualized.   He first presents a series of random examples.   Thus, from the history of criminal enforcement of the Sherman Act he deduces the proposition that "penal legislation ought to avoid elastic prohibitions where the difference between the exercise of a valuable right and the commission of a proposed criminal of-

[63] *Id.* at 135.

[64] *Id.* at 254.   [65] *Id.* at 255.

fense is entirely one of degree and effect."[66] But the larger part of his analysis concerns two much more comprehensive concepts: the principles of correlation and of standardization.

By correlation, Freund means the interdependence of rights and obligations. "In so far as it is recognized it compels the legislator to examine a relation, if the term may be used, from the debit as well as the credit side, and it works against the assertion of absolute and unqualified right."[67] It is the failure "to perform the difficult task of adequately surveying and covering the entire aggregate of rights and obligations involved in new legislation which accounts for much of the alleged unreasonableness of modern statutes, and has been particularly conspicuous in labor legislation."[68] Thus, can the state without the sacrifice of justice require an employer to institute a hiring policy that does not discriminate against union labor without protecting him from the abuses of union power? Or (to use an example much discussed in Freund's centennial year) may the community impose penalties on the citizen who fails to come to the aid of one being made a victim of crime without offering compensation to the citizen or his family in the event that the required interven-

---

[66] *Id.* at 222. Freund had made the same point in his earlier work: "It cannot be maintained that this principle is part of the general American constitutional law; but it seems to be in accordance with sound legislative policy, that the exercise of a right intrinsically useful and indispensable should not become criminal by overstepping a line which the law refuses to define and which is not defined by custom." Pol. P. at 25. See also Freund, "The Use of Indefinite Terms in Statutes," 30 Yale L. J. 437 (1921).

[67] S.A.L. at 248.   [68] *Id.* at 240.

tion results in injury or death? It will be clear to the reader, as it was to Freund, that the principle of correlation is impossible of complete realization. The ramifications of legislative regulation are so numerous and pervasive that no effort or foresight on the part of legislators can assure a perfect balancing of privileges and obligations. "The claim," says Freund, "is not that legislation shall be perfect, but that it shall approximate perfection so far as actual conditions will permit. Only to this extent is the principle of correlation contended for. It is easily demonstrated that much legislation falls short even of the attainable standard."[69]

The principle of standardization is Freund's second major concept. "If correlation means more carefully measured justice, standardization serves to advance the other main objects of the law, namely, certainty, objectivity, stability, and uniformity."[70] Whatever improvements may have occurred in legislative practice during the past half-century, sheer caprice and inconsistency still characterize much of American legislation. In Freund's view, these failures threaten the legitimacy of statutory law. "Permanence and uniformity are in themselves elements of strength . . . Conversely, lack of standardization must weaken the authority of statutes."[71] Modern illustrations of Freund's position come readily to mind. It was discovered, for example, that the criminal statutes operative in Illinois before the enactment of the Criminal Code

[69] *Id.* at 246.
[70] *Id.* at 248.   [71] *Id.* at 261.

of 1961[72] employed more than a dozen different terms to
describe the mental elements of the various crimes defined.
The difficulty was that the legislature had used some fifteen or sixteen undefined statutory terms to express not
more than five or six distinct ideas. The wholly avoidable
confusion that resulted advanced neither the interests of
the state nor those of the individual citizen. But the problem encompasses more than the capricious use of language.
Certain features of regulatory legislation, such as those
relating to enforcement and administration, present common problems and, in Freund's view, should be made to
express a consistent policy. "If policies regarding subsidiary clauses are determined anew for each measure as a
mere matter of habit or as a consequence of the absence
of a general rule, it means for the legislature the waste and
wear of responsibility for new decisions, for the administration the inefficiency which results from lack of consistent purpose, and for the individual lack of uniformity
and therefore something that approaches the deprivation
of the equal protection of the [laws]."[73] No doubt, in some
degree modern American legislation reveals greater fidelity
to the principle of standardization than in the period in
which Freund wrote; and it is also probably true that
further improvements may be expected from the expanded
operations of such devices as the legislative reference
bureau, of which Freund was one of the earliest and most
effective proponents. But Freund's discussion demon-

[72] Ill. Rev. Stat., ch. 38, §§ 1-1—35-1 (1962).
[73] S.A.L. at 269.

strates that some of the causes of the unfortunate "ad
hocness" of our statutory law reflect basic characteristics
of American legislative bodies. "The striking difference
between legislation abroad and in this country is that
under every system except the American the executive
government has a practical monopoly of the legislative
initiative."[74] This extraordinary diffusion of legislative
initiative among all members of the legislature breeds irresponsibility and resists standardization and uniformity
where consistency of practice is most desirable. But the
privilege of legislative initiative does much to enhance the
power and prestige of the individual legislator; and its
speedy surrender is hardly to be anticipated.

Although the *Standards* is first and foremost an investigation into the nature of principle of legislation, it also
serves as a vehicle for a variety of Freund's reflections on
the problems of the modern world. These dicta remain
one of the principal attractions of the volume. Much of
Freund's thought was devoted to the complexities of
preserving individual freedom in the emerging welfare
state. He approached these problems with a strong initial
bias in favor of the basic freedoms of expression. In *The
Police Power* he had written: "[T]he constitutional guaranty of freedom of speech and press and assembly demands
the right to oppose all government and to argue that the
overthrow of government cannot be accomplished otherwise than by force; and the statutes referred to, in so far
as they deny these rights, should be considered unconstitu-

[74] *Id.* at 288.

tional."[75]   In the *Standards* he says: "That immediate
political advantage is so readily sacrificed to the conviction
that free expression of opinion is in the long run more
wholesome to the constitution of the body politic is one of
the most remarkable achievements of democracy and of
education in public affairs."[76]   Although he was not unaware of certain illiberal tendencies of his time, his confidence in the security of the rights of free expression seems
to have prevented his foreseeing the continuing crisis of
individual freedom that first beset the United States and
all Western civilization in the years immediately following
the First World War.   Perhaps more surprising was
Freund's failure to anticipate the complexity of the specifically legal problems presented by certain kinds of civil
liberties litigation, particularly that involving charges of
obscenity.   "The offense of lewdness and obscenity," he
wrote, ". . . is a matter of circumstance, spirit, and purpose, but these are on the whole so well understood that
in the great majority of cases it is clear enough whether
acts or conditions fall under the criminal law."[77]   But if
some of Freund's particular comments on the civil liberties
have only limited application to modern problems, much
of his general analysis has greater relevance.   One of the
preoccupations of American legislatures in the present
century has been the enactment of statutes that define
"political" crimes: offenses that adversely affect or are
believed to affect the security of the state.   Since the
legislative objective is to frustrate subversive activity be-

[75] Pol. P. at 513.   [76] S.A.L. at 16.   [77] *Id.* at 78.

fore it becomes an unmanageable threat to the government, the statutes typically attempt to reach, through
the conspiracy concept or other devices, conduct that is
not immediately dangerous but which is believed to be potentially dangerous.[78]   Although Freund's comments were
not specifically directed to legislation defining political
offenses, his remarks constitute an unusually effective and
succinct description of the problems in this area: "[I]n
the absence of scientific certainty it must be borne in mind
that the farther back from the point of imminent danger
the law draws the safety line of police regulation, so much
the greater is the possibility that legislative interference is
unwarranted."[79]   And again: "If free action is as essential
to the interests of the community as protection from harm,
the remoteness or conjectural character of the danger is in
itself a strong argument against the policy of legislative
interference and, if libery is held to be a constitutional
right, against its validity."[80]

It is apparent that Freund was fascinated by the para-
doxes of freedom in the modern world.   Certainly, the
conditions of an industrialized society require police power
regulation, which is to say, the limitation of freedom.   In
this connection Freund delivers one of his best known
observations: "Living under free institutions we submit
to public regulation and control in ways that would appear
inconceivable to the spirit of oriental despotism; it is well
known what deep-seated repugnance and resistance of the

[78] Allen, The Borderland of Criminal Justice 128 (1964).

[79] S.A.L. at 83.   [80] *Id*. at 84.

native population to the invasion of their domestic privacy
and personal habits English health officers in India have to
overcome in order to enforce the sanitary measures necessary to prevent the spread of infectious or contagious
disease."[81]   Even the notion of freedom from regulation
"has become unmeaning in so far as adequate freedom in
the sense of free scope of endeavor and of action demands
regulation in support of it."[82]

But Freund also identifies another range of problems:
those encompassed by the paradox that there are certain
kinds of freedom peculiarly vulnerable to invasion by the
political agencies of a democratic community. "A strong
sense of civil liberty affords no guaranty of tolerance for
practices conceived to be immoral, especially where the im-
morality bears on social as distinguished from business and
political relations; on the contrary, the enlightened democratic community is apt to be more intolerant than that
which is despotically governed."[83]   These problems are
still very much a part of American life, and, insofar as
their practical aspects are concerned, it is doubtful that the
modern polemics have advanced the discussion much
beyond the point at which Freund left it in the *Standards*.
Freund does not begin with a doctrinaire insistence that
there are areas of private morality that may under no circumstances be invaded by legislative power.   Instead, he
explores the American experience with sumptuary legislation, particularly that involving liquor control and gam-

[81] *Id.* at 21. See also Pol. P. at 109.
[82] Freund, *op. cit. supra* note 28, at 116–117.
[83] Pol. P. at 172, n. 1.

bling, and concludes that such attempts have in general
resulted in unfortunate consequences. "We may start with
the obvious observation," he says, "that not every standard of conduct that is fit to be observed is also fit to be
enforced."[84]   And the discrepancies between the legal
norms and their enforcement are where many of the difficulties arise.   In *The Police Power* Freund observes: "It
[legislation for the protection of morals] is the tribute
which the organized community pays to virtue, and the
tribute is willingly paid so long as it involves nothing more
than the enactment of a statute."[85]   And in the *Standards:*
"The formal declaration of policies is insisted upon irrespective of whether they can be carried out faithfully or
even with tolerable success; indeed, the advanced policy is
sometimes consented to only upon the tacit understanding
that in actual administration it will be somewhat relaxed."[86]   It is perhaps here that a sound sense of "the
limits of the attainable" is particularly required.   "There
is an obvious unwillingness to abandon abstract moral
standards once established, and the evil effect of disharmony between legislation and administration is not
sufficiently appreciated."[87]   Freund's essential teaching is
that before legislative intervention in these areas is sanctioned there should be a careful and dispassionate calcula-
tion of the costs involved.   It is a message of as great a
relevancy today as it was in Freund's time and one sub-

[84] S.A.L. at 106.

[85] Pol. P. at 172, n. 1.

[86] S.A.L. at 19-20.   [87] *Id.* at 105.

stantially ignored by the makers of American legislation during the half-century since he wrote.

Freund's views on American legal scholarship and American legal education require brief attention, because they constituted an integral part of his thought and contributed in some measure to his continuing influence. The Law School of the University of Chicago was opened on October 1, 1902. An agreement had been reached with Harvard Law School for Professor Joseph H. Beale, Jr., to serve as the first dean of the new school. There is some evidence that President Harper of the University of Chicago originally conceived of the new school primarily as an institute for scholarly research rather than as a school for the training of professional practitioners. Freund resisted this concept, and argued that the effectiveness of the new school depended upon its being placed on a sound professional basis;[88] and his view of the matter ultimately prevailed. Nevertheless, only six months before the law school was scheduled to open, a letter from Dean James Barr Ames of Harvard to President Harper protested Freund's views of legal education and suggested that if they were to prevail, Professor Beale ought not to undertake the temporary deanship at Chicago.[89] "I understand it to be your wish and purpose," wrote Dean Ames, "to

[88] Van Hecke, "Ernst Freund as a Teacher of Legislation," 1 U. Chi. L. Rev. 92, 93 (1933).

[89] Letter from James B. Ames to William H. Harper, March 31, 1902, Archives of the University of Chicago. See Comment, "Ernst Freund—Pioneer of Administrative Law," 29 U. Chi. L. Rev. 755, 763–770 (1962), where the letter is set out as well as a letter of similar tenor from Professor Beale to President Harper, dated April 2, 1902.

establish at your University a law school resembling as closely as possible in its curriculum, methods of study, and quality of its Faculty, the Harvard Law School." But a recent conversation with Professor Freund had raised serious doubts about the latter's commitment to these goals. Dean Ames lists three principal areas of disagreement. First, Freund had "suggested that 2/9 of the work leading to the degree should consist of subjects belonging properly in the departments of Political Science or Sociology." Second, Freund would admit non-lawyers to the faculty to teach non-legal subjects, whereas the success at Harvard was "due in no small degree to the solidarity of our Faculty and to its concentration upon the work of teaching the law pure and simple." Finally, Dean Ames suspected that Freund's commitment to the case method of instruction was something less than wholehearted. Appropriate assurances were apparently provided, since Professor Beale came to Chicago as dean of the Law School and made an important contribution to the School's establishment and early development.

Consideration of Dean Ames's concerns provides a convenient device for examining Freund's views on legal education. Sometime early in 1902, Freund prepared a proposed three-year curriculum for the new school.[90] Some of the proposals were entirely conventional, but others must have seemed at the time to involve startling innovations. In the second and third years, the students

[90] Proposed Curriculum of Ernst Freund, Archives of the University of Chicago.

would have been required to elect five or six units from among such course offerings as criminology, experimental psychology, relation of state to industry, and finance. It was this proposal which seems to have particularly alarmed Dean Ames and Professor Beale. But perhaps more significant was Freund's emphasis on the public law subjects. He proposed instruction in constitutional law and international law as part of the required first-year curriculum, and would have offered administrative law and federal jurisdiction among the second- and third-year electives. Freund's proposed courses in non-legal subject matter did not survive the opening of the Law School, but his impact on the school's instructional program was, nevertheless, clear. Thus, the 1902 catalogue states the second objective of the school to be the cultivation and encouragement of "the scientific study of systematic and comparative jurisprudence, legal history, and principles of legislation." Administrative law became an established feature of the curriculum, and courses in international law were taught by members of the University's political science faculty.[91] In the years that followed, Freund's own courses and the particular emphasis of his interests strongly affected the character of the institution. Indeed, the nature and extent of Freund's influence led Mr. Justice Frankfurter to identify him as "the father of the Law School."[92]

[91] Comment, "Ernst Freund—Pioneer of Administrative Law," 29 U. Chi. L. Rev. 755, 769 (1962).

[92] Frankfurter, Some Observations on Supreme Court Litigation and Legal Education 1 (The Ernst Freund Lecture, The Law School, University of Chicago, February 11, 1953).

There is no evidence that Freund at any time advocated complete abandonment of the case method of instruction in the American law schools. In the *Standards* he recognizes it as "a method superior to the German system as a training for the future practitioner. . . ."[93] But Dean Ames's suspicions that Freund entertained reservations about the case method seem to have been well founded. As early as 1915, Freund was quoted as doubting the effectiveness of the method after about the middle of the student's second year in law school,[94] an observation expressed by many modern teachers of law. But more seriously, Freund was concerned about case study as the exclusive mode of law school instruction, because of its impact not only on legal education but on legal scholarship as well. He regarded the influence of the case method as being "as unfavorable as possible from the legislative point of view; for the ideals of case law will tend to be those of the system in which judge-made law had its highest development . . . and the case method will foster the common-law attitude toward legislation, looking upon it as an inferior product of the non-legal mind to be tolerated and minimized in its effects."[95]

Freund made no secret of his dissatisfactions with the state of legal scholarship in his time. In the *Standards* he remarks: "Unfortunately, hardly any systematic thought has been given to problems of jurisprudence in their constructive aspect. . . . In America the critical treatment of

[93] S.A.L. at 311–312.
[94] Van Hecke, *op. cit. supra* note 88, at 93.
[95] S.A.L. at 312.

technical legislative problems is . . . meager and unsystematic."[96]   Freund must have suffered at times from the
loneliness of an intellectual pioneer; and he was probably
expressing more than the natural resentment of an author
for his critics when he confessed that he had never read an
understanding review of one of his books.[97]   There is evidence that he believed that legal scholars had not sufficiently immersed themselves in the problems of social
policy and had failed to master the materials necessary for
sound policy judgments.   At a meeting of the Association
of American Law Schools, he is reported to have "compared the wanderings of the social scientist through the
trackless wilderness of fact and official action with the
smooth road of the law teacher, whose way was made clear
. . . when he found the appropriate key number" in the
legal digests.[98]   It is apparent that the preoccupations
of legal scholarship have substantially changed since
Freund's day and, from Freund's point of view, for the
better.   It would not be accurate to suggest that Freund's
influence was primarily responsible for these changes. The
logic of events made it inevitable that the law schools
could not forever confine themselves to the elaboration
and rationalization of common-law doctrine, important as
that undertaking undoubtedly is.   But Freund foresaw
the path that much modern legal scholarship would be
required to follow, and he is entitled to recognition for his
vision and his constructive example.

[96] *Id.* at 251–252.
[97] Van Hecke, *op. cit. supra* note 88 at 92.
[98] *Id.* at 93–94.

Standards of American Legislation remains after half a century one of the most stimulating books ever to come out of an American law school. It is not without its weaknesses. One may justly complain, for example, that much of Freund's discussion of legislative principle is too general and too little related to particular areas of legislative regulation to be wholly meaningful. On the other hand, the need for general theory in at least certain areas of legislative policy is clear and compelling. Penal sanctions appended to regulatory statutes constitute one of these areas, and Freund's argument for consistency of policy in the interests of efficiency and individual rights is highly persuasive.[99] Much greater attention is given to legislative materials in legal education today than formerly; but many of the difficulties confronting courses in legislation that Freund identified remain largely unsolved.[100] In short, the *Standards* does not solve all the problems it exposes. "It is not for the student of . . . law to offer a solution for every problem in his field," Freund wrote, "but he should help others to understand why some problems are as yet unsolved."[101] Tested by Freund's own criteria, the book must be judged an impressive achievement.

FRANCIS A. ALLEN

THE LAW SCHOOL
UNIVERSITY OF CHICAGO

[99] S.A.L. at 270. See also Freund, Legislative Regulation 339–340 (1932).

[100] S.A.L. at 314.

[101] Freund, "Historical Survey" in Growth of American Administrative Law 41 (1923).

Selected Bibliography of the Works of Ernst Freund

BOOKS

The Legal Nature of Corporations. (University of Chicago Press, Chicago, 1897.)

The Police Power: Public Policy and Constitutional Rights. (Callaghan and Co., Chicago, 1904.)

Cases on Administrative Law. (West Publishing Co., St. Paul, 1911. 2d ed., 1928.)

Elements of Law. (University of Chicago Press, Chicago, 1912.)

Standards of American Legislation. (University of Chicago Press, Chicago, 1917.)

Illegitimacy Laws of the United States: Analysis and Index. (U.S. Government Printing Office, Washington, 1919.)

Illegitimacy Laws of the United States and Certain Foreign Nations. (U.S. Government Printing Office, Washington, 1919.)

"Historical Survey" in Freund, Fletcher, Davies, Pound, Kurtz, and Nagel, The Growth of American Administrative Law. (Thomas Law Book Co., St. Louis, 1923.)

Administrative Powers over Persons and Property. (University of Chicago Press, Chicago, 1928.)

"Legal Aspects of Philanthropy" in Faris, ed., Intelligent Philanthropy. (University of Chicago Press, Chicago, 1930.)

Legislative Regulation: A Study of the Ways and Means of Written Law. (The Commonwealth Fund, New York, 1932.)

ARTICLES AND REPORTS

The Effect of the Norman Conquest on English Law, 1 Colum. L.T. 232 (1888).

Contracts and Consideration in Roman Law, 2 Colum. L.T. 167 (1889).

Historical Jurisprudence in Germany, 5 Pol. Sci. Q. 468 (1890).

The Study of Law in Germany, 1 Counsellor 131 (1892).

The Law of the Administration in America, 9 Pol. Sci. Q. 403 (1894).

Malice and Unlawful Interference, 11 Harv. L. Rev. 449 (1898).

The Control of Dependencies through Protectorates, 14 Pol. Sci. Q. 19 (1899).

Government and Law in America, 34 Am. L. Rev. 16 (1900).

The New German Civil Code, 13 Harv. L. Rev. 627 (1900).

Jurisprudence and Legislation, Congress of Arts and Science, Vol. 7, p. 1, Universal Exposition, St. Louis (1904).

Constitutional Aspects of Employers' Liability Legislation, 19 Green Bag 83 (1907).

Jurisprudenz und Gesetzgebung, 1 Jahrbuch des öffentlichen Rechts der Gegenwart 137 (1907).

The Problem of Intelligent Legislation, 4 Proceedings of Am. Pol. Sci. Assoc. 69 (1907).

Some Legal Aspects of the Chicago Charter Act of 1907, 2 Ill. L. Rev. 427 (1908).

A Proposed Uniform Marriage Law, 24 Harv. L. Rev. 548 (1911).

The Enforcement Provisions of the Sherman Law, 20 J. Pol. Econ. 462 (1912).

Unifying Tendencies in American Legislation, 22 Yale L. J. 96 (1912).

Report of Standing Committee on Legislative Methods, Proceedings of the Am. Pol. Sci. Assoc., 1913–1914, p. 271.

Constitutional Aspects of Hour Legislation for Men, 4 Am. Lab. Leg. Rev. 129 (1914).

The Problem of Adequate Legislative Powers under State Constitutions, 5 Pub. of the Academy of Pol. Sci. 98 (1914).

Supplemental Acts: A Chapter in Constitutional Construction, 8 Ill. L. Rev. 507 (1914).

Classification and Definition of Crimes, 5 J. Crim. L. and Criminology 807 (1915).

The Substitution of Rule for Discretion in Public Law, 9 Am. Pol. Sci. Rev. 666 (1915).

Correlation of Work for Higher Degrees in Graduate Schools and Law Schools, 11 Ill. L. Rev. 301 (1916).

Principles of Legislation, 10 Am. Pol. Sci. Rev. 1 (1916).

Report of the Special Committee on Legislative Drafting: Provisions for Licensing and Certification, 2 A.B.A. Jour. 454 (1916).

Interpretation of Statutes, 65 U. Pa. L. Rev. 207 (1917).

Prolegomena to a Science of Legislation, 13 Ill. L. Rev. 264 (1918).

The Debs Case and Freedom of Speech, 19 New Repub. 13 (1919).

The New German Constitution, 35 Pol. Sci. Q. 177 (1920).

Three Suggestions Concerning Future Interests, 33 Harv. L. Rev. 526 (1920).

Abstract of Statutory Precedent Material Collected and Available for a Manual of Legislative Drafting, 46 Rep. Am. Bar. Assoc. 417 (1921).

The Right to a Judicial Review in Rate Controversies, 27 W. Va. L.Q. 207 (1921).

Use of Indefinite Terms in Statutes, 30 Yale L.J. 437 (1921).

Memorandum to Serve as a Basis for a Round Table Discussion of a Course on Statutes, 1 N.C.L. Rev. 104 (1922).

A Uniform Illegitimacy Law, 49 The Survey 104 (1922).

Commission Powers and Public Utilities, 9 A.B.A. Jour. 285 (1923).

Search and Seizure, 56 Chi. Leg. N. 211 (1924).

Administrative Law—Appeal from Administrative Decisions, 21 Ill. L. Rev. 378 (1926).

Deportation Legislation in the Sixty-ninth Congress, 1 Soc. Ser. Rev. 46 (1927).

Administrative Law—Due Process in the Revocation of Licenses, 21 Ill. L. Rev. 493 (1927).

Administrative Law, 1 Ency. Soc. Sci. 452 (1929).

Some Inadequately Discussed Problems of the Law of City Planning and Zoning, 24 Ill. L. Rev. 135 (1929).

United States v. Schwimmer, 7 N.Y.U.L. Rev. 157 (1929).

Operation of the Rule Against Perpetuities, 24 Ill. L. Rev. 727 (1930).

Responsabilité de l'État en Droit Interne (Mémoires de L'Académie Internationale de Droit Comparé, 1932).

ARTICLES ABOUT ERNST FREUND

Note, 26 Am. Pol. Sci. Rev. 1103 (1932).

Woodward, Ernst Freund, 19 The University Record 39 (January, 1933).

Addams, The Friend and Guide of Social Workers, 19 The University Record 43 (January, 1933).

Wormser, Legal Learning Dedicated to the Progress of Society, 19 The University Record 45 (January, 1933).

Kent, Ernst Freund (1864–1932)—Jurist and Social Scientist, 41 J. Pol. Econ. 145 (1933).

Kent, The Work of Ernst Freund in the Field of Legislation, 1 U. Chi. L. Rev. 94 (1933).

Van Hecke, Comment, Ernst Freund as a Teacher of Legislation, 1 U. Chi. L. Rev. 92 (1933).

Note, 49 Law Quarterly Review 177 (April, 1933).

Frankfurter, Some Observations on Supreme Court Litigation and Legal Education (The Ernst Freund Lecture, The Law School, University of Chicago, February 11, 1953).

Comment, Ernst Freund—Pioneer of Administrative Law, 29 U. Chi. L. Rev. 755 (1962).

CONTENTS

INTRODUCTION

There have been few judicial decisions so disconcerting to believers in the progressive development of the law as that rendered in 1911 by the Court of Appeals of New York against the validity of the first workmen's compensation act of that state. Differing in this respect from most other constitutional decisions in labor cases, it did not reflect the judicial view of the wisdom or justice of the legislation which it condemned but merely its view of the rigidity of the law under existing American constitutions. While the decision did not, as subsequent developments have shown, stop the onward course of the type of legislation which it checked only slightly, yet as the unanimous expression of the most important of state courts it could not be regarded otherwise than as extremely significant. It seemed quite inadequate to apply to such a decision the usual methods of legal criticism; for even if it were possible to demonstrate conclusively the unsoundness of the conclusion reached by the court, the question would remain how it was possible that so narrow a view of legislative power could command such eminent support and what theory of judicial control or of constitutional limitation it indicated.

A clue to the situation may be discovered in the opinion itself. The court speaks of the cogent economic and sociological arguments urged in support of the work-men's compensation law; it admits the strength of the appeal to a recognized and widely prevalent sentiment; but, the opinion adds, "it is an appeal which must be made to the people and not to the courts." Here, in other words, is a law that can be made by the people, but not by the legislature. It is well known that the appeal was successfully made, and that a new compensation law was enacted under express constitutional authority which the Court of Appeals has since sustained (*Jensen* v. *So. Pac. R. Co.*, 215 N.Y. 514).

To the Court of Appeals, then, the due-process clause of the constitution, upon which it based its decision, was not, as the similar clause in the federal Constitution appeared at least in one case to the Supreme Court, a clause intended to secure the immutable cardinal principles of justice (169 U.S. 387). It is unthinkable that the court should have suggested an appeal to the people to subvert those principles. It was rather a fundamental policy of distributive justice which the New York Court saw fixed upon the state by the guaranty of due process —fundamental, but after all only a policy, likely to be changed by the progress of economic and social thought.

It is an interesting and significant fact that the attitude of the courts toward social legislation which culminated in the Ives case gave rise to the demand for a right to recall judicial decisions which was inscribed upon the platform of a political party. The demand represented, in addition to the dissatisfaction with the judicial resistance to policies indorsed by progressive and insistent popular sentiment, a strong political reaction against the claim of judicial power to fix upon the state by way of constitutional interpretation policies which were merely implied and upon which the people had never had a chance to declare themselves explicitly. If the movement for the recall of judicial decisions is severely condemned—and there is no intention here to defend it—it should at least be understood how it arose, and it should help us to discriminate between policies and principles.

The popular objection to the attitude of the courts in opposing to social legislation alleged constitutional policies was, however, not merely that these policies were implied and therefore judge-made; more serious was the fact that they were entirely indefinite. It would be possible to read into our constitutions, as essential to republican government, a right of political association in analogy to the explicitly guaranteed right of assembly. Such a right could be easily formulated and its limits judicially defined without great difficulty. It is otherwise with the rights that are supposed to stand in the way of advanced social legislation. We have heard much of freedom of contract. Would anyone be prepared to place this right by the side of freedom of press and religion without definition or qualification? Legislative regulation of the right of contract can obviously be questioned only by reason of the manner and extent, not by reason of the mere fact, of its exercise. But then, from a legal standpoint, the essential thing is not the right, but its qualification, and an undefined claim to freedom of contract presents in reality no justiciable issue.

What then have the courts done to define the issue? Have they said that the freedom of contract may be impaired only for the protection of public health and safety? No, for they always also make a reservation for the vague interest designated as public welfare. Do they concede to the state the right to interfere on behalf of economically inferior classes? There is as yet no clear doctrine to that effect. After all, the courts offer us nothing more definite than the idea of reasonableness, a criterion which lacks both precision and objectiveness. What should we say to a similar criterion in the law of property? A family settlement has been said to be much like an act of Parliament, and, not unlike public legislation, it impairs the freedom of property. The courts have therefore established a rule against perpetuities. In an early leading case (*Duke of Norfolk's case*, 3 Chancery Cases 1 [1682]) Lord Chancellor Nottingham, who had sustained a settlement which made property inalienable for a number of lives in being, was asked to indicate the bounds of a lawful limitation: What time? Where are the bounds of that contingency? Where will you stop if you do not stop here? "I will tell you," he said, "where I will stop: I will stop wherever any visible inconvenience doth appear." It took the courts one hundred and fifty years to define this visible inconvenience with precision; before that time they operated with the principle of reasonableness; thereafter they discarded it and placed the law upon a certain footing. The criterion of reasonableness may be the only one available; but if so, it means that adequate scientific or conventional tests have not yet been developed. To oppose legislative discretion by undefined judicial standards of reasonableness is to oppose legislative by judicial discretion, and constitutional doctrines so vaguely formulated cannot be expected to command confidence.

Apart from this the question will remain whether the extent of legislative power over personal and property rights not covered by specific constitutional guaranties is a legal or a political issue. The prevailing doctrine of constitutional law treats the issue as a legal one and thus assigns its determination to judicial authority; but if it is in its nature political, the purely judicial attitude of mind brought to the task must constitute a limitation and a handicap rather than a superior qualification. It is therefore worth while to examine the relation of law to individual rights from a broader point of view than precedent and implication from abstract formulas, and to see whether a survey of historic changes will not give a fairer basis for estimating the legitimacy of statutory policies.

Such a survey will therefore form the starting-point in the attempt to differentiate policy and principle in legislation. In order to simplify the task, the reference will be mainly to social policies, which will be traced in common-law doctrines, in the legislation enacted to meet common-law deficiencies, and in constitutional provisions.

It will appear that the prevailing concepts of principle are in the main due to judicial action, and on the basis of both legislative and judicial experience the meaning of principle should be made clear. The result of the examination should enable us to estimate the factors by the aid of which a system of constructive principles of legislation may be built up.

CHAPTER I

HISTORIC CHANGES OF POLICY AND THE MODERN CONCEPT OF SOCIAL LEGISLATION

The main phases of evolution which are summarized in the catalogue of changes which follows are perfectly familiar; they are restated simply in order to bring out pointedly the drift of modern legislative thought and its significance.

They arrange themselves naturally under a few principal heads: the recognition of the right of personality; the establishment of freedom of thought; the repression of unthrift and dissipation; the protection of public health and safety; and the relief from social injustice.

I. THE RIGHT OF PERSONALITY

It is a commonplace of legal history that the importance of status as something differentiated from personality diminishes as we proceed from primitive to modern law. We have almost attained to a wiping out of personal differences in relation to legal rights; but the leveling process is in many respects quite recent, and, so far as it goes, has in the main been fully accomplished only in the course of the nineteenth century.

Let us briefly review the principal phases in the establishment of free and equal personal status.

a) The abrogation of personal slavery and serfdom.—
These have practically disappeared from the face of the
civilized earth. By the beginning of the nineteenth
century all personal unfreedom had ceased to exist in
Western Europe, and Russian serfdom was abolished
in the early sixties. About contemporaneous was the fall
of negro slavery in the United States, which was made
legally perfect by the Thirteenth Amendment, proclaimed in December, 1865; the emancipation of negro
slaves held by whites had begun in 1833 in the British
colonies, and was completed by the act of Brazil in 1888.
European powers still tolerate customary forms of
domestic slavery within their spheres of influence in
Africa; but even here the slave trade is suppressed by
the Brussels convention of 1890.

b) The disappearance of legal class distinctions.—If we
ignore the anomalous and rapidly waning status of our
own tribal Indians as wards of the nation, Russia alone
of the Western nations continues to divide her people into
classes having different legal capacity (nobility, clergy,
citizens, peasants, besides Asiatics and Jews). France
did away with class disabilities as a result of the great
Revolution in 1789, while in Germany the last traces
of peasants' disabilities did not disappear until 1867.
Blackstone gives in his *Commentaries* a list of classes of
the community which (barring the political privileges of
the peerage) impresses us as formal and practically
insignificant; it has indeed been one of the chief merits of
the common law that for many centuries past it has been

singularly free of class distinctions. This rule of equality was inherited by the American law. Because the principle of equality had never been a great issue in the constitutional history of the English people it received only a perfunctory recognition in the early bills of rights; its deliberate and distinct formulation by the Fourteenth Amendment was due to the race conflict of the South and came only after the Civil War. The practical acceptance of the principle thus long preceded its formal declaration. The principle encounters difficulty only in its application to the colored race; and in the legal enforcement of reciprocal discrimination and segregation in marriage, in education, and in transportation in public conveyances (quite recently also in residence) denies the principle in substance, while claiming to respect it. The demand for legal penalties shows that the social sanction is not believed to be sufficiently strong to maintain a separation strongly supported by the sentiment of the dominant class.

Apart from this anomaly, however, in the modern world the accident of birth as a member of a social class neither carries privilege nor entails disability in the capacity to acquire or hold legal rights.

c) *The recognition of the legal rights of aliens.*—In the ancient Roman law alien and enemy were, alike, covered by the same term—*hostis*—and were entirely without legal rights. Today by comity or treaty the alien enjoys practically the same civil capacity as the citizen. The common law attaches to alienage certain disabilities in the matter of land tenure which have not been everywhere or altogether removed by legislation, and which in some instances have been added to, particularly with reference to non-resident aliens. By an anomaly of our constitutional law this matter is in America still under state control, subject to the supremacy of treaty stipulations. It is noteworthy that the guaranties of the Fourteenth Amendment apply to all persons within the jurisdiction of the states, and not merely to citizens.

The important right of immigration and settlement is not necessarily included in the civil capacity of the alien. In many countries the matter is not of sufficient importance to have called for special regulation, but where immigration assumes considerable dimensions the right has been qualified by restrictive legislation. Our own legislation is typical in that respect. In the absolute exclusion of Chinese laborers disabilities of race, class, and alienage are combined, and this legislation serves as a warning that the modern principle of equality is by no means of absolute operation.

d) *The emancipation from domestic subjection.*—The law of ancient Rome and the law of modern Japan are typical of legal systems in which members of the household are subjected to the dominion of the male head and are individually of imperfect legal capacity. In Rome the wife became in course of time relieved from this subjection, and in the case of the child it survived mainly as a formal rule of law, practically nullified by important modifications and exceptions. The Continental nations which received the Roman law repudiated this entire branch, and related institutions of their own (mundium) gradually died off. In the modern civil law the wife is an inferior partner, but still a partner, in the marital community.

The common law of England practically reproduced for the wife the dependent status which the older Roman law assigned to all the members of the family except the head. It even aggravated the dependency by denying to the wife the capacity to perform disposing or binding acts (coverture; feme covert). It is significant that the old law of serfdom furnished to English lawyers analogies for the relation of husband and wife. The courts of equity managed, however, to give to the married woman a very considerable protection in the enjoyment of her property.

The law of coverture was taken over by the American states, together with such practical modifications as the system of equity jurisprudence had developed in England. Legislative reform began about 1840, and in the beginning did little more than adopt and enact into statute law the doctrine of the courts of equity. Gradually it made the wife entirely independent of the husband. In this legislation England followed America, beginning her reform in 1870. In America the course of legislation extended over a very long period; Tennessee, as the last state, did not abandon the system of coverture until 1913. In those states which have on the whole adopted the Continental system of marital community of property rights the peculiar disabilities of coverture are likewise unknown.

It should be remembered that the coverture applied only to women living in marriage; that, in other words, the common law recognized no sex disability in the matter of civil rights.

In considering domestic subjection it is also necessary to refer to the status of the child, that is, the infant child, for parent and adult child are in law, except for purposes of inheritance, practically altogether strangers to each other. As a holder of property the infant child occupies a position of peculiar independence in the common law, for the father has neither usufruct nor guardianship (except the "socage" guardianship with regard to land which terminates when the infant attains the age of fourteen);[1] on the other hand, the father is entitled to the earnings of the child, and to this absolute right to the earnings corresponds no similarly absolute duty to support, for from this the father may relieve himself by emancipating the child and thereby surrendering the right to earnings.

The personal control of the father over the minor child is at common law almost unlimited; even an effectual criminal liability probably did not exist except in case of homicide, the policy of the law being very decidedly not to interfere with the exercise of domestic authority. There was thus a domestic subjection of the

[1] The father was formerly regarded as the guardian of the child's personal property; see Blackstone, I, 461, and the act of 1670, which gave him the right to appoint a guardian for the child by deed or will.

severest and most unqualified kind. This has been broken in upon only by very modern legislation, beginning with the criminal punishment of cruelty, and more recently establishing a system of public care of juvenile dependents. The development of this phase of law, which may be said to have started with the Illinois law of 1899, is in its very beginning, and the rights of the parent will undoubtedly more and more assume the character of a trust.

This completes the series of legal changes through which personal status has gone. Liberty and equality have received practically universal recognition, but this has come only in the nineteenth century. Race alone remains a sinister distinction which the law has not fully overcome, and which in some respects it even tends to emphasize, owing to the greater menace of foreign race invasion in modern times. The disability of the child, a transitory status, must of course remain, but the emancipation from the abuse of domestic power constitutes perhaps the most marked triumph of the right of human personality.

2. FREEDOM OF THOUGHT

All American bills of rights give prominent places to religious liberty and the freedom of the press. The guaranties incorporated both the achievement and aims of constitutional struggles and philosophical theories of natural right. They represent political ideas directly contrary to the maxims of earlier statecraft. Until far into the seventeenth century it had been a commonplace of public policy that the safety of the state demands the control of opinion. The view that religious dissent was a factor of political disintegration found expression in the English Conformity Acts (reign of Elizabeth), in the maxim accepted in the Peace of Westphalia (1648), *cuius regio, eius religio,* and in the revocation of the French Edict of Nantes (1685). Though the American colonists had sought refuge from religious oppression, Rhode Island alone of all the colonies proclaimed the principle of toleration. To the present day Russia regards heterodoxy as inimical to her national unity. With these historic facts in view we can better appreciate the step in advance which religious liberty represents, and yet in the course of the nineteenth century toleration, if not religious equality, has been established all over the civilized world, and belief and worship are nowhere any longer the subjects of penal repression.

As regards the press, Blackstone tells us that the art of printing, soon after its introduction, was looked upon in England as well as in other countries as "merely a matter of state" (*Commentaries,* IV, 152, note). Its control was part of the freely conceded jurisdiction of the Star Chamber. After the fall of the latter, its control simply passed to Parliament, which exercised it on similar principles. The essence of this control was that nothing was to be printed without previous license, and by the removal of this requirement in 1694 the liberty of the press was supposed to be established.

In the course of the eighteenth century, however, a further struggle took place for greater freedom from responsibility, which resulted in the liberalization of the law of libel. Our bills of rights reflect this stage of development: they guarantee impunity for true matter published, but only if published with good motives. Here most of our constitutional guaranties stop; but the practice of the nineteenth century has proceeded far beyond this, and now, generally speaking, not only is truth an absolute justification, but the defense of privilege is recognized to the widest extent in every kind and form of public criticism.[1]   The free expression of opinion on political subjects is guarded with possibly even greater jealousy than the freedom of art, literature, and science and of social thought and agitation.

In view of the wide toleration of freedom of political agitation which public opinion demands, the law of sedition, even where not formally abrogated, has lost much of its practical importance; when in 1886 in England, in consequence of strong public labor demonstrations, prosecutions were instituted against prominent leaders, the instructions as to the constituent elements of sedition were so qualified that the jury could hardly do otherwise than render a verdict of not guilty (*Reg.* v. *Burns*, 16 Cox 355; *Reg.* v. *Cunningham*, 16 Cox 420; Russell on *Crimes*, I, 557–65). The law is equally obscure in America, where, as in England, the conditions under

[1] See Schofield, "Freedom of the Press in the United States," *Publications of the American Sociological Society*, IX, 67.

which government has been carried on for the last hundred years have rendered political repression unnecessary or inexpedient.

We have here a complete reversal of the public policies of former times, which yet had a show of plausibility in their favor; the experience of a great war shows how effectually after all for a time at least public opinion can be controlled by authority, and how much the action of the state in a certain direction can be strengthened thereby. That immediate political advantage is so readily sacrificed to the conviction that free expression of opinion is in the long run more wholesome to the constitution of the body politic is one of the most remarkable achievements of democracy and of education in public affairs. That the achievement is not altogether safe from attack and impairment is shown by the public attitude toward anarchistic agitation, as evidenced by the short-lived red-flag law of Massachusetts, an attitude comparable to that of those of our state constitutions which temper their toleration of religious dissent by creating certain disabilities for atheists.

The establishment of the right of personality and of freedom of personality and of freedom of thought are accomplished in the main by the removal of legal and other restraints, and the positive function of legislation is relatively slight; the advances in the protection of human interests which follow involve, on the other hand, a constant enlargement of the field of legislative activity and control.

3. THE REPRESSION OF UNTHRIFT AND DISSIPATION

Certain phases of this legislative policy are old or even antiquated; thus the formerly prevailing type of sumptuary legislation has disappeared. On the whole, however, the activity of the state against the three great forms of unthrift—gambling, drink, and vice—has gained in incisiveness and extent, and its greatest development has taken place in the American democracy.

The relation of the state and the law to moral ideals is complex and peculiar. The main motive power of every political organization is self-preservation, which produces the type of the state best fitted for the maintenance of communal integrity. After some type has once successfully established itself and led to the predominance of one element of the body politic, the instinct for self-preservation again makes the interest of that element the ruling factor of state policy. Morality as represented in law thus becomes subordinate to, and an instrument of, the established order of things; and in all communities it tends to be identified with authority, the family, and property. The canons of justice and equity presuppose respect for these institutions, and purely ethical standards of conduct lie outside of the range of civil obligations.

In European systems of polity the place of morality was further determined by the position and the claims of the church. The Christian religion was based on ethical ideals; ethical thought and ethical aspiration were in consequence entirely dominated by religion, and the state considered that the preservation of public morals was not a secular function, but belonged to the church.

The common forms of moral laxity and dissipation were thus regarded as sins to be visited by spiritual penalties, and almost the entire law of sex relations, including marriage, fell in England to the province of ecclesiastical jurisdiction, and the marriage law has to the present day not been entirely secularized. It is also to be noted that non-forcible injuries were only gradually drawn within the cognizance of the King's courts; defamation (which was first an ecclesiastical offense) not until the seventeenth century, while fraud became a tort only toward the end of the eighteenth century.

It was only after the Reformation and the attendant relaxation of church discipline that evil practices not directly invading other persons' rights or public authority were drawn within the range of legislative policy; the first attempts to repress gambling and prostitution date from the reign of Henry VIII, and from the reign of Edward VI on the liquor trade is subjected to the régime of the licensing system.

The attitude of the English law (and that of Continental countries is similar) toward gambling, drink, and vice has remained tolerably fixed for centuries; the liquor business has been the subject of constant restrictive regulation, while gambling and vice were placed beyond the pale of legal protection, but otherwise tolerated as long as outwardly disorderly practices were avoided. An attitude of indulgence toward the common human weaknesses became part of the established order of things.

It is interesting to observe how with the advance of democracy the legislative policy toward these evils becomes gradually more aggressive. The mass of the people struggling for material prosperity prize the "middle-class" virtues of habits of industry and domestic regularity, and they seek to impress their ideals upon the legislation which they control. Thus liquor becomes a conspicuous issue in politics; absolute prohibition, a radical interference with personal liberty, is first introduced as a legislative policy; the same policy is applied to gambling, and particularly to lotteries, previously used freely as a means of raising funds for public purposes, and in many states the prohibition is made part of the fundamental law; and for the first time a determined crusade is instituted to suppress prostitution.

The standards of this "morals" legislation are perhaps all the more advanced, as the standards of enforcement are not equally high. This may be due to our peculiar governmental organization, which divorces legislative power entirely from administrative responsibility. The formal declaration of policies is insisted upon irrespective of whether they can be carried out faithfully or even with tolerable success; indeed, the advanced policy is sometimes consented to only upon the tacit understanding that in actual administration it will be somewhat relaxed. The result is inevitably a certain demoralization of governmental standards, but the system makes possible an insistence upon high abstract moral ideas, which in other countries is deemed impracticable, and which all the time operates as an educative influence.[1] Even with its imperfect operation, however, this phase of legislative policy carries with it encroachments upon personal liberty which would not have been ventured upon by less democratic systems of government.

4. THE PROTECTION OF PUBLIC HEALTH AND SAFETY

The large amount of health and safety legislation which fills modern statute books represents less a change of legislative policy than a change of conditions that had to be met by an extension of state control. In principle the exercise of public power for the protection of life and limb is old-established, but prior to the nineteenth century there was relatively little occasion for its practical application. The nineteenth century brought two conditions which revolutionized the need for public control: the pressing of newly invented mechanical forces into the service of industry and the progress of science in discovering the causes of disease and their remedies.

---

[1] Under the German ideal of scrupulously correct statutes strictly enforced legislation is likewise an educating influence, but of a different type; it is not meant to represent an ideal to be ultimately attained, but a practical norm of conduct; just and fixed rules, the most powerful and insistent expression of the social conscience, are to operate as a sort of secular catechism, and the sense of formulated boundaries is relied upon to check the impulses of unsettled character—an education that consists in the subordination of individual tendencies to general standards. This point of view is admirably developed in a recent German treatise (F. W. Förster, Schuld & Sühne, 1911).

The imperative necessity of developing economic resources retarded adequate protection against mechanical dangers until it was possible to combine safety with the effective carrying on of industry; the former had to yield to the latter; this is well illustrated by the history of mining legislation.[1] Sanitary legislation encountered resistance on the part of personal and property rights as well as of business interests by reason of the widespread skepticism regarding the reality of the alleged dangers or the efficacy of the proposed remedies, but the English law of 1848 and the New York law of 1857 firmly established the principle of an elastic administrative control, and the recent American so-called eugenics legislation indicates the long distance that we have traveled in the direction of state interference with private affairs. Living under free institutions we submit to public regulation and control in ways that would appear inconceivable to the spirit of oriental despotism; it is well known what deep-seated repugnance and resistance of the native population to the invasion of their domestic privacy and personal habits English health officers in India have to overcome in order to enforce the sanitary measures necessary to prevent the spread of infectious or contagious disease. Oriental systems of polity act more powerfully upon the habits of individual life than modern governments do; the primal need of the community for the perpetuation of its own existence through marriage and offspring is more effectually secured in India and China than in Western Europe;

[1] R. G. Galloway, *History of Coal Mining in Great Britain*, 1882.

but the sanction is custom and not law; and in the same way the sanitary régime of the Old Testament seems to have been enforced by spiritual threats and not by secular penalties. Modern policy makes legislative compulsion coextensive with the reciprocal dependence of men upon each other's standards of conduct for the preservation of the health and safety of all, and with the progress of invention and of science there seems to be hardly any limit to that independence. Our modern sanitary laws are laws in the real sense of the term, enforced by the power of the state. As such they represent, if not a new policy, yet a new legislative activity and function.

5.   THE GROWTH OF SOCIAL LEGISLATION

The development of phases of legislative policy thus far traced shows two main tendencies: the steady growth in the value placed upon individual human personality and the shifting of the idea of the public good from the security of the state and established order to the welfare of the mass of the people. The growth of social legislation combines those two tendencies. By the term social legislation we understand those measures which are intended for the relief and elevation of the less favored classes of the community; it would thus be held to include factory laws, but hardly legislation for the safety of passengers on railroads.

The lower classes (as the term was formerly commonly used) became the object of special legislation in England after the Great Plague; but the policy of this early legislation was repression and not relief. The first great systematic relief measure was the English Poor Law of 1601 (43 Elizabeth, ch. 2); it is worth noting that the principle of taxation by state authority for the relief of the poor was not introduced into France until three hundred years later, in 1905, antecedent to the separation of church and state. In the beginning of the nineteenth century England inaugurated a new phase of social legislation by her child-labor law of 1802, followed by a series of other factory laws.

Yet until about twenty years ago the term social legislation was generally unfamiliar and conveyed little meaning even to students of reform movements. The word came from Germany, and there originated about the beginning of the eighties.

More particularly the new term social legislation was associated with the workmen's insurance measures announced by the message of November 17, 1881, submitted by the German Emperor to the Reichstag, which provided relief in form of pensions for sickness (1883), accident (1884), and invalidity and old age (1889).

The purpose of these measures as proclaimed by the imperial message was to counteract social democratic agitation and to supplement the repressive law of 1878 by positive and constructive state action. Other European countries gradually enacted similar legislation; in England compensation for industrial accident was introduced in 1897, old-age pensions in 1908, and insurance against sickness and unemployment in 1912. The American states have so far approached only the problem of compensation for industrial accident; since 1910 about three-fourths of the states have enacted measures of that kind.

What was the special feature of this new legislation that marked it as a new departure in legislative policy? It was that relief changed its character. Poor relief had been a matter apart from industry; it had stigmatized the recipient and placed him under disabilities; the policy of the English poor-law reform of 1834 had been to make it in addition distasteful and repellent (indoor relief). The new pension or compensation system carried no stigma or disability, and by its conditions or terms rather seemed to be in the nature of the discharge of a debt that the community owed to its members, a deferred payment for previous inadequately rewarded services, or a compensation for some kind of injustice suffered. It realized the idea of a "respectable provision unattended with degradation" first put forward in 1837[1] and again advocated in the Minority Report on poor-law reform under the name of an "honorable and universal provision." In Germany the entire legislation, moreover, incorporated important features of insurance. The recipient of pensions or other allowances upon an insurance basis takes them, morally as well as legally, as a matter of right, and would be beholden to the community merely for setting the plan in operation and administering

[1] See Rose, *Rise of Democracy*, p. 100.

it. Every contribution from the employer or from the community alters the nature of the allowance, and the tendency in England and America has been to relieve the beneficiary from any contribution and to throw the entire burden either upon the community (old-age pensions) or upon the employer (workmen's compensation). However free from stigma, the provision is thus yet in the nature of relief.

In Europe relief legislation of the advanced type is at present as firmly established as sanitary or safety legislation, the defects of which it in part supplies, while America is only just beginning to develop that part of the system which connects most closely with the remedial methods of the common law.

Even in Europe a sharp line is still drawn between relief and the larger policy of using the power of the state to alter the economic terms of the labor contract. An entire readjustment or reconstruction of the economic relation between the classes is not as yet, generally speaking, considered as part of a practical legislative program.

Not so very long ago this larger program would have been sufficiently condemned by being characterized as socialistic, and even at the present time there is an instinctive perception that the most liberal policy of relief is in principle still very far removed from an attempt to control economic relations under normal conditions.

We are, however, quite accustomed to one form of relief which is really undistinguishable from social reconstruction, and that is the legislation dealing with children. It is well to remember that factory laws began everywhere with the regulation of child labor, and that that regulation always went hand in hand with efforts to secure to the child some measure of education and instruction. And with regard to education, the American states, at a period when they represented the most individualistic type of political and economic organization, pursued a progressively socialistic policy, shifting more and more the financial burden of education from the family to the community. While the existence of universal suffrage has given to this form of communism a political justification, the present movement for vocational instruction is significant in frankly abandoning this basis and embarking upon schemes of economic reconstruction, the consequence of which can hardly be foreseen.

As factory legislation in England began with the regulation of the employment of children, so it advanced farther along the line of least resistance by restricting the hours of labor of women. When the bill which resulted in the act of 1844 was agitated, the men desired the like reduction for themselves, but were satisfied that the legislation should be confined to women in the hope, which events justified, that the legal reduction of women's work would accomplish without legislation the same purpose for men.[1]   The act of 1844 had been preceded by a report calling attention to the special physical considera-

---

[1] Hutchins and Harrison, *History of Factory Legislation*, p. 186.

tions which made the restriction desirable for female employees.[1] Whether exclusively on this ground or not, the state from now on extended its guardianship in the matter of industrial labor over both women and young persons. A similar development took place in Germany, where a maximum work-day for women in factories was established in 1892.

In the United States the regulation of women's hours of labor has furnished the main battle ground for conflicting theories of constitutional right and power. The course of decisions proved on the whole favorable to state control. Of the two adverse holdings, that of Illinois, rendered in 1895 (*Ritchie* v. *People*, 155 Ill. 98), was greatly weakened if not nullified in 1910 (*Ritchie* v. *Wayman*, 244 Ill. 509), and that of New York, relating to night work (1907), was directly overruled in 1915 (*People* v. *Williams*, 189 N.Y. 131; *People* v. *Charles Schweinler Press*, 214 N.Y. 395). There has, however, been considerable inclination to support this legislation on the stricter theories of the police power. A vast array of material was presented to the Supreme Court to prove the detrimental effect of prolonged industrial work upon the female organism, and the attempt has been made to connect, not only the prohibition of night labor, but also minimum-wage laws with the protection of morals. It is therefore significant that in the Oregon case (208 U.S. 412) Justice Brewer referred to female peculiarities of disposition and habits of life which remove woman

[1] *Ibid.*, p. 84.

from equality of competition and justify special protection to secure her a real equality of rights (p. 422).

As legislation for women advances from the ten-hour day to the Saturday half-holiday, to the eight-hour day (established for the District of Columbia in 1915), to the total prohibition of night work, and to the regulation of wages, the narrow foundation of the old-established grounds of the police power will become more and more untenable, and courts will be forced to recognize in such laws measures of social and economic advancement, and not merely measures for the protection of health or morals. It will then become necessary to scrutinize the ground of differentiation between men and women, and particularly to examine whether such differentiation implies inferiority, as the words used by Justice Brewer may seem to indicate. At a time when women are demanding equal political rights it does seem incongruous to insist unduly upon infirmities inherent in sex, and it will be fairer to support legislative discrimination for their protection by arguments not derogatory to other claims. Such arguments can well be brought forward without specious pleading.

Both from an economic and from the historical point of view the status of women is constitutionally different from that of men: economically, because the temporary and adventitious character of women's industrial work, due to the effect of marriage upon their industrial status, handicaps their capacity for combination, and hence their capacity for efficient self-help, and further because the state has a distinct interest in conserving part of a woman's time and strength to enable her more adequately to perform her non-industrial functions, her duties to the home and the family, and to render her indispensable aid in the furtherance of the state's child-welfare policies; historically, because centuries of economic dependence and the universal conventional discouragement of habits of self-assertion necessarily removed women from those ideals of individualism which were in America supposed to have crystallized into constitutional rights and limitations upon the legislative power. It is true that these conventions with regard to women have partly been altered; but coincident with their advance toward greater independence has been a general modification of the ideals of individualism. Nothing could be more characteristic of that coincidence than the fact that the legislature of Illinois, on March 22, 1872, passed an act declaring that sex should not be a bar to any occupation or employment, and five days thereafter, on March 27, 1872, passed another act forbidding the employment of women in mines—enactments opposed to each other upon a mechanical view of liberty, and yet quite harmonious in spirit as making for a larger freedom of women. It is obvious that upon any large view women stand on a different footing from men as regards the exercise of legislative protection. In all European countries and by the international conventions regarding industrial labor this has been recognized. It follows that a very much farther reaching control over women than we have at

present would leave unprejudiced the problem of legislative policy with reference to adult men.

Germany, whose program of social legislation has been
more systematic and comprehensive than that of any
other country, has yet so far firmly adhered to the
principle of non-interference of the state in the terms of
the wage contract between employer and adult male
employee except for the purpose of preventing abuses
in methods of payment (truck acts). Reduced hours of
labor and increased pay are left to free bargaining between
the parties. France has been, if possible, even more
individualistic than Germany in this respect. Until
recently English legislation pursued the same policy, but
departed from it in establishing the eight-hour day for
coal mines in 1908 (distinctly not a sanitary measure)
and in applying the trade-board system for fixing minimum wages in sweated trades to men as well as women,
and enacting a similar wage act for coal miners (Acts of
1909 and 1912), while constitutional scruples have confined similar legislation in America to women. England
has indeed entered upon a deliberate policy of economic
reconstruction in an entirely distinct field of legislation,
that of land tenure, and has undertaken to alter fundamentally the status of an entire class of the population.
The agrarian legislation for Ireland culminating in the
measures of 1881 and 1897, dictated by political considerations, was in 1912 upon purely economic grounds
applied to Scotland, and the extension of a similar
system to England will perhaps be hastened by the

necessity of making the national food supply less dependent upon foreign imports.

Here is legislation of a purely socialistic type showing the liability of even apparently most firmly fixed policies to be revolutionized by change of conditions or change of sentiment.

Why should industrial legislation be exempt from like revolutionary change? It is true that the state has thus far departed very little from its attitude of neutrality in the struggle between capital and labor. Of the things that labor most desires, naming them in the order of the strength of the desire—chance of employment, security of employment, better remuneration, lessened toil, fairness of methods, safe and sanitary conditions, and relief in distress—it appears that even the most advanced type of European social legislation undertakes to secure less than one-half, being the half less prized by labor. If the reason for this is that the conditions for radical improvement are or are believed to be beyond legislative control, or that the effectual remedy is unknown, legislative inactivity cannot be said to be a matter of deliberate policy of self-imposed limitation, but merely the consequence of imperfect power and knowledge, and advance in legislation would merely wait upon advance in knowledge and efficiency. At any rate, the possibility of embarking upon new policies seems to be foreshadowed both by the growing insistence of what is called the new social conscience and by the fact that the widest possible scope of state control is the avowed

demand of a political party which is constantly growing in strength.

If this brief outline has correctly characterized the
various aspects of social legislation and the stages in its
progress, it is also easier to understand the position of
American courts. In their hostile or suspicious attitude
toward legislation regulating hours of labor and payment
of wages which they regarded as involving merely
economic issues they resisted the beginnings of a novel
function of state control, and if they nullified even
reasonable and necessary measures it was perhaps
because they were unwilling to concede the first steps in
a development the scope of which they could neither
define nor foresee, and the full course of which must
justly have appeared to them as revolutionary.

But a larger view of changes and developments than
courts are in the habit of taking must also make us
extremely skeptical with regard to the fundamental
assumption underlying their method of approaching
legislation. Into the general clauses of the constitutions
they have read a purpose of fixing economic policies
which, however firmly rooted in habits of thought or
structure of society, are by their very nature unfit to be
identified with the relatively immutable concept of due
process. Where the makers of constitutions did intend
to establish policies, they did so in express terms: freedom
of speech and press, religious liberty, the favor to the

accused in criminal proceedings—these we find guaranteed in specific clauses; and nothing was guaranteed that had not at some time been a live issue.   It was foreign to their minds to foreclose issues that no one could foresee.   Due process was an idea centuries old and meant to last for centuries; the idea that it should be subject to amendments, qualifications, or exceptions is utterly incongruous. That the clause should have been seized upon to protect policies which to the courts seemed essential to the social structure they were used to was perhaps not unnatural; but it was certainly an extreme step for the Court of Appeals of New York to identify the constitution with a policy which it recognized as standing in need of a change.   In any event, the attempt of the courts to check modern social legislation by constitutional principles can be properly estimated only if we recognize in it the exercise of a political, and not a strictly judicial, function.

CHAPTER II

THE COMMON LAW AND PUBLIC POLICY

It has been said that our legal system might be conceived as existing without the statute book, but not without the common law.[1] The statement implies, not merely that legislation constantly presupposes the existence of common-law rules to aid in its operation, but also that the common law contains in itself, though imperfectly, the essential elements of justice and policy. By the common law we should then have to understand the entire aggregate of unwritten principles and rules.

At an earlier stage of legal history it would have been less possible to identify unwritten law and common law. The latter term indicated a distinction from local law, the vitality of which declined with the centralization of justice in the King's courts, until local customs as well as municipal by-laws became negligible factors in the legal system, in strong contrast to the development in Germany, where municipal custom and regulation originated much that became subsequently incorporated in state- or nation-wide institutions.[2]

---

[1] Geldart, *Elements of English Law*, p. 9.

[2] Gierke, *Genossenschaftsrecht*, II, sec. 28. The present German system of land-title registration, similar to the so-called Torrens system, seems to have originated in the German cities (Stobbe, *Privatrecht*, sec. 94). The English Act of 1535 for the enrolment of bargains and sales (27 H. 8., ch. 16) contains

Long after the decline of local law there remained, however, two strong rivals of the common law of the King's courts in the royal prerogative and the church. Apart from the important matter of testamentary jurisdiction, the church not only guarded the integrity of faith, but looked after public morals, civilly by its jurisdiction over marriage and divorce, criminally by punishing bigamy, adultery, and incest, while crimes of violence, such as rape, and for some reason also the crime against nature, fell under secular cognizance. The gaps left by the disappearance of the punitive jurisdiction of the church in 1640 were filled by legislation, but in a somewhat haphazard manner, so that in England not only adultery, but even incest, was not brought under the criminal law—the latter omission clearly not the result of deliberate policy, and cured in 1908.

EQUITY

The royal power was for a long time regarded as an organ of supplementary justice—a theory which now survives in the pardoning power, and to which also the former practice of special remedial legislation may be traced. The exercise of the royal power for the purpose of modifying the rigor of the common law by less formalistic principles giving effect to intent, good faith, and

a saving for cities, boroughs, or towns corporate wherein the mayors, recorders, chamberlains, bailiffs, or other officers have authority or have lawfully used to enrol any evidences, deeds, or other writings within their precincts or limits. We know nothing further of these recording systems, and so far from exercising any influence upon general practice, they seem to have disappeared.

trust grew at a relatively early period into a distinct and co-ordinate system of remedial justice under the name of equity. When Blackstone speaks of the High Court of Chancery as in matters of civil property by much the most important of any of the King's courts, he might have added that equity contributed practically nothing to English law outside the sphere of property interests. The jurisdiction exercised over charitable trusts was avowedly limited to maintaining the original purposes of the founder unimpaired, and it was a deliberate and probably wise construction of judicial powers that kept the court from meddling with the terms of endowments; even where a power of regulation was expressly given it was said that alteration still belonged to Parliament (2 Bro. C.C. 662), but the doctrine of cy pres was for a long time overscrupulously applied, particularly in the matter of the instruction permissible in grammar schools (cf. *A.-G.* v. *Whiteley*, 11 Ves. 241, 1805, with the more liberal doctrine recognized in *A.-G.* v. *Dixie*, 3 Russ. 534, n. 1825), and the failure to develop principles for dealing with schemes which, without having become incapable of execution, had outlived their usefulness[1] eventually led to legislative interference and to the creation of administrative organs of control. And while no one could justly expect that prior to the nineteenth century modern ideas of charity should have been entertained or promoted by the Lord Chancellor in the exercise of his sporadic

---

[1] Neither the consent of all members of the parish nor even that of the heir of the founder warrants a departure from the original scheme (1 Vern. 35, 45).

jurisdiction, it still must be noted that equity never gave expression to a single opinion on the personal idea of charity administration; it is very probable that no application was ever made to the court on that score.

The jurisdiction of equity over married women is likewise characteristic for its close confinement to property interests. It was only the wife with invested wealth who was protected against the husband's control and against his creditors. It should not have been impossible for equity to extend the like protection to the married woman's independent earnings, but this step was never taken. It was this defect, more strongly felt in England than in America, which led to the first English Married Women's Act in 1870. With regard to infants the court of equity represented the sovereign as *parens patriae*, and the possession of an estate has been held not to be indispensable as a foundation of equitable jurisdiction (1892, 2 Ch. 496, 512). Judicial protection was thus afforded against the abuse of paternal authority before the legislature intervened for that purpose (10 Ves. 52). But equity did not as a rule concern itself with children who had no property, and the modern advances in the protection of children's personal rights and interests owe nothing to equitable principles. There is a striking contrast between the strong influence which equity has had on property legislation, which often simply copied its doctrines, and the almost entire absence of any influence upon modern legislative policy outside of the domain of property rights.

ROYAL POLICE POWER

While the royal power of granting equitable relief soon became merged in a regular judicial power, the royal power of controlling the internal police of the realm continued for a long time as a prerogative outside and independent of the ordinary tribunals. The power was exercised by the King through his council sitting in the Star Chamber, a name that has come to be associated with arbitrary and despotic methods of inquiry and punishment in consequence of the political struggles in which the Crown found itself engaged in the seventeenth century. But for a long period of its existence the Star Chamber exercised what was at the time considered a normal and legitimate function of state, namely, an inherent executive police power. The duty and power of guarding the public welfare did not necessarily have to wait upon legislative or judicial action, even though repression involved punitive processes. The theory is now otherwise, but when it flourished it was no usurpation and was frequently of beneficent operation; it was an integral factor in the system of public policy. It was also a result of prevailing ideas of public policy that the welfare of the realm seemed more identified with the maintenance of established order than with the advancement of the condition of the people. In historic retrospect, at least, political agitation and disturbance seem to engage a large share of the attention of the Star Chamber, and riot, sedition, seditious libel, and the license of the printing press play a considerable part in its jurisdiction. After the fall of the Star Chamber in 1640 the censorship of the press was first placed on a statutory basis and then abolished. If the censorship of plays remained in the hands of the King's Chamberlain, this was due to the historic attachment of the profession of actors to the court, and not to any theory of royal power. The law of libel, sedition, and riot came to be administered by common-law courts. The law of libel became politically conspicuous through the conflict as to the respective provinces of court and jury which was settled by Fox's Libel Act of 1792 and left its traces in the bills of rights of American constitutions; the law of sedition lost its practical importance through the growing freedom of political agitation. The public policy for which the Star Chamber stood has given way to different governmental purposes and ideals.

CORPORATIONS

Another phase of public policy was controlled by the royal power as a consequence of the legal theory of corporate capacity. In its various forms of ecclesiastical bodies and foundations, gilds, municipalities, trading companies, or business organizations, the corporation has always presented the same problem of how to check the tendency of group action to undermine the liberty of the individual or to rival the political power of the state. The somewhat vague theory of the later Middle Ages that communal organization not sanctioned by prescription or royal license was illegal was at least from the fifteenth century on supplemented by the technical doctrine, developed under canonist influences, that there is no capacity to act as a body corporate without positive authorization. To grant this authority has remained in England an attribute of the royal prerogative, though extensively and, where coupled with other privileges inconsistent with the common law, necessarily exercised in concurrence with Parliament; in America the necessary authority is granted by the legislature through special charters or general laws.

It is hardly possible to overestimate the theory that corporate existence depends on positive sanction as a factor in public and legislative policy. It is natural that the charter or incorporation law should be made the vehicle of restraints or regulations which might not be readily imposed upon natural persons acting on their own initiative, and the course of legislative history bears this out. So far as the businesses of banking and insurance have been carried on under corporate charters they have been the subject of thorough and detailed regulation, while private banking and the unincorporated forms of fraternal insurance remain to the present day in the main unregulated and uncontrolled. Railroads have been built and operated from the beginning by corporate enterprise; thus legislation was called for and was made the instrument of exercising public power over operation service and in some cases over rates; the express business, on the other hand, which happened to be carried on chiefly by unincorporated concerns, or at least did not seek special charters, practically escaped regulation and was not placed under administrative jurisdiction until the Rate Act of 1906; this tends to show that it was not merely the fact of being a common carrier subject to special power, but more particularly the fact of being a corporation asking for powers, which subjected the railroad company to the extensive and intensive legislative régime which it has experienced.

Moreover, a corporation once organized is, without positive legislation, subject to peculiar remedies at the hands of the state. Both common-law courts and courts of equity can entertain proceedings brought by the attorney-general to inhibit corporate misdoings. The information in the nature of a quo warranto is well established, and the proceeding in equity was used in 1874 in the notable case of the railroad companies of Wisconsin (35 Wis. 425–608). That case reviewed the history of the law very fully and concluded (whether correctly or incorrectly does not matter for the present purpose) that irrespective of statute the courts of equity had power to deal with the illegal conduct of corporations, and this without the showing of any specific injury to the public. There are also later American cases in which the corporate character of an offender has been held to justify a resort to equitable relief where the same would be denied against an individual (compare 143 Ind. 98 with 155 Ind. 526). Considering the great value which is now commonly attached to the possibility of the enforcement of law through the equitable process of injunction, so much more familiar and less technical than the proceeding in quo warranto, the doctrine that corporations are peculiarly subject to the exercise of the power need not be very firmly established or ancient to be availed of with eagerness, and the precedents are sufficient to support a liberal exercise of jurisdiction. It would of course be impossible to contend as against individuals for an equally comprehensive power to restrain illegal conduct in equity. In the case of a corporation it will also often be possible to construe charter limitations in conformity to public policy, and thus to identify injury to public interests with illegality; corporations organized for the purpose of holding or dealing in real estate were thus dealt with in Illinois. Altogether, if there lurks in corporate organization a special danger to the public, it also affords the legal ways and means for public control of exceptional strength.

LAW OF THE COURTS OF COMMON LAW

We finally come to that portion of the unwritten law which was administered in the King's courts, and which constitutes the common law in the narrower sense of the term. Like equity, and unlike the jurisdiction of the King in council, it is a system of justice rather than of policy, and its policy is not always easy to discover. Custom and precedent frequently stand in place of reason and expediency. Justice in some cases means merely a rule justly, i.e., impartially, administered, and not a just rule; thus it would be difficult to imagine a more flagrant injustice than that a husband should have absolute power to will away from his widow the entire personal estate which she brought into the marriage and leave her penniless; and yet that was the law of England.[1] Particularly in the domain of family law the peculiar common-law doctrines elude rational explanation. For the rule of primogeniture and the husband's property in the wife's chattels—both foreign to the Continental systems and contrary to almost universal notions of equity—Pollock and Maitland suggest no better reason than that the courts chose a "short cut" in preference to complex and involved arrangements (*History of the Common Law*, II, 272, 430).

It is not inconceivable that a highly centralized and powerful court should set the considerations of easy administration of justice above the highest type of substantive justice and should prefer symmetry and simplicity of the system to its close adjustment to varying conditions. Such a tendency certainly manifests itself in some of the most characteristic phases of judge-made law, although it is also possible to cite instances to the contrary. The rule against perpetuities furnishes illustrations in point. The rule sets a limit in point of time to the tying up of property. The period was finally fixed at the duration of lives in being at the creation of the

[1] Lord Ellenborough in *Doe* v. *Barford*, 4 M. & S. 10: "I remember a case some years ago of a sailor who made his will in favor of a woman with whom he cohabited, and afterwards went to the West Indies and married a woman of considerable substance, and it was held, notwithstanding the hardship of the case, that the will swept away from the widow every shilling of the property."

interest and a gross term of twenty-one years in addition thereto. The period clearly indicates that the rule was intended to apply to family settlements, and analogous rules in other legal systems have no other application. Yet after the rule had become established, it was held to control an option agreement entered into by a corporation —a purely commercial transaction. The criterion of lives in being is quite unsuitable in such a case, and the economic value of the rule so applied, if any, is extremely slight. It is a case of a purely mechanical application of a doctrine; yet no question has been made of the propriety of the extension (*L. & S. W. R. Co.* v. *Gomm*, 20 Ch. D. 562).

After it had once been settled that the transgression of the limits of the rule by so little as the fraction of a year or month would avoid the entire settlement, the same rigorous principle was applied to cases where, without violation of the essence of the scheme, a cutting down of the period to its permissible limit would have served every end. The question whether the existence of powers of sale making the concrete property, as distinguished from the fund, freely alienable should not legitimately affect the operation of the rule has not even been discussed. The rule has ceased to be a principle, and the courts have lost all control over it.

A centralized system of justice is naturally unfavorable to differentiation of legal rules. The common law differs from other modern systems in having no distinct commercial law. The doctrine of market overt is, however, practically a relic of old commercial custom. It recognized in favor of the purchasing public the principle that the possession of the selling merchant should be equivalent to title. It applied to sales at fairs and in open shops in the city of London,[1] and thus covered a substantial proportion of retail sales. But with the practical disappearance of fairs and the systematic discouragement of local customs the doctrine has ceased to be of importance in England and never gained any footing in America, while it has become the principle of the French and German codes. The rule caveat emptor, whereby the purchaser assumes the risk of hidden defects, may be a proper rule between persons dealing at arm's length, but it can hardly be defended as between the professional dealers selling in the way of trade. In the Roman law the difference was recognized by the reversal of the general rule in the case of market transactions, and gradually the special rule thus established by the market police, the aedilician edict, became part of the common law and of the modern civil codes, while the caveat emptor rule remains the rule of the English common law with only very slight qualifications. If the protection of the bona fide purchaser is thus much more adequate in the civil law than in the common law, it is because the common law eliminated, while the civil law generalized, a more favorable rule demanded by special conditions.

We should guard against too readily ascribing rules to a distinct policy. A rule analogous to that of caveat

[1] Pease, "Market Overt in London," 31 *Law Quarterly Review* 270.

emptor applies to leases, the landlord not being bound in any way to let the demised premises in a suitable condition for the purposes for which he knows the tenant intends to use them.   It might be tempting to attribute this rule to a conscious or unconscious bias in favor of the land-holding class.[1]   But it would be quite impossible to prove such a bias.   The rule apparently did not receive distinct judicial expression until 1843 (*Sutton* v. *Temple*, 12 M. & W. 52; *Hart* v. *Windsor*, 12 M. & W. 68), and then was rather assumed than argued, the only reason given being a purely juristic one, namely, that the term demise carried only a warranty of title, and therefore not any assurance of quality.   If we concede, however, that favor to the landlord class did not even subconsciously bias the judicial mind, we should also notice that there was quite remote from the judicial mind the thought of the poorer classes of dwellers in city tenements, whose interests demanded that the obligation thus judicially denied should be placed upon the landlord.

A similar observation may be made with regard to the establishment of the fellow-servant doctrine.   It was reserved for the ingenuity of an American court to discover in the doctrine that a servant cannot recover from the master for the negligence of a fellow-servant a public policy in favor of increased safety, since servants would be thereby induced to watch each other mutually (Ch. J.

---

[1] Class-bias, even unconscious, is likely to be very much overestimated as a factor in the modern common law (see Burdick, "Is Law the Expression of Class Selfishness?" 25 *Harvard Law Review* 349); of deliberate favor to economically dominant interests there is practically none.

Shaw in *Farwell* v. *Boston & Worcester R. Co.*, 4 Metc.
49, 1842). The case by which the doctrine was established in England (*Priestly* v. *Fowler*, 3 M. & W. 1, 1837)
concerned a butcher boy, and the court considered the
problem entirely from the point of view of the hardships
that might result to the head of a small business or of a
private household. That point of view is not without
merit. The civil law does not make the master liable
for the servant's fault unless the master was at fault in
selecting or supervising him (*culpa in eligendo*), while the
common law makes the master liable irrespective of such
fault if the servant's negligence was in the course of his
employment (*respondeat superior*). The fellow-servant
doctrine, which refuses to apply this rule where another
servant in the same employ is the victim of the negligence,
is thus the illiberal offshoot of a very liberal doctrine.
The fellow-servant stands in our law as unfavorably as,
but not more unfavorably than, any other person under
the civil law. The difference is that in the civil law his
rule is the normal and general rule, while in the common
law it is an exception from a rule which has come to be
accepted as the rule of ordinary justice. No wonder
then that workingmen felt and feel aggrieved.

Mr. Asquith, explaining in Parliament the law of
employer's liability, ascribed the exceptions from normal
rules which prejudiced the workmen to the consideration
that if the ordinary rule were enforced in such cases it
would operate to check the development of industry and
the investment of capital (8 Hansard 1943, 1893). But

if any such idea operated on the minds of the judges, no
trace of it is to be found in reported opinions, and the
judges were probably quite unaware of it. The trouble
was here, as in other cases, that they considered the
problem as if it concerned abstract relations between convertible human personalities, while it was a problem concerning industry and a class. The law did not take
cognizance of this fact until the multiplied effects of the
rule reflected themselves in class-reaction and class-
consciousness.

Most of the common law has developed in that
atmosphere of indifferent neutrality which has enabled
courts to be impartial but also keeps them out of touch
with vital needs. When interests are litigated in particular cases, they not only appear as scattered and isolated interests, but their social incidence is obscured by
the adventitious personal factor which colors every
controversy. If policy means the conscious favoring of
social above particular interests, the common law must
be charged with having too much justice and too little
policy. It has fallen to the task of modern legislation to
redress the balance.

While public policy is thus subordinate and elusive as
a factor entering into the law of property and contract,
it is also somewhat vague and unsatisfactory where it
appears as a distinct doctrine, as it does when we speak
of acts or agreements contrary to public policy or of torts
or crimes in violation of general public interests. The
courts appear to have kept the notion flexible on purpose.

AGREEMENTS CONTRARY TO PUBLIC POLICY

It is a commonplace that an agreement for the doing of a thing immoral or forbidden by law will not be enforced. An agreement in consideration of the doing of such a thing stands, generally speaking, on the same footing, though in England a bond given in return for past illicit cohabitation has been held valid as a voluntary bond (*Gray* v. *Mathias*, 5 Ves. 286, 1800). The only serious controversy that has arisen in this branch of the law is whether betting or wagering contracts are unlawful, and the rule in England has come to be that in order to render them void there must be something about the particular subject-matter or object of the wager that is objectionable or prejudicial to public or private interests (see Cowper, pp. 37 and 729; also 2 Term Rep. 610). In some of the American states this lenient doctrine has been repudiated, and betting or wagering contracts, irrespective of any particular features, have been declared unenforceable (3 N.H. 152, 1825; 2 Vt. 144, 1829; 1 Strobh. S.C. 82, 1846). The unsettled state of the common law should be contrasted with the very pronounced legislative policy against gambling of any kind.

Much greater interest attaches to those cases in which agreements are held to be contrary to public policy, although the law looks with unconcern upon their being carried out. Agreements in restraint of marriage and many forms of agreements in restraint of trade are the most conspicuous instances in point. A person may refuse to marry if he chooses, but a bond conditioned upon remaining unmarried will not be enforced. A person may decline to sell below a certain price, but a price-maintenance agreement is invalid; he may limit his output, but cannot legally bind himself toward another to do so.

It is tempting to say that what the law discountenances in these cases is the premature binding of a freedom of decision which ought to remain unfettered until the time of action has arrived. This would represent a pronounced policy in favor of personal rights, subordinating the abstract freedom of will as expressed in the binding obligation of contract to the concrete freedom of action where the latter seems material to the freedom of social movement or to the conservation of other social values. But the study of English decisions hardly supports this otherwise attractive theory and reveals a much more utilitarian view of public interest. Much attention has always been given to the exceptions to the rule against agreements in restraint of trade. A reasonable restraint is allowed, and the most important application of the exception is found in covenants not to compete, which are incidental to the sale of a good-will or to a contract of employment. Such a covenant must not exceed the bounds of reasonableness. What is the criterion of reasonableness? If we examine the English decisions down to a very recent date, we find that the criteria are adequate protection to the covenantee and the leaving of ample facilities for the service of the public. The consideration that the covenantor shall not be hampered unduly in pursuing his means of livelihood represents a larger policy, identifying public interest, not merely with facilities for public service, but with the largest opportunity for individual usefulness. This aspect of the matter seems hardly to have been considered in the earlier cases, which allow lifelong restraints upon an employee against setting up in business or accepting employment with rival firms anywhere within a large metropolis or other district (*Mattan* v. *May*, 11 M. & W. 653, 1843, surgeon-dentist's assistant, entire city of London; *Mumford* v. *Gelking*, 7 C.B.N.S. 305, 1859, midland district of England, commercial traveler) on the ground that such covenants are proper securities for the protection of the employer and encourage rather than cramp the employment of capital in trade and the promotion of industry. Four very recent cases are, however, very much more favorable to the employee,[1] and the observation of Lord Haldane in one of these, that "the practice of putting into these agreements anything that is favorable to the employer is one which the courts have to check," seems to mark a turning-point in this phase of the English law. Similar restraints upon employees seem to be unusual in America, where undoubtedly a

---

[1] *Mason* v. *Provident, etc., Co.*, 1913, A.C. 724; *Nevanas, etc., Co.* v. *Walker*, 1914, 1 Ch. 413; *Eastes* v. *Russ*, 1914, 1 Ch. 468; *Herbert Morris, Ltd.* v. *Saxelby*, 1915, 2 Ch. 57; 1916, A.C. 688, particularly the opinion of Lord Shaw of Dunfermline: "Under modern conditions, both of society and of trade, it would appear to be in accord with the public interest to open and not to shut the market of these islands to the skilled labour and the commercial and industrial abilities of its inhabitants, to further and not to obstruct for these *les carrières ouvertes*."

strong public sentiment would condemn such a hampering of the freedom of individual action.

A similar question is presented by the attitude of the law toward what is called "contracting out," that is to say, agreements by which the benefit of a rule of law imposing some liability is waived in advance of the liability arising, by the person intended to be benefited by the rule. The question has practically arisen in England in connection with the Employer's Liability Act of 1880, in America in connection with stipulations of railroad companies for exemption from liability for the negligence of their employees.

The English decision has been in favor of the right to contract out (*Griffiths* v. *Earl of Dudley*, 9 Q.B.D. 357, 1882). The employer had in that case been a liberal contributor to an employees' pension fund, and no contracting-out stipulation appears to have come before English courts in which that was not the case. This element undoubtedly entered as an important factor into the decision that the contract did not violate public policy, and it would therefore be unwarranted to draw the general conclusion that an advance exoneration from tort liability is valid under the English law. If the silence of the books upon the subject is due to the fact that bald stipulations for immunity from liability for personal injury have not as a matter of fact been brought to judicial test, this rather points to a popular belief that such agreements are illegitimate. The practice of railroad companies exempting themselves from liability for injury to property led to the enactment of legislation leaving it to the trial judge to determine the reasonableness of the condition (Railway and Canal Traffic Act, 1854, sec. 7); but no similar legislation exists with regard to passengers or other persons.

In America we find it strongly held that the rule of employer's liability cannot be avoided by contract between employer and employee (*Johnston* v. *Fargo*, 184 N.Y. 379); but the decision related to an unqualified contract of exemption supported by no other consideration than the employment itself. The American reports also show a number of important cases passing on the validity of stipulations by railroad companies against their liability for injuries to persons carried by them. In all these cases there was some special consideration, if only a reduced rate, and in New York the agreement was sustained, while the Supreme Court of the United States adopts a stricter rule (*Bissell* v. *R. Co.*, 25 N.Y. 443; *Railroad Co.* v. *Lockwood*, 17 Wall. 357; but see *B. & O. S.W. Ry. Co.* v. *Voigt*, 176 U.S. 498). If on the whole the American courts seem less inclined to recognize a right to contract out than the English courts, the explanation may perhaps be found in part in the character of the cases which have arisen in the respective jurisdictions, and in neither of the two countries is the doctrine entirely settled.

Again, however, particular notice should be taken of the judicial concept of public policy. New York supported the validity of the exemption in the case of gratuitously carried passengers by the argument that their number was so small that the inducement to adopt safeguards could not be materially affected by non-liability to them (24 N.Y. 185). The English court, in permitting exoneration from the Employer's Liability Act of 1880, said that it was at least doubtful whether, where a contract is said to be void as against public policy, some public policy which affects all society is not meant, and that in the present case the interest of the employed only could be affected.

The idea that the policy of the law is opposed to a freedom of contract which results in the bargaining away of bodily safety and the lowering of strict standards of care does not appear conspicuously until a very recent decision of the New York Court of Appeals (*Johnston* v. *Fargo*, 184 N.Y. 379, 385, 1906). We find, on the contrary, strong intimations of a theory that the defenses of assumption of risk and of common employment which in the majority of cases negative any liability on the part of the employer are the result of implied contract, that is to say, of the employee contracting himself out of the benefit of a normal rule making for safety, and that the strict employers' liability legislation merely negatives the implied contract, thus leaving room for the reinstatement of the defenses by express agreement (9 Q.B.D. on p. 363). The two defenses become far more objectionable, if based upon the fiction of an agreement, than if they are derived from the nature of the relation. A classical expression of the older view, which sounds to us

like a travesty on common-sense, may be found in the
dissenting opinion of Lord Bramwell, one of the most
distinguished of Victorian judges, in the case of *Smith* v.
Baker (1891 A.C. 325), and his words should be quoted
in full:

It is a rule of good sense that if a man voluntarily undertakes
a risk for a reward which is adequate to induce him, he shall not,
if he suffers from the risk, have a compensation for which he did
not stipulate. He can if he chooses say: "I will undertake the
risk for so much, and if hurt you must give me so much more or
an adequate equivalent for the hurt." But drop the maxim.
Treat it as a question of bargain. The plaintiff here thought the
pay worth the risk and did not bargain for a compensation if hurt;
in effect he undertook the work with its risks for his wages and no
more. He says so. Suppose he had said, "If I am to run this risk
you must give me six shillings a day, and not five shillings," and
the master agreed, would he in reason have a claim if he got hurt?
Clearly not. What difference is there if the master says, "No, I will
only give you five shillings?" None. I am ashamed to argue it.

But *Smith* v. *Baker* is generally regarded as marking a
turning-point in the law. The doctrine of freedom of
contract flourished during the greater portion of the reign
of Queen Victoria, and in its extreme form was stated by
Sir George Jessel in 1875:

It must not be forgotten that you are not to extend arbitrarily
those rules which say that a given contract is void as being against
public policy, because if there is one thing which more than any
other public policy requires, it is that man of full age and competent
understanding shall have the utmost liberty of contracting, and
that their contracts when entered into freely and voluntarily
shall be held sacred and shall be enforced by courts of justice.

Therefore, you have this paramount policy to consider—that you are not lightly to interfere with this freedom of contract. Now, there is no doubt public policy may say that a contract to commit a crime, or a contract to give a reward to another to commit a crime, is necessarily void. The decisions have gone further, and contracts to commit an immoral offense, or to induce another to do something against the general rules of morality, though far more indefinite than the previous class, have always been held to be void. I should be sorry to extend the doctrine much further. I do not say there are no other cases to which it does apply; but I should be sorry to extend it much further.[1]

In the same year, 1875, a new phase of social legislation, the first Agricultural Holdings Act (38 & 39 Vict., ch. 92), made its provisions expressly subject to be set aside by agreement, "freedom of contract" being the ruling consideration. But the Ground Game Act of 1880 for the first time introduced a distinct clause invalidating contrary agreements, and in 1883 the same rule was applied to the amended Agricultural Holdings Act of that year, reversing the policy of 1875. In the workmen's compensation legislation of 1897 careful provision is made for substitute schemes, and they are not left to a general right of "contracting out." The American Federal Employers' Liability Act of 1908 contains a strong clause annulling contrary agreements, and it may be assumed that even without express provision such agreements would at present be held to be invalid. If agreements to avoid the operation of mechanics' lien legislation are held valid or are expressly sanctioned by

[1] L.R. 19 Eq. 462, 465.

statute, this is an exception due to the doubts entertained concerning the principle of that legislation (see 251 Ill. 135, and Laws of Illinois, 1913, p. 400). The more recent legislation reflects altered views regarding the freedom of contract, but Sir George Jessel was probably right when he declared that freedom to have been the paramount policy of the common law.

PUBLIC POLICY IN THE LAW OF TORTS AND MISDEMEANORS

The legal status of agreements in restraint of marriage or of "contracting out" under the more recent judicial doctrine shows that an act contrary to public policy is not necessarily illegal in the sense in which the term is used in the law of torts and crimes, so as to give occasion to positive measures of redress, either by way of penalty or by way of damages. Where the law is systematically classified, crimes belong to public law and torts to private law; but that the illegality of torts has also a public aspect is shown by the fact that practically every tort when committed under aggravating circumstances becomes a crime.

The more serious crimes touch the very foundations of social order; the Anglo-Saxon or early Anglicized terms of the more important felonies—murder, mayhem, rape, robbery, burglary, arson, larceny—indicate old-established and firmly settled notions, while in the law of torts only the term trespass suggests ancient and customary origins. The very simplicity of the underlying standards seems to remove these branches of the law from the domain of public policy, which as usually understood refers to interests either controversial or at least more or less openly opposed by considerable elements of the community. We should hardly refer to murder as a crime against public policy, and although problems of prosecution and punishment raise profound issues of policy, these issues are in a manner foreign to the community at large, which looks upon criminal procedure as a thing apart and outside of the sphere of common interests.

It is otherwise with regard to less evil and lawless practices endangering social interests, forms of misconduct, or machinations devoid of violence and not constituting either trespass, breach of peace, or felony. Negligence, nuisance, and conspiracy are the principal categories of wrong which, whether as torts or as misdemeanors, involve considerations of public policy— negligence, as endangering safety; nuisance, as a menace to health and comfort; and conspiracy, on account of its connection with forms of economic oppression and exploitation. The limitations of the common law in connection with these three branches of the law of torts and crimes have had important bearings upon modern legislation.

The manifold dangers to life and limb resulting from the employment of great mechanical forces in industry and transportation have raised causes of action for negligence to the first place in civil litigation. In Prussia the introduction of railroads was followed almost immediately (in 1838) by the establishment of a rule of liability irrespective of negligence, and subject only to the defense of force of nature or the injured person's own fault, and this law was subsequently extended to the German Empire (Act of June 7, 1871). This step was not taken either in England or in America; but the courts uniformly applied to railroad companies as carriers of passengers an extremely high standard of care, and it is probably true that the rigorous enforcement of strict rules of liability has contributed more than any other factor to the present standard of safety in railroad transportation. A marked contrast is presented by the law of negligence in its internal industrial aspect. The principles of liability which operate between railroad companies and the public at large are almost nullified in the relation between railroad companies and their employees as a consequence of the defenses which qualify the liability of the employer.

These defenses (assumption of risk and common employment) operate in all industries, and the utterly unsatisfactory character of the law of negligence in the field of industry has produced the demand first for safety legislation, then for a modification of the common law of employer's liability, and finally for workmen's compensation. The fact that negligence does not constitute a tort in the absence of actual damage suffered has also barred the way to effective preventive relief; there seems to be no case in which an injunction has been sought or granted against unsafe or unsanitary working conditions. As regards dangers to health, the law of negligence, indeed, affords no adequate relief even by way of redress, for in nearly all cases of occupational disease it is impossible to establish the chain of causation between some particular employment and loss of health resulting in injury, or if the causation is established, it is counteracted by assumption of risk or contributory negligence.[1] Where disease is contracted through insanitary dwellings, the common law of landlord and tenant relieves the former of any duty, and negligence can therefore not be predicated. The difference made by the common law in the protection accorded to the public at large (passengers) and to dependent groups (employees, tenants), to the disadvantage of the latter, is obvious.

Nuisance as a tort covers in part the same ground as negligence; but the law of nuisance has in so far a narrower application, as it is regularly confined to injuries concerning the enjoyment of property. Under circumstances an unsafe or insanitary factory, mine, or tenement might give a cause of action for nuisance to the owner of an adjoining property, but not to employees or mere occupiers. Thus nuisance counts for less than negligence as a civil weapon for the protection of social interests; it concerns itself with persons only as landowners and through the medium of property rights (*Kavanagh* v. *Barber*, 131 N.Y. 211).

[1] The difficulties are well set forth by Professor F. H. Bohlen in 63 *University of Pennsylvania Law Review* 183. There is also the additional difficulty of apportioning liability between different establishments in which the employees may have worked while contracting the disease. This is taken care of by sec. 8*c*. (3) of the English Workmen's Compensation Act of 1906.

The law of conspiracy in its civil aspect might have been expected to play some part in the struggle against monopolistic combinations. It is therefore interesting to learn from the opinions rendered in a leading English case (*Mogul S.S. Co.* v. *McGregor*, 1892 A.C. 25) that no damages had ever previously been recovered in English courts by a trader against a trade combination cutting off his trade on account of his refusal to join the combination. The decision in that case denied the actionability of injurious practices designed to insure the success of the combination. The American reports likewise fail to show successful actions for damages against capitalistic combinations, until such a cause of action was created by the anti-trust legislation of the last decade of the nineteenth century.

It is true that common-law actions have been sustained against labor combinations, and that injunctions against picketing and boycotts have been granted repeatedly by courts of equity; and it is also characteristic that the most conspicuously successful of civil actions for damages under the federal anti-trust act has been brought against a labor union (*Lawlor* v. *Loewe*, 235 U.S. 522). Even if the object of such actions were more commonly than it actually is the protection of the rights of labor rather than the protection of the property of the employer, the civil law of conspiracy cannot be said to have coped successfully with the great problem of combination. The line between lawful persuasion and coercion remains largely undefined, and the extent to which collective effort and power may be carried legitimately is as yet uncertain; no doctrine of defenses comparable to that of privilege in the law of libel has been developed. The very fact that the courts have begun to discuss these questions only within the last twenty years shows how little the freedom of economic action owes to the civil law of conspiracy.

CRIMINAL ASPECT OF OFFENSES AGAINST PUBLIC POLICY

The relative importance of negligence, conspiracy, and nuisance changes as we approach them from the point of view of the criminal law.

If negligence results in the death of another, it constitutes manslaughter, which is a felony. Looking merely at constituent elements, it takes in some respects less to make a case of criminal guilt than of civil liability; for it is not necessary to show any pecuniary loss or damage to a representative of the person killed, nor would assumption of risk or contributory negligence on his part be recognized as defenses to a criminal prosecution (21 Cyc. 766). Nevertheless, criminal responsibility has been a negligible factor in comparison with civil liability as an incentive to raising standards of safety; for the requirements for establishing criminal guilt, as regards proof of causation, are stricter than in civil cases. The instructions given in the trial of the Triangle Waist Fire case in New York[1] illustrate the difficulties that have to be overcome in the way of evidence and which are so likely to lead to acquit-

[1] See *Chicago Legal News*, January 20, 1912.

tals or mistrials. The conviction obtained in the case of the fire which destroyed the steamboat "General Slocum" was a conspicuous exception to a general rule (*U.S.* v. *Van Schaick*, 134 Fed. 592).

Apart from homicide through carelessness, the common law knows no offense of criminal negligence, nor any offense of negligent injury to person or property. Unless the conditions due to the neglect or carelessness amount to a nuisance, there is no power to prosecute, and the fear of criminal responsibility will fail entirely as an inducement to the taking of necessary precautions to avoid accident. In the relation between employer and employee this defect of the common law is of particular significance.

Criminal conspiracy.—The law of conspiracy is as unsatisfactory in its criminal as in its civil aspect. The Mogul Steamship Company case was an action for damages, but the arguments by which the court disproves the existence of an actionable tort are equally applicable to dispose of the contention that a combination in restraint of trade constitutes a crime; and they are so understood and accepted by an authoritative text-writer.[1] A hundred years earlier the understanding of the law would probably have been different, and the charge of criminal conspiracy might have been maintained.

American states, in codifying the common law of crimes, have not hesitated to include in the enumeration

[1] Russell on *Crimes*, I. 492.

of the objects of a criminal conspiracy "acts injurious to public health, to public morals, or to trade or commerce" (New York Penal Law, sec. 580), and in 1893 a capitalistic combination was successfully prosecuted under this very general provision (*People* v. *Sheldon*, 139 N.Y. 251). Both in England and in America the law of criminal conspiracy in its application to trade had as a matter of history become associated in the public mind with attempts to repress labor combinations and strikes, and in the early part of the nineteenth century prosecutions of labor organizations for conspiracy had resulted in convictions in New York and Pennsylvania.[1] A decision of the Supreme Court of Massachusetts rendered in 1842 (*Com.* v. *Hunt*, 4 Metc. 111) marks a turning-point in the judicial attitude toward combinations of labor; but the law of criminal conspiracy has become unfortunately tainted with the suspicion of being an instrument of class-oppression.

As regards combinations of capital, they do not in America appear to have become the subject of criminal prosecution for common-law conspiracy; and authoritative treatises exhibit the greatest uncertainty as to the existence and scope of common-law crimes in restraint of trade;[2] hence it is safe to say that in 1890, when the Sherman anti-trust law was enacted, no person in or out of Congress could have stated with any confidence what

---

[1] Carson, *Criminal Conspiracy; Documentary History of American Industrial Society*, Vols. III, IV; Freund, *Police Power*, sec. 331.

[2] Bishop, *New Criminal Law*, secs. 518–28.

constituted a criminal conspiracy in restraint of trade at common law, and in penalizing unqualifiedly all combinations in restraint of commerce Congress took a leap in the dark and set a task to the courts with which they are still wrestling.

While, in so far as we can speak of a common-law policy, there appears to be no discrimination in theory between combinations of labor and of capital, unquestionably the common law, as distinguished from the recent anti-trust legislation, has been used chiefly, if not exclusively, against the former. At the same time it has proved entirely inadequate to cope with the great economic and social problems involved in labor troubles, even more so than the legislation framed upon the same lines has failed to cope with the problem of capitalistic combination and consolidation. The vagueness of the offense, so far from being an advantage in dealing with controverted issues, has placed criminal prosecution under the suspicion of meddling or arbitrariness, and has condemned it to ultimate failure.

Common nuisance.—The scope of nuisance is as vague and elastic as that of conspiracy. Blackstone, in discussing it, speaks of an offense against public order and the economical regimen of the state, and of neglecting to do a thing which the common good requires. A statute of Oklahoma paraphrases the common law not inaptly by defining the offense as unlawfully doing any act or omitting to perform any duty required by the public good which annoys or injures the comfort or safety of the people, or offends public decency, or renders life uncomfortable.

Both conspiracy and nuisance are offenses of degree, with this difference, that the former relates to acts which so long as they are legitimate are inoffensive, and even useful, while the acts and things which if carried to excess become nuisances are even this side of that line offensive and ordinarily (except in the case of trade nuisances) matter of mere indulgence. The law of nuisance is therefore not likely to become an instrument of oppression or mischief. It might, on the contrary, be urged that wisely used it should constitute an effective check against the tendencies toward new forms of danger and evil that unregulated life in the community constantly develops. Theoretically, it might be said, the law of nuisance is the common law of the police power, striking at all gross violations of health, safety, order, and morals. Indeed, the English and American reports show sporadic cases in which what may be called police offenses have been proceeded against successfully as common nuisances: the exposing of infected persons on public streets (*King* v. *Burnett*, 4 M. & S. 272); the exhibition of indecent pictures for money (*Com.* v. *Sharpless*, 2 S. & R. 91); the maintenance of notorious adulterous relations (*Adams* v. *Com.*, 151 S.W. 1006); acrobatic performances on the street (*Hall's case*, Ventr. 169); a house for slaughtering horses (*R.* v. *Cross*, 2 C. & P. 483); the carrying on of other physically offensive trades or industries (Bishop, *Crim. Law*, sec.

1143); or the exposure of unwholesome provisions for sale in a public market (Bishop, sec. 491). In 1629 the judges expressed the opinion that the use of carriages of excessive weight on the public roads constituted a public nuisance (Rymer's *Foedera*, 19, p. 130). It was sought at one time to proceed against unincorporated companies as public nuisances, but without success (Lindley on *Companies*, p. 180). Perhaps the most remarkable attempt to extend the law of common nuisance was made in Indiana in 1907, when a criminal prosecution was instituted charging the keeper of a licensed place for the sale of intoxicating liquors with maintaining a public nuisance, on the ground, not only that the sale of such liquors was indictable at common law, but that to authorize such an injurious business was unconstitutional. Notwithstanding the plain unsoundness of both propositions, the court thought it necessary to devote extended arguments to their refutation (*Sopher* v. *State*, 169 Ind. 177–204).[1] The cases are cited merely to illustrate the imagined potentialities of the idea of a nuisance at common law.

It is obvious, however, that the law of nuisance is inadequate as a substitute for modern police regulation: it takes cognizance of practices only when danger passes into actual mischief. A factory without safeguards against fire or accident; a tenement house without sanitary conveniences; an unfenced railroad track or an unguarded grade crossing; offering for sale fruit

[1] The claim that a saloon, though licensed and conducted in an orderly manner, may constitute a private nuisance had been sustained by a divided court somewhat earlier, *Haggart* v. *Stehlin*, 137 Ind. 43.

deceptively packed; a bucket shop; a white phosphorus
match factory; betting on elections—all these fall as
short of a common-law nuisance as the place for the sale
of intoxicating liquors; nor do they offend against any
other common-law principle. On the other hand, however, the common law is not sufficiently considerate of
the requirements of industry, for the law of trade nuisances takes no account of the value or benefit of offensive
manufacturing processes. That a nuisance at common
law cannot be predicated upon dangers due to purely
natural conditions, without human action or default,
would perhaps not materially impair its availability from
a social point of view; it is more serious that a nuisance
must be alleged to be to the injury of all the persons
residing in a given neighborhood (6 Cushing 80); for that
requirement negatives the offense where merely definite
groups of persons are affected by the danger or mischief,
as, e.g., the workers in a factory or the occupants of a
tenement house.

Thus for many of the modern conditions requiring
control or relief not even the very elastic and comprehensive law of nuisance affords an adequate or appropriate
remedy, and we are forced to the conclusion that the
common law of torts and crimes does not furnish the
protection called for by present needs.

SHORTCOMINGS OF THE COMMON LAW AS A SYSTEM OF PUBLIC POLICY

If the foregoing survey has on the whole been rather
a summary of defects, and should appear to place too low

an estimate upon the serviceability of the common law, it should be remembered that the point of view has been that of modern social needs and interests, and that in consequence that aspect of the common law has been ignored to which the labors of courts and lawyers have been mainly devoted, namely, its function in adjusting conflicts of interests in which the contending parties appear simply as representatives of purely private interests and generally as holders of property dealing with each other on equal terms.

Not only would other systems of private law, developed mainly on the basis of custom and of adjudication, notably the Roman and the Germanic systems, yield but little different results if subjected to a like test, but even a modern codification like that of Germany, undertaken at a time when the social functions of legislation were fully realized, did not attempt to make the civil code the vehicle for carrying into effect every desirable social reform,[1] but constructed it with a primary view to abstract and equal justice between private and presumably equivalent interests.   While this individualistic attitude has been criticized, it represents a perfectly intelligible method and principle, and the expansion of the civil and the common law over practically the entire civilized world demonstrates the success of those systems in meeting the needs of the prevailing economic constitution.

[1] There are conspicuous exceptions; see, e.g., secs. 138, 296, 530, 544, 617-19, 624, 671, 1245, 1654.

Judged from the standpoint of modern demands, the shortcomings of the common law, as it stood in the early part of the nineteenth century, may be recapitulated as follows:

First, its standards had failed to keep pace with advancing or changing ideals; it was most emphatic in maintaining order and authority, least emphatic in relieving social weakness and inferiority; it developed no principles of reasonableness regarding economic standards or equivalents (oppressive practices of employment, landlords' obligations, reasonableness of price); its ideal of public policy was too exclusively the advantage of the many and not sufficiently the regard for the claims of individual personality; equity was absorbed with property interests to the neglect of non-material human rights.

Secondly, the system of rights and obligations was too abstract and undifferentiated; as illustrated by the well-known story of the deserted husband who was driven to bigamy because he could not afford the expense of a divorce by special act of Parliament, the law made no difference between the rich and the poor and virtually became a law for the rich; the fundamental social and economic changes brought about by the industrial revolution remained unreflected in common-law principles.

Thirdly, in matter concerning social security (represented chiefly by the law of nuisance and fraud) the common law hewed too close to the line of actual mischief to afford effectual protection; the law of nuisance proved inadequate for the purpose of sanitation or safety in industry or transportation; the law of fraud was too lax to insure commercial fair dealing, and with regard to liquor and gambling, common-law illegality begins only with disorderly practices.

Fourthly, in the common-law offenses against public policy, especially nuisance and conspiracy, the concept of public injury was too vague for practical guidance and, in consequence, fatally defective for impartial and vigorous criminal enforcement.

Finally, the spirit of the common law was too neutral for an effective offensive against practices injurious to the weaker elements of society. There was no adequate organization for initiating criminal prosecution, and civil remedies were expensive and dilatory and unduly favored pecuniary resource and professional skill. While this aspect of the common law has not been discussed in the foregoing survey, it would have to enter largely into any discussion of modern administrative and procedural reform, and it accounts for important phases of the recently enacted workmen's compensation legislation.

CHAPTER III

THE TASKS AND HAZARDS OF LEGISLATION

If the tasks of legislation are set by the traditional shortcomings of the common law or by its failure to adjust itself to changing conditions, we should expect to find in modern regulative statutes a general endeavor to define vague restraints or prohibitions, to strike at antisocial conditions at a point more remote from actual loss and injury, and to give effect to altered concepts of right and wrong and of the public good. Such, in fact, is the scope and content of modern welfare legislation.

Not only, however, is it inevitable that the legislature should not always clearly comprehend its task and therefore perpetuate, instead of correcting, common-law defects, but it must also happen that, in narrowing the bounds of toleration, legislation will now and then antagonize important and powerful interests, and will be challenged for having taken its new stand upon insufficient justification.

The problems thus created should be considered somewhat in detail.

A. LEGISLATION AND THE VAGUENESS OF COMMON-LAW STANDARDS

1. *Restraint of trade and monopoly.*—The failure to correct common-law inadequacies has been most conspicuous in dealing with the problem of combinations in

restraint of trade. The common law of conspiracy was notoriously uncertain as to the nature and extent of illegal practices, whether as a matter of tort or of crime, whether applied to labor or to capital. When toward the end of the eighties of the last century a strong apprehension seized the nation with regard to the dangers and evils of monopolistic combination, a demand for new legislation arose, and the absence of a federal common law of crimes made legislation for interstate commerce necessary if repressive action was to be taken by the national government. In the great mass of anti-trust legislation practically nothing was done, however, to specify forbidden practices with adequate certainty. The federal act of 1890 is typical in that respect. It declared unlawful and actionable, and penalized, any combination in restraint of commerce between the states, and also any monopoly or attempt at monopoly. Any doubt under the common law as to whether such a combination constituted a tort or crime was thereby removed, but not the doubt as to the precise practices which the act intended to cover.

In the first important cases in which the Supreme Court interpreted the act (*Trans-Missouri case*, 166 U.S. 290, 1897; *Joint Traffic case*, 171 U.S. 505, 1898) it was held that every agreement which the common law rendered merely void, i.e., any agreement restraining competition between two separate concerns, except certain covenants incidental to the sale of a good-will or to an employment, was now liable to prosecution, irrespective of its economic purpose and effect. If the law thus interpreted worked out unreasonably—and its unreasonableness as regards railroad-traffic understandings was convincingly demonstrated by the dissenting opinion of Justice White (166 U.S. 363, 364, 370, 371)— the act in its sweeping prohibition left at least little room for uncertainty so far as agreements were concerned as distinguished from monopolistic consolidations; for the illegality of the latter was entirely a matter of degree, undefined and undefinable. In the Standard Oil and Tobacco cases, however (221 U.S. 1, 106, 1911), the Supreme Court, speaking through the Chief Justice who, as Associate Justice, had dissented from the first interpretation of the act, made certain observations which have been generally understood as meaning that the test of prejudice to the public would be applied to combinations if proceeded against by the government. The result of this more liberal view was that the line separating immune from condemned practices was again one entirely of degree and effect. At once it was contended that if the commission or non-commission of the offense depended upon criteria thus vague and governed by subjective differences of opinion, there was a denial of due process. The contention was rejected by the Supreme Court which pointed out that similar uncertainty had characterized a number of common-law offenses, and that it would be difficult to condemn traditional common-law standards as inconsistent with due process (*Nash* v. *U.S.*, 229 U.S. 373, 1913). The law thus stands unrepealed at the present day, although by the supplementary Clayton Act of 1914 a number of practices are specifically defined as unlawful. More significant is the new departure which the Trade Commission Act, passed at the same time, makes in dealing with unfair methods of competition. There is likewise an entire absence of definition in this act, but the act creates no new criminal offense. The Trade Commission investigates practices and forbids them if they are found contrary to the act, its orders being subject to judicial review, and disobedience to these orders being liable to punishment. There will thus be a gradual definition of unlawful practices by administrative and judicial rulings without, however, penalizing conduct preceding such definition. In view of the controverted issues beclouding the notion of unfair competition, there is force in the contention that there is a delegation of a truly legislative function, and it may be that a conservative interpretation of the act will disappoint those who expect that the act will develop a code of rules for the checking of various undesirable practices, such as price-cutting and similar methods of doing business. But at least a rational attempt has been made to improve upon the method of the anti-trust legislation, which in the matter of restraint of trade achieved very little, if any, progress beyond the common law.

2. *Legislation and the common law of fraud.*—It is not without significance that when in 1896 Germany undertook to legislate against unfair competition the resulting act confined itself to dealing with certain distinctly

fraudulent practices, such as false representations regarding quality or prices of goods or sources of supply, misleading trade names, etc. In making fraud a necessary element the law chose as a criterion of illegality a form of intrinsically wrongful conduct, which is also as capable of definition as most other abstract legal notions, whereas an offense of restraint of trade, if left by the statute without any qualification, is an economic absurdity, and if qualified by requiring injury to the public, is too indefinite for purposes of criminal enforcement. If the common law of fraud was inadequate, it was because on the civil side its standard of commercial truthfulness and care in making statements was not sufficiently high (*Derry* v. *Peek*, 14 App. Cas. 337, 1889), and because on the criminal side it took cognizance only of aggravated forms of fraud (false tokens)—in other words, because a lenient view was taken, not because the concept was inherently too vague for adequate judicial definition.

To a considerable extent this leniency had been supplemented and remedied from a very early period, as far as commercial dealings were concerned, by elaborate systems of trade regulation, proceeding first from corporate authorities and subsequently from Parliament. All these regulations purported to be made in the interest of honest workmanship and trade; but they were likely to suffer from the tendency to officious intermeddling resented by trade as a hindrance to its development. The English Statutes of the Realm show a considerable number of acts, beginning in the reign of Edward III, and particularly numerous in the fifteenth and sixteenth centuries, concerning the true making and vending of certain commodities (wool, linen, worsted, cloth, leather, wax, tiles, malt, oil, etc.), and the work of certain artisans and manufacturers (painters, plasterers, upholsterers, etc.). After the reign of James I this legislation disappears for over one hundred years, but a few isolated acts recur in the eighteenth century (1738, woolen cloths, 11 George II 28; 1769 and 1777, brick and tile, 10 George III 49, 17 George III 42). A long list of these statutes, apparently covering the entire series, was repealed in 1856 (19 and 20 Victoria, ch. 64). In the first revision of the statutes of New York the provisions for the regulation of trade are of almost equal number and prominence with those regulating the internal police of public order, safety, and health; but the constitution of 1846, by abrogating the old inspection offices and forbidding their re-establishment, deprived the formerly well-known New York system of trade regulation of its most characteristic feature. Here, then, we have the exceptional case of a distinct dropping of previous legislative restraint, due in England to a strong economic current against state regulation of industry, and in New York to dissatisfaction with the multitude of officials and their perquisites. Legislation for securing high commercial standards has never regained the importance which it formerly had, and at present there is an inclination to support if possible the regulation of trade on grounds of safety or health rather than on the ground of the prevention of fraud.

3. *Legislation and the common law of nuisance.*—A comparison of the great mass of modern health, safety, and morals legislation with the common law of nuisance illustrates both the substitution of precise for undefined restraints and prohibitions and the more effectual protection afforded by moving the line of illegality farther away from the point of actual mischief.

As regards the former point, however, nuisance does not stand quite on the same footing as conspiracy in restraint of trade. The law of nuisance, it is true, penalizes noxious and offensive conditions without indicating precisely the point at which criminality begins; but that constitutes a hardship only where the offensive condition represents at the same time some legitimate and valuable interest. The significance of this qualification appears when we compare the nuisance of lewdness and obscenity with what is called a trade nuisance.

Lewdness and obscenity: The offense of lewdness and obscenity (the terms are not carefully distinguished from each other) is a matter of circumstance, spirit, and purpose, but these are on the whole so well understood that in the great majority of cases it is clear enough whether acts or conditions fall under the criminal law. The lack of precise demarcation has never presented any danger or inconvenience to the essential interests of truth as represented by scientific teaching and publication, for the traditions of science have always found the propagation of truth compatible with the selection of channels by which scandal and offense to the community are avoided. For the legitimate claims of art and literature a reasonably safe guide is found in established convention, which concedes very considerabl.: license and cannot be charged with intolerance. If the analogy of the law of libel may be used, it might not be incorrect to say that no less than an absolute privilege will satisfy the needs of science, while art and literature enjoy a qualified privilege that should depend, not only upon the genuineness of the alleged motive and appeal, but also upon its conformity to recognized canons.

Undoubtedly some difficulty has been experienced in reconciling supposed common-law inhibitions with certain phases of social propaganda (particularly in connection with attacks upon the confessional and the agitation for birth control), and there have been illiberal decisions in isolated cases. The privilege afforded by genuineness of motive and appeal ought to be at least as wide as in the case of art and literature, and if we judge the "living law" by established practice and not by exceptional cases which are disproportionately conspicuous in the recorded history of the law, this seems to be recognized. Legislation could probably do no more than circumscribe with more or less elaborateness limitations and qualifications, which are generally understood and accepted. A clear and explicit authoritative statement of the law might be desirable; but an attempt at legislation would involve the risk of narrowing the existing domain of freedom in deference to sentiment or prejudice.

Trade nuisances: It is probably also true that an exclusive reference to adjudicated cases gives us an incorrect view of the operation of the common law of nuisances in its criminal aspect so far as it applies to noxious trades. Both English and American reports down to very recent times show cases in which valuable industries have been condemned as nuisances, and the number of cases in which the charge of nuisance has been held to be made out, or at least, assuming the facts to be true, to have been stated with legal sufficiency, is perhaps greater than the number of cases in which the court concluded as a matter of law that there was no nuisance. An altogether different picture of the situation presents itself, however, when we consider the enormous number of offensive establishments which are known to exist and the small number of cases that have come before the courts. But while in the matter both of offensive publications and of trade nuisances cases of conviction where there is a genuine claim of a legal interest are the exceptional cases, the difference is that in some of the cases of publications held to be obscene it is possible to contend that the law was misapplied, while it can hardly be denied that the law of trade nuisances without misapplication clearly prejudices valuable and essential interests and is quite inconsistent with the legitimate demands of industry. Not only danger to life, limb, and health, but mere offensiveness to the senses, makes an enjoinable, abatable, and technically a punishable nuisance, and this irrespective of the economic benefit to

the community; for it has been said that there will be
no balancing of public benefit and public inconvenience
(*The King* v. *Ward*, 4 A. & E. 384), and that there can be
no such thing as a reasonable nuisance (*Attorney-General*
v. *Cole*, 1 Chancery 205, 1901)—a phrase which really
prejudges the case, for the question should be whether
there can be lawful annoyance or discomfort, a question
which special legislation has in numerous cases answered
in the affirmative.

The difficulty does not lie, however, as in the case of
restraint of trade, in the vagueness of the test, but in the
legal subordination of the countervailing interest. If
anywhere, there is here a case for legislative adjustment,
and as a matter of fact there has been a great deal of
legislation of a regulative character. The common type
is that of licensing offensive or dangerous trades or
assigning places where they may be carried on: this was
done for gunpowder and other explosives in England in
1772 (12 George III 61); for all noxious trades in Massachusetts in 1785, and in England by the Public Health
Act of 1848 (sec. 64; now Act of 1875, sec. 112). Where
local bodies and administrative boards are authorized in
general terms to deal with nuisances, the difficulty is
that they cannot by their subordinate power supersede
the general criminal law or the criminal codes which
re-enact the common law of nuisance in general terms so
as to include everything that is noxious and offensive.
Where, however, statutory power is given expressly to
license noxious trades, the license ought surely to give

immunity from prosecution, and this seems to be conceded in Massachusetts (*Com.* v. *Rumford Chemical Works*, 16 Gray 231; *Com.* v. *Packard*, 185 Mass. 64; 69 N.E. 1067). But England, while penalizing the establishment of certain trades without the consent of the proper authorities, expressly refrains from legalizing anything that would be a nuisance at common law. The same policy is pursued by the series of the so-called Alkali Acts extending from 1863 to 1906, which save any remedy by action, indictment, or otherwise, for what would be deemed a nuisance if it were not for the act. The Alkali Act of 1906 is the most conspicuous example on the English statute book of legislation standardizing a trade that is inevitably noxious to a certain extent, and it seems to be without exact parallel in American legislation. It illustrates not only the most appropriate but the only adequate method of dealing with necessarily offensive industries, and logically such legislation ought to supersede the common law. Indeed, for purposes of criminal enforcement that must practically be the result of well-constructed legislation, any saving clause to the contrary notwithstanding. It is a well-known canon of construction that a legislative intent to abrogate the common law will not be readily assumed or implied, and the unwillingness to supersede common-law standards is a marked and common feature of legislative policy. Yet it is just as true that where the defects of the common law have induced legislation, and legislation has dealt with the problem in a superior manner, the more effective must drive out the less effective rule. A perfunctory statutory denial of this principle will be of little avail against its actual operation.

Health and safety legislation: Our entire legislation for the promotion of health and safety is, as it were, a code partly elaborating, but to a much larger extent supplementing, the common law of nuisances. The call for legislation has been due in part to the conviction that the common law left too narrow a margin between illegality and actual injury, and, so far as health and safety were concerned, there was also ample occasion to meet dangers previously unknown and to apply to many of them newly discovered remedies. The progress in public sanitation bears testimony to the beneficial effects of legislation largely based upon the discoveries of science.

But this scientific foundation is by no means equally secure and uncontroverted in all phases of health and safety legislation, and it fails almost entirely where legislation deals with problems in which moral and psychological factors predominate. And in the absence of scientific certainty it must be borne in mind that the farther back from the point of imminent danger the law draws the safety line of police regulation, so much the greater is the possibility that legislative interference is unwarranted. We may apply to the relation between common law and police regulation the simile of the citadel and its outworks which Professor Jhering used in order to characterize the relation between morality and convention. Protective works placed well in advance of the main defenses diminish the chances of a successful assault upon the latter, but they also enlarge the zone which is withdrawn from normal and more profitable occupation. So when the law combats tendencies in order to check evil it may easily hinder legitimate activity. If free action is as essential to the interests of the community as protection from harm, the remoteness or conjectural character of the danger is in itself a strong argument against the policy of legislative interference and, if liberty is held to be a constitutional right, against its validity.

B. THE PROBLEM OF DEALING WITH APPREHENDED TENDENCIES AND CONJECTURAL DANGERS

Until the nineteenth century this problem was not acute. The modern legislation against gambling began in the middle of the eighteenth century when a statute of George II (12 George II, ch. 28) prohibited and penalized certain exploiting schemes and games of chance; but while this legislation was broad enough to bring now and then rather innocent pastimes under the ban of the law, the interests affected were on the whole not such as were likely to put forward open claims for consideration. The method of dealing with the abuse of intoxicating liquors had from an early period (1552) been the system of licensing the trade, which was tolerant both of traffic and consumption.

Liquor.—The outstanding legislative problem in connection with intoxicating liquors is presented by the policy of prohibition. Prohibition is the extreme type of police legislation; prohibition, written into the Constitution, seeks to fix this extreme type by protecting it from repeal by the exercise of ordinary legislative power. Practically, however, the Constitution will depend upon auxiliary legislation. Mere words of prohibition in the Constitution will outlaw the liquor traffic, but will not penalize it, and while penalization by the Constitution itself is not absolutely impossible, it is unlikely, and the details of enforcement will in any event have to be left to the legislature. Constitutional prohibition will therefore not entirely remove the liquor issue from the domain of legislative policy; and a great deal will be left to legislative discretion if the constitution, by speaking merely of intoxicating liquors, leaves the way open for varying statutory definitions of the alcoholic content that makes the liquor intoxicating. Moreover, toleration of alcoholic liquor for non-beverage purpose will call for the continuation of some system of licensing. Enforcement under a régime of prohibition will require greater effort than where legalization admits of regulated supervision and administrative directing powers. The whole matter will be thrown necessarily into the machinery of criminal justice. Drastic measures of repression (search and seizure) will form a conspicuous feature of enforcement. These will encounter the difficulties presented by the attempts to enforce any law not supported by practical unanimity of what may be called "respectable" public opinion. The difficulty is greatly enhanced, if prohibition stops short of outlawing liquor entirely, and leaves both possession and consumption lawful. This will necessarily add to the public confusion as to the right and wrong of the entire matter, and will complicate the problem of enforcement, both from a moral and from a technical point of view. A policy having so many drawbacks would probably not be ventured upon if it had not at the same time the character of a moral crusade. If it can be justified on rational grounds, it must be as a long-distance policy, as an educational measure, the benefits of which will be reaped by the coming generation; but if that view is admissible, it is also true that the price paid in temporary demoralization of the law is a high one. Perhaps the time has not arrived for passing final judgment.

Gambling.—With regard to gambling the legitimacy of the policy of prohibition is generally conceded. In Prussia the state makes a concession to the gambling spirit by conducting a state lottery, but prohibits private lotteries except under special permit granted for public or quasi-public purposes. In a number of foreign countries municipal bond issues are permitted which carry chances of large premiums. The keeping of public gambling-places, such as existed in many of the European resorts, has been prohibited in the course of the last fifty years, last by Belgium upon payment of compensation to the municipalities interested. The Prince of Monaco derives his revenues from a gambling establishment, but interdicts its use to his own subjects.

In the United States the prohibition of all forms of gambling is universal, and some states express it in their constitutions. The federal government supports this policy by excluding all matter concerning lotteries or "other enterprises offering prizes dependent upon lot or chance," not only from the mails, but from interstate and foreign commerce, and it has been decided that even foreign government premium loans are within this prohibition (147 U.S. 449). While English legislation confines itself to games of chance, lotteries, and the keeping of places for betting, American statutes strike at all playing or betting for money, permitting rewards for skill only if they are offered by third parties, and otherwise allowing playing only for pleasure or recreation where no party can have any contingent loss or gain.[1] The terms of some statutes make the prohibition perhaps more sweeping than intended and appear to penalize common practices which it would be impossible to suppress; but in the absence of any attempt to enforce the law according to its letter this phase of it presents no problem of any significance.

Horse racing.—Important interests are, however, affected by the application of the statutes against betting and gaming to horse races. In view of the connection of this sport with the improvement of the breed of horses, a certain measure of legislative toleration has been accorded to it, resulting under the laws of some states in systems of licenses with incidental restrictions. In New York early statutes declared all races not expressly authorized by law to be public nuisances (1 Rev. Stat.

[1] Freund, *Police Power*, sec. 192.

672, sec. 55). The constitution of 1894 (I, sec. 9) prohibited pool-selling and bookmaking in express terms and
directed the legislature to pass appropriate laws to
prevent offenses against the provision. The legislature
thereupon in 1895 (ch. 570) passed an act authorizing and
regulating horse racing, which prohibited betting upon
the result of any race and forfeited any money or property
staked to the other party or to the depositor, but failed
to make betting a penal offense. The practice of betting
thus remained virtually unchecked. Governor Hughes
considered that this legislation was not a compliance
in good faith with the constitutional mandate, and in a
memorable legislative campaign succeeded in having
a stringent statute enacted which makes pool-selling,
bookmaking, the receiving or recording of bets, and any
act in aid thereof a misdemeanor punishable by imprisonment in the penitentiary or county jail, and does not
even permit the alternative of a fine (Laws of 1908, ch.
570). This measure was reinforced in 1910 by the repeal
of a section of the existing law relating to trotting associations (Membership Corporation Law, sec. 291) that
had secured to directors complying with the law immunity from liability for acts done on the racetrack. It is
understood that this drastic legislation has effectually
done away with the previous system of legalized gambling,
but that it has also been prejudicial if not fatal to the
raising of thoroughbred horses in the United States.[1]

[1] *Outing*, CLXII, 188. A partial revival of horse racing is said to be
due to a decision holding that betting without the professional element of
bookmaking is not punishable (*People* v. *Gettem*, 137 N.Y. Supp. 670, 1912).

Stock dealings, options, and futures.—Another interest to which gambling practices attach themselves, of far greater importance than horse racing, is the dealing in stocks. Even in France and Germany, where stock exchanges are institutions under government supervision, a considerable proportion of the transactions is nothing but betting on the rise or fall of prices. In 1896 a German statute undertook to make the validity of dealings of this character dependent upon the registration of the parties in an exchange register, with the result that speculation was largely diverted to foreign exchanges, and it was deemed necessary in 1908 to abrogate the requirement. The prohibition of private non-professional dealings had proved impracticable.

In America no systematic regulation of stock or other exchanges has been attempted by legislation, but places which are not regular exchanges for legitimate business, being kept merely for the pretended buying and selling of stock, produce, etc., without any bona fide intention of actually transferring or accepting the securities or commodities, are prohibited in a number of states, and apparently no difficulty has been found in distinguishing the legitimate exchange from the "bucket shop." Definitions of these places are found in statutes of Illinois, Missouri, and Massachusetts, and in a subsequently repealed act of Congress of 1901 (Vol. 31, St. at L., p. 943).

The prohibition of fictitious transactions on regular exchanges is theoretically a simple matter and is quite

common in America,[1] but the proof of the character of
the transaction is attended with difficulty. Proceeding
upon the theory that the great majority of option sales and
sales for future delivery are forms of disguised gambling,
legislation has been enacted repeatedly making these
transactions altogether illegal. This was done by an
English statute of 1737, and a statute of New York of
1812, forbidding contracts for the sale of securities not
owned by the seller, and by a qualified provision to the
same effect of the French Penal Code (sec. 422). Illinois
made it a misdemeanor to make options of purchase or
sale of any commodity (Crim. Code, sec. 130), and
California placed a provision in the state constitution
making void all contracts for the sale of shares of stock
on margin or to be delivered at a future day (IV, 26).
It is obvious that in outlawing all contracts for options
or "futures" legislation strikes at transactions which
under some circumstances may well be necessary for the
protection of valuable interests. Is it reasonable thus
to interdict legitimate business because it fosters a pro-
pensity to gambling and frequently serves as a cover
for it? The Supreme Court of Illinois held that this
was a matter for legislative discretion—in other words,
that it is not in the constitutional sense unreasonable—
and the Supreme Court of the United States has affirmed
this view (186 Ill. 43; 184 U.S. 425). In like manner the
Supreme Court sustained the equally sweeping prohibition contained in the constitution of California (187 U.S.

[1] Freund, *Police Power*, sec. 201, note 35.

606), again expressing its deference to the legislative judgment. The prohibition thus being "vindicated" from the point of view of constitutional law, it is extremely instructive to observe its failure to vindicate itself by the test of practical experience. The New York law was repealed in 1856, the English statute in 1860, the French provision in 1885. Illinois amended the Criminal Code in 1913 by confining the prohibition of option contracts to cases where it is intended to settle by payment of differences only, and in California a constitutional amendment to the same effect was adopted in 1908 (printed in 123 Pac. 278). Thus in practically all communities containing important centers of trade there has been a deliberate recession from the policy of outlawing a legitimate business because it encourages gambling, and if the lessons of history are worth considering in determining the bounds of legislative power, we should conclude that such a policy is unenforceable, and therefore intrinsically unsound.

Oleomargarine legislation.—The problem of conjectural dangers has also been conspicuously illustrated by the legislation against oleomargarine. Pure-food laws are directed against unwholesome and against fraudulently prepared products. The justification is stronger when health is involved. All imitation has in it an element, slight though it may be, of deception, yet it would be unreasonable to prohibit customary imitations or to restrict familiar trade designations to products of a prescribed quality when settled usage is thereby interfered with. To such legislation the observation may easily become applicable that was made with reference to the strict wine law enacted for Germany some years ago, that the consumer knows now what he gets, but can no longer get what he wants. However, legislation seeking to inculcate a stricter standard of commercial honesty than purchasers or consumers desire, while it may be unwise, can hardly be called illegitimate unless established usage has ripened into vested interest.

Oleomargarine legislation which confines itself to prohibiting the manufacture of oleaginous products in semblance of butter, or which requires distinct labeling or packing, is common in this and in other countries, and, whatever its motives, has been uniformly sustained by American courts; it is particularly to be observed that oleomargarine thus made in imitation of butter is held, not to be a legitimate commercial product, but subject to state law, though imported from other states and sold in original packages (*Plumley* v. *Massachusetts*, 155 U.S. 461). Perhaps the same would be true of a law forbidding oleomargarine not deceptively made to be designated as butter.

It is an entirely different matter for legislation to prohibit the manufacture out of any oleaginous substance other than that produced from milk or cream of any article *designed to take the place* of butter, that is to say, to prohibit honest substitutes as well as imitations, as was done by the statutes of several states. The statute of New York was declared unconstitutional (*People* v.

Marx, 99 N.Y. 377), while that of Pennsylvania was
sustained, not only by the highest court of the state, but
also by the federal Supreme Court (*Powell* v. *Pennsylvania*,
127 U.S. 627). The decision in New York proceeded
upon the principle that an industry may not be prohibited in order to protect another industry from competition—a principle to which the federal Supreme Court
would have readily subscribed. The federal Supreme
Court, on the other hand, relied at least in part upon the
possible injuriousness to health of oleomargarine which
presented a question of fact for the legislature to decide,
so that the court below was held justified in refusing
testimony to disprove the legislative finding, while the
courts in New York admitted such testimony and satisfied
themselves that oleomargarine was not unwholesome.
The question whether a valuable and useful industry
may be entirely suppressed in order to stop fraudulent
practices connected with it which the legislature feels
unable to deal with effectually by a system of regulation
is thus not dealt with by the New York decision, and in
the federal decision is entirely subordinated to the consideration that the manufactured product was possibly
injurious, and that its entire suppression was called for on
that ground. Yet that was the real question at issue
and one of fundamental importance, and the decision of
the federal Supreme Court at least seemed to incline to
an affirmative answer. But subsequently the Supreme
Court vindicated for the product which it had thus
permitted to be outlawed as a matter of domestic state

legislation the status and immunity of an article of commerce, thus denying for the purposes of interstate commerce the validity of a prohibition of the substitute product (*Schollenberger* v. *Pennsylvania*, 171 U.S. 1), while it had conceded the validity of the prohibition of the imitated product. It is true that Congress subsequently withdrew from oleomargarine the protection of the original-package doctrine by express legislation (Act of May 9, 1902), thus apparently again abandoning the substitute product to prohibitory state laws. But since the Supreme Court now takes judicial notice of the wholesomeness of oleomargarine, most of the reasoning of the earlier decision has lost its force, and it is more than doubtful whether that decision would stand at the present day. As a matter of fact the decision has become substanceless. As far as can be gathered from compilations made by the Department of Agriculture, the states which prohibited the manufacture of oleomargarine were New York, Pennsylvania, Maryland, and Minnesota. The act of New York was annulled by judicial decision, that of Pennsylvania was repealed in 1899, that of Maryland in 1900, and the present statutes of Minnesota no longer show the prohibition. As in the matter of the prohibition of options and futures, the history of legislation must be read as a supplement to the history of judicial decisions. That the fight is won in the courts settles nothing if the principle is unsound. The courts tell us that valuable interests may be sacrificed to conjectural apprehensions, but the practical needs of the community reject and finally overthrow the conclusion.

That the legislature should even attempt to suppress altogether an economic function of undeniable utility, as was done in the case of options and futures, and again in the case of oleomargarine, must be an altogether exceptional occurrence; such isolated other instances as we may find in the history of legislation, as, e.g., the prohibition of peddling in New York and in Pennsylvania toward the end of the eighteenth century, have been of only temporary duration. No sane legislative policy would allow an even serious danger to human safety to stand in the way of real economic utilities. The legend on the old town hall of the Hanse town of Lubeck, *Navigare necesse est, vivere non est necesse,* has found manifold applications since great mechanical forces have been pressed into the service of transportation and manufacture. Thus the suppression of useful industries, while it illustrates admirably the triumph of principle over judicial doctrine, presents no problem of great practical importance.

Conjectural dangers and the question of fact.—Where the basis of legislation is some wrong to be remedied or some danger to be averted, the rightfulness of a law may depend upon a question of fact. However, in legislation, as in the administration of justice, error due to human fallibility has to be reckoned with, and it would be impossible to maintain that a mistake of fact as to underlying evils should affect the validity of a statute.

Such a doctrine would invest the courts with a revisory function which they were not intended and are not qualified to exercise. Courts are without adequate facilities for the re-examination of the complex social and economic phenomena of which the legislature is supposed to have taken cognizance, and it is not likely that they will be furnished with investigating machinery that will equal in effectiveness the sources of information at the disposal of a legislative body or of a well-equipped administrative bureau or commission.

Questions of fact have furnished important issues in sanitary and in labor legislation. Apart from the alleged injuriousness of oleomargarine, which has already been referred to, controversies have arisen with regard to the qualities of certain food ingredients and preservatives. The use of alum in the manufacture of bread was at one time prohibited in Missouri (*State* v. *Layton*, 150 Mo. 474), but the prohibition was subsequently removed (Laws of 1905, p. 130), while it is still in force in England. The use of boric acid in the preparation of food is now forbidden by some laws, while others are silent or permit its use in small quantities; the prohibition has been sustained by the Supreme Court of the United States (*Price* v. *Illinois*, 238 U.S. 446). The limitation of hours of labor has been defended for men engaged in certain occupations, and for women more generally, on the ground that unduly prolonged work is physically harmful, a contention which in that general form is certainly not uncontroverted. Quite recently the adequate foundation in fact of the so-called full-crew laws has been vigorously contested.

In most of these cases there has been room for genuine difference of opinion, and in the most conspicuous case in which injury was clearly disproved, that of oleomargarine, the legislative ban was lifted after a relatively brief period. Mistakes may also occur where there is practically no difference of opinion. The old saying that common error makes law applies to the effect of widespread beliefs concerning scientific matters; thus sanitary authorities were originally invested with their extensive powers over property and industries upon the theory then prevailing that sewage, garbage, and the exhalations from slaughterhouses and other offensive industrial establishments poison the air and that the noxious vapors thus produced cause disease; this theory is now rejected, but while it was universally accepted it furnished a valid ground for legislation, and the offensive conditions justified interference in any event. So long as there is respectable opinion holding that miscegenation or marriage between near relatives is physiologically undesirable, legislation can hardly be successfully questioned; indeed, a strong and universal sentiment may in itself furnish a sufficient foundation for law, as is demonstrated by the illegality of marriages universally regarded as incestuous, which certainly does not depend for its justification upon ascertainable biological dangers.

The courts have repeatedly professed their ignorance of the complex scientific, sociological, or economic factors with which legislatures have to deal and have disclaimed the power to question legislative findings of fact; but the practice has not always been according to the profession, and, unfortunately in the one case in which the Supreme Court of the United States took it upon itself to override the legislative judgment as to conditions and needs, the well-known New York Bakeshop case (*Lochner* v. *N.Y.*, 198 U.S. 45), the general opinion is now that the legislature was right and that the court was wrong. The protest against this judicial blunder was such that courts have since been more reluctant than ever to set their impressions against those of the legislature and have reversed previous rulings in which the legislative conclusion had been repudiated (*People* v. *Charles Schweinler Press*, 214 N.Y. 395).

The problem of doubtful facts is one that only the legislature itself can handle adequately, but it can hardly be denied that a proper regard for constitutional rights demands more careful legislative methods than have been used in many cases in the past. If error of fact does not vitiate judicial judgment, it is because due process in judicial proceedings means some assurance of careful consideration before a conclusion is reached. Due process is now treated as a requirement applicable to legislation, and it is significant that our courts have not accepted the mere compliance with the constitutionally prescribed steps in the enactment of a law as satisfying the requirement. On the other hand, the courts cannot well prescribe for the legislature a method of procedure that will insure a specific evidential basis for legislative conclusions, for it is inevitable that now and then measures should have to be adopted upon less than convincing proof. Legislation is not yet pure administration of justice. What can be justly insisted upon at the present time is only, first, that conclusions should not be reached in the face of undisputed evidence to the contrary, and, secondly, that in the absence of evidence the assumed basis of legislation should not be opposed to understandings and beliefs so general and so strong that the courts are compelled to take judicial notice of them. And as a matter of fact the basis of legislation is to this extent controlled by the courts. The time may come when courts will be justified in demanding that the legislature shall act only upon some evidence somewhere placed on record, but that time has hardly yet arrived. In the meanwhile it is well to bear in mind that the legislative practice accords in substance with what must be laid down as the present minimum requirement, and that if there have been instances of conclusions reached upon a totally unsatisfactory basis the courts have sinned in that respect no less than the legislatures.

Conjectural dangers and the question of good faith.— Another kind of difficulty is presented by the many license requirements of recent years. The breaking away from the old system of apprenticeship and qualification tests which resulted in closed trades, and the substitution of the untrammeled right to engage in lawful business must be regarded as one of the great gains of the nineteenth century. This right has been proclaimed as a principle by the German Trade Code, and our courts tend to regard it as a constitutional right, though it is not specifically recognized as such by any American state constitution. Yet it is a right everywhere subject to many exceptions, established for businesses or professions the improper conduct of which may touch the public interest in some prejudicial manner. And it is impossible to confine these exceptions to any specific grounds, as, for instance, the danger to health or morals, for the law imposes qualification tests relating to character where the only danger to be guarded against is that of possible fraud, as in the case of peddlers. The justification of the exceptions lies entirely in the degree and not in the kind of danger which unlicensed activity carries with it. The old system was by no means inherently irrational, for the community has a very positive interest in the quality of industrial or professional service. The former policy has merely yielded to the conviction that systematic restriction of trade is in the long run more prejudicial to industrial development than occasional inconvenience or abuse due to incompetence or irresponsibility. If in recent years license requirements have been established for plumbers, barbers, undertakers, and horseshoers, a plausible ground was undoubtedly advanced for each category, and it would not be impossible to make a case for licensing grocers, tailors, or shoemakers. Apart from general principle any license requirement may be rendered constitutionally objectionable by special features, as, for instance, by a qualification test which is manifestly irrelevant (e.g., requiring an undertaker to show skill in embalming when he does not propose to carry on the business of embalming with his general business, *People* v. *Ringe*, 197 N.Y. 143; *State* v. *Rice*, 115 Md. 317), or by an apprenticeship requirement which allows the trade to restrict its numbers when the necessary qualification can be as well obtained in other ways (*State* v. *Walker*, 48 Wash. 8).   But in the absence of such specific objections the courts have generally felt obliged, though with reluctance, to sustain the legislation.

The truth is that it is difficult to question such laws upon any other ground than the genuineness of their avowed purpose.   Some time ago it was proposed in Chicago to provide by ordinance that no motorman should be employed on a street-car line unless he had had twenty-one days' instruction from some motorman who had been employed for the preceding twelve months on a street-car line in the city.   The ordinance was proposed on the outbreak of a strike, with the conceded object of keeping strike breakers from the city, and upon the settlement of the strike it was quietly dropped.   It would not be easy to find in any existing statute a parallel to this barefaced perversion of power.   But it is generally charged and not denied that much of the new legislation is sought for the purpose of allowing the trade to control its members and, if possible, its numbers.   In connection with the legislation for plumbers the Supreme Court of

Washington said (*State* v. *Smith*, 42 Wash. 237): "We are not permitted to inquire into the motive of the legislature, and yet why should a court blindly declare that the public health is involved when all the rest of mankind know full well that the control of the plumbing business by the board and its licensees is the sole end in view?" Yet the court, while declaring the license requirement for plumbers on this ground invalid, sustained a similar requirement for the barber trade (*State* v. *Sharpless*, 31 Wash. 191).

In view of the absence of a sharp line of demarcation between business that should be free and business that may be placed legitimately under qualification tests, it would be almost impossible to make a satisfactory constitutional issue upon the result of legislative judgment fairly invoked and fairly exercised. Practically the entire difficulty lies in the diversion of legislative power to improper ends. No other phase of legislation presents this sinister aspect as strongly as this one. It is not generally a question of legislative good or bad faith, but in most cases it is evident that the legislature has yielded too readily to specious arguments advanced by interested parties and has not sufficiently appreciated the more remote but more important general interest of the freedom of pursuit of livelihood. So long and in so far as courts refuse or feel unable to inquire into the motives that have induced legislation the present unsatisfactory state of the law must continue, but indications are not lacking that in flagrant cases, at least, the courts may be relied upon to judge motive by effect and to refuse judicial sanction to legislation serving private ends.

C. THE PROBLEM OF CONTESTED AND UNMATURED STANDARDS

Unavowed purposes of legislation are not always intrinsically objectionable or contrary to public interest. Under systems of limited powers, such as American constitutions have established, it has happened now and then that a generally desired object could be attained only by indirection. Thus the United States has occasionally resorted to the taxing power for the purpose of accomplishing objects not otherwise within the general legislative power of Congress. In one instance of this kind, the suppression of the white phosphorus match industry by a prohibitive tax, there was no pretense that the law was in any sense a revenue measure. Such instances of perversion of power are regrettable, and yet we have to take cognizance of the fact that legal development now and then takes this devious course.

Hence it happens occasionally that objects are pursued ostensibly upon the familiar or well-established grounds of the police power because the real purpose sought to be attained is in advance of prevailing ideas of what the state ought to undertake, though conceded to be intrinsically desirable, as, for instance, when billboards are attacked upon the ground of safety, or when an eight-hour law for women is advocated upon the ground of public health. It is quite natural that new ideals should seek to establish themselves by claiming identity or close relationship with those that are unquestioned until public opinion is won over to the new standard. It is true that under the theory upon which the law relies the conjectural character of the alleged danger involves likewise a stretch of legislative power, but the controversy is at least shifted from the ground of principle to that of controverted fact. A legislative policy can hardly be worked out in a satisfactory manner if it has to sail under a false flag, and sooner or later the new standard will be openly asserted.

The difficulty also exists only if legislative action is in advance of what may be called the average public sentiment, and it is to be observed that where public opinion has been fully won over to new standards legislation is more likely to accept these than to relax established standards in response to growing public indulgence. One hundred years ago public opinion in America saw little evil in public lotteries and looked upon the use of intoxicating liquors with considerable toleration. On the other hand, it demanded the strict observance of the Sabbath and frowned upon such amusements as dancing or the stage. The attitude is now reversed. But while the growing strictness of standards has been registered in legislation, it is curious how little the greater indulgence is reflected upon the statute books. Sunday laws and municipal charter powers over amusements (for there is little direct state legislation upon the latter subject) are left standing much as they were seventy-five years ago. Massachusetts (R.L., ch. 98, sec. 4) permits Sunday licenses only for sacred, charity, and open-air concerts; and all amusement licenses may still be revoked at the pleasure of the local authorities (ch. 102, sec. 172), so that valuable and perfectly legitimate interests are sub-jected to an arbitrary and unregulated power, totally at variance with the spirit of our institutions or even with the idea of government by law.   Such powers are relics of the past and are continued upon the understanding that they will not be exercised, just as Sunday laws are maintained with an expectation of non-enforcement. There is an obvious unwillingness to abandon abstract moral standards once established, and the evil effect of disharmony between legislation and administration is not sufficiently appreciated.

While there is at present a practically universal acquiescence in the greater strictness enforced with re-gard to such practices as gambling or the use of intoxi-cating liquors, there are a number of other standards that are still fighting their way into legislation and the status of most of which is as yet unsettled.   Liability for industrial accident, unsightliness, exploitation and oppres-sion, unfair competition, and discrimination are the principal categories which represent new types of statutory restriction or requirement.   In all of them we find conduct and duty measured by an advanced sense of social obliga-tion, and the first inquiry should therefore be whether any attempt has been made to carry a general concept of social obligation into statute law.

1. *The violation of social obligations: malice, wantonness, and sharp practices.*—We may start with the obvious observation that not every standard of conduct that is fit to be observed is also fit to be enforced. Acts establishing boards of health or medical boards with disciplinary powers over medical practitioners have attempted to give to the idea of unprofessional conduct a legal status which some American courts have rejected as too indefinite for penal enforcement (*Kennedy* v. *Board of Health*, 145 Mich. 241; *Mathews* v. *Murphy*, 23 Ky. L.R. 750; *Hewitt* v. *Board of Medical Examiners*, 148 Cal. 590). But it is safe to say that no American legislator would be willing to establish as a statutory norm even for civil purposes the notion of ungentlemanly or antisocial conduct, or whatever might be regarded as an equivalent term. Yet something approaching this has been done by the German Code of 1900. By its provisions the violation of the accepted standards of right conduct ("Verstoss gegen die guten Sitten") is made not only a ground of nullity of legal acts (sec. 138), but an actionable tort (sec. 826). The effect of so extremely general a provision must be that practically the law leaves it to the courts to develop a new code of enforceable standards, and merely indicates by its declaration that the specific criteria of legal wrong established by the old law are not to be treated as exclusive, and that an adjustment to advancing standards is permissible. Perhaps this is wiser than to

specify in advance standards of conduct in connection with as many particular relations as possible, even if such an undertaking were practicable. A provision of this nature is likely to be interpreted conservatively and may for a time find its chief application in the nullification of contracts which our law likewise regards as contrary to public policy. But the Imperial Court has gone farther: it has held the stipulation of an unconscionable attorney's fee to be void and has allowed a recovery of the amount paid, and in a series of decisions it has laid down the rule that the exaction of a pledge of honor to secure the performance of a pecuniary obligation renders the entire contract void as placing the party thus pledged under an unfair duress of conscience. Such a decision foreshadows great possibilities of lifting moral to the plane of legal standards of conduct.

The attitude of our law is perhaps somewhat indicated by the treatment of malice when disconnected from any specific tort, such as libel. It may be stated as the predominant view that malice does not constitute an independent general tort. Even if the case of *Allen* v. *Flood* (1898 A.C. 1) is read in connection with the later case of *Quinn* v. *Leathem* (1901 A.C. 495), and if the determining element in holding the conduct in the former case nonactionable should be held to be the existence of an ulterior purpose of self-protection or of advancement of legitimate interests, the result would merely be that malice is actionable only if it assumes the form of unjustifiable interference with the relations of other parties. The malicious exercise of rights of ownership or of contractual rights gives no cause of action except in one or two jurisdictions in connection with what are known as spite fences (Michigan, Montana), whereas the German Code expressly declares such exercise to be unlawful (sec. 226).

The only instance in which there has been occasion for singling out a specific form of malice for legislative condemnation has again been that of "spite fences." Legislation dealing with that subject has been apparently confined to few jurisdictions (New England states California, Washington) and is of slight importance.

Of great significance, however, is a new departure in legislation which is found in the English Agricultural Holdings Act of 1906. The Irish Land Act of 1881 had established the principle of fixity of tenure, according to which a tenant can be deprived of his holding only upon the breach of one of six statutory conditions laid down in the act. Parliament was not willing to go to that length in England. The landlord is left master of his property. But the arbitrary exercise of the right of ownership is qualified by giving the tenant a right to compensation if the landlord "without good and sufficient cause and for reasons inconsistent with good estate management" terminates a tenancy by notice to quit or refuses to grant a renewal (sec. 4). In similar manner the Scotch Small Landholders' Act of 1911 (sec. 32) gives a right to renewal unless there is reasonable ground of objection to the tenant. In these cases, then, opportunity is given to the courts to develop rights upon the basis of what was before an obligation amenable to purely social and moral standards, and a beginning is made of carrying into the law a category of considerations totally different from those hitherto regarded as characteristic of jurisprudence. It would be hazardous, however, to generalize upon so slight a basis of legislation, and it should also be observed that by centuries of tradition the ownership of agricultural land in Europe has been a tenure practically qualified by social obligation, from which the ownership of industrial capital and also of city tenement property has been unfortunately divorced, until in very recent times great corporations have made a beginning in acknowledging similar duties. The obligation which the Agricultural Holdings Act makes legally enforceable is therefore one which is of old standing in social custom.

2. *Liability for industrial accident.*—It has been pointed out before that the German system of workmen's insurance inaugurated a new phase of legislative policy by making honorable provision for relief from suffering and dependence. Industrial accident was dealt with, like sickness, invalidity, and old age, as a social phenomenon requiring remedial treatment, and relief was given by insurance, the cost of which was in part assessed upon the employer by requiring him to contribute to the invalidity fund. This obligation of the employer, which extends also to sickness and old-age insurance, is quite divorced from any idea of fault. In England and in America the normal form of workmen's accident compensation is a liability placed upon the employer

exclusively, and thus appears in form as an extension of old principles of liability for negligence.

It is well known that to the Court of Appeals of New York the extension appeared so radical and unwarranted that it declared the Act of 1910, the first of its kind passed in America, unconstitutional (*Ives* v. *So. Buffalo R. Co.*, 201 N.Y. 271, 1911). A few months later the Supreme Court of the state of Washington sustained an act which was an insurance law, though modeled upon a type somewhat different from that of Germany (*Davis-Smith Co.* v. *Clausen*, 65 Wash. 156). The New York decision, though it has never commanded the assent of the best legal thought of the country, has had the effect of retarding compulsory compensation legislation unless sanctioned by express constitutional provisions, but in the compromise form of pseudo-elective laws the principle of compensation has spread through the United States in a manner almost unparalleled in American legislative history.

It is perhaps easier to criticise the decision of the Court of Appeals of New York than to explain how the highest court of the greatest state of the Union could have possibly reached the conclusion it did by a unanimous vote. The fatal defect of the position taken by the court probably was that it looked upon the law simply as a measure of employer's liability with the element of fault eliminated. In its opinion the court paid no attention to the fact that workmen's compensation legislation does not, like the employer's liability legislation which pre-

ceded and in part accompanies it, simply create a liability
fashioned on common-law analogies and attended by all
the chances of miscarriage of justice which made the
cause of action for damages at best a speculative affair.
The entire structure of carefully measured obligations
and safeguards counted for nothing in the reasoning of
the court. Yet the essence of the new law was that it
did not attempt to redress acts or omissions, but to
relieve a situation, not, as the court seemed to think,
upon an arbitrary basis, but upon a new principle which
perhaps should be designated as that of social solidarity.
The nexus of employer and employee in a common
undertaking, the inevitable risk of accident, and the
apportionment of loss through a system of measured
benefits not aiming to give absolutely full indemnity—
these are the elements of solidarity which are entirely
absent from the common-law principle of liability. It
is obvious that the court failed to comprehend the new
departure in legislation which it was called upon to
judge.

The principle of social solidarity is by no means confined to workmen's compensation for accident. In
Germany it extends to invalidity, sickness, and old age;
in England to unemployment. How in each case rights
and obligations are to be adjusted, who can equitably be
made contributories, must be a matter of careful consideration in each case. But it is safe to say that the
only adequate form of liability based on social solidarity
is a provision for insurance. And it is interesting to

observe how the logic of the principle forces in a constantly increasing number of states the adoption of insurance requirements, so that in course of time undoubtedly workmen's compensation will be enforced everywhere through some system of compulsory insurance.

3. *Disfigurement or unsightliness.*—Of the novel and contested grounds of legislation none perhaps has had a wider appeal than the unsightliness produced by outdoor advertising. The state of the problem in this country and of the judicial decisions and suggested remedies is set forth in a report of a New York City commission which was published in August, 1913. This commission proposed an amendment to the constitution of the state worded as follows: "The promotion of beauty shall be deemed a public purpose, and any legislative authority having power to promote the public welfare may exercise such power to promote beauty in any matter or locality or part thereof, subject to its jurisdiction." In suggesting so wide a power the commission opened up issues which are not at present involved in any practical proposition. It is true that in European cities we find municipal regulations which prescribe certain styles of building with a view to securing symmetry and artistic effect in prominent thoroughfares or squares, and the results of such regulations appear very clearly in the show streets of Continental towns. But it is said that the practice of prescribing styles is declining, and in many cases such regulations have probably taken the form of conditions imposed by the city or state as vendor upon purchasers

of property which had been acquired by the public in connection with street widenings under the power of eminent domain.   In any event, official dictation of this kind has not yet been seriously suggested in this country, and this aspect of the matter may therefore be dismissed as not calling for present discussion.

Perhaps it is also a rather theoretical question whether outdoor advertising is not a matter over which the public may legitimately claim an absolute control.   It might well be urged that the public at large should have a right to determine whether its attention is to be practically compelled in undesired ways, just as the freedom of speech does not mean the liberty to address an individual against his will.   However, this aspect of the matter has not been put forward as a basis of legislation.

It is safer to discuss the problem upon the basis of actual or proposed regulations.   Several acts have been passed in Germany and England since the beginning of this century which deserve consideration.   A Prussian act of 1902 authorizes the prohibition outside of cities and villages of billboards or other advertising signs which disfigure the appearance of a district distinguished by beauty. Another act of 1907 directs the denial of building permits for structures which will grossly disfigure a street or place or the general aspect of a locality, and also confers power on municipal authorities, in connection with places of historic or aesthetic interest, to reject plans for building which impair the character of the scene, and to deny licenses for placing advertising signs; it also permits special building regulations for districts with detached houses, summer resorts, and "show" streets. An English act of 1907 permits local by-laws forbidding billboards exceeding twelve feet in height, and controlling advertisements calculated to affect injuriously the amenities of a public park or pleasure promenade, or to disfigure the natural beauty of a landscape.

It will be noticed that these acts emphasize the idea of disfigurement: the English act meddles with advertising only when it impairs the amenity of public pleasure grounds, and the Prussian act permits regulations in the nature of an aesthetic control only where a place is already, as it were, dedicated to beauty. The term "amenity" which is used in the English act recurs in broader application in the Housing Act of 1909, in which (sec. 54) sanitary conditions, amenity, and convenience are mentioned together without any difference of power. There has been neither judicial interpretation nor, so far as ascertainable, any other authoritative discussion of the term "amenity," and it is perhaps futile to speculate how far the concept can be carried. Its introduction into statutory language, however, indicates at least the possibility of developments in a new direction.

American legislation has been more commonly in form of local ordinances than of statutes, but courts have made no distinction upon that basis. As a rule the attempted restrictions have been directed against billboards, sky signs, and similar structures expressly erected for advertisements and only in very few cases against signs painted or posted on house walls or fences (*Com.* v. *Bost. Adv. Co.*, 188 Mass. 348, 1905; *People* v. *Greene*, 85 App. Div. N.Y. 400). Except in these last cases the regulations have been framed with a view to justification on other than purely aesthetic grounds, such as measures designed against fire or wind hazards, or against nuisances in the commonly accepted sense of the term. Where they have been sustained by the courts, these latter grounds were chiefly or altogether relied upon, and, on the other hand, where it appeared that the use for advertising rather than the structure itself was the objective point the regulation was held invalid (*People* v. *Murphy*, 195 N.Y. 126; *Chicago* v. *Gunning System*, 214 Ill. 628). Cases involving the use of streets and highways stand upon a different basis (*Fifth Ave. Stage Coach case*, 194 N.Y. 19, 221 U.S. 467). Aside from a few dicta the very decided judicial view in this country is that the police power of the state cannot be exercised on aesthetic grounds (see also *Haller Sign Works* v. *Physical Culture School*, 249 Ill. 436, 1911).

While it must be conceded that the present trend of authority is opposed to even such legislation as has been enacted in Prussia, yet it is perhaps unfortunate that the issue has been generally stated too broadly, and particularly the proposition made in New York to place by constitutional amendment beauty on a par with morals and safety is to be deprecated. Apart from considerations of abstract power it is undesirable to force by law upon the community standards of taste which a representative legislative body may happen to approve of, and compulsion with that end in view would be justly resented as inconsistent with a traditional spirit of individualism. But it is a different question whether the state may not protect the works of nature or the achievements of art or the associations of history from being wilfully marred. In other words, emphasis should be laid upon the character of the place as having an established claim to consideration and upon the idea of disfigurement as distinguished from the falling short of some standard of beauty. It is quite possible that the approval of American courts may yet be won for regulations placed upon that basis if the measures prescribed observe a proper degree of discrimination.

4. *Unfair competition.*—The Trade Commission Act of September 26, 1914, has given the concept of unfair competition, previously used only in somewhat loose fashion to indicate various practices falling below the average standard of business ethics, a legal status in American law, but has deliberately refrained from defining the term.[1] Unless Congress will further legislate upon the subject, its meaning will depend upon administrative and judicial rulings, and past experience may aid us in forecasting future development.

There is a German act of 1896 dealing with what is generally regarded as the German equivalent of unfair

---

[1] See *Yale Law Journal*, XXV, 20, for review of opinions expressed during debate in Congress.

competition; but the German term *unlauter* has a connotation of uncleanness, which makes it stronger than the "unfair" of our language. Accordingly the practices forbidden lie within the narrow compass of actual deception, misleading designations, and the betrayal of trade secrets learned in the course of employment.[1]

American legislation has in the past confined itself in the main to two forms of unfair competition, each of which had risen to the status of a distinct business: the scalping of railroad tickets and the issue of trading stamps.[2] Since the established policy of railroad-rate regulation negatives the principle of free competition in any event, an attempt to regulate the sale of transportation in such a way as to check ruinous or underhand competition can hardly be held illegitimate. Where the legislation has been attacked successfully (157 N.Y. 116; 71 N.Y.S. 654, 168 N.Y. 671), it has been on the ground of the supposed monopolistic features of the regulation; but in the majority of states (Illinois, Indiana, Minnesota, Pennsylvania) the legislation which confines the sale of railroad tickets to railroad companies or their agents has been sustained.[3]

On the other hand, the attempt to suppress the trading-stamp business by forbidding the issue of such

---

[1] A recent American treatise (E. S. Rogers, *Goodwill, Trademarks and Unfair Trading*) likewise discusses under the head of unfair competition in the main deceptive practices in using names, in advertising, etc.

[2] I leave aside fire and bankrupt sales which are aimed at fraudulent practices.

[3] Freund, *Police Power*, secs. 291, 673.

stamps in connection with the sale of merchandise has generally been held to be an unjustifiable exercise of legislative power.[1]   The courts were unable to discover in the device an element of fraud; and the majority of courts also thought that at least if the element of uncertainty was eliminated there was nothing in the nature of an appeal to the gambling spirit (95 Md. 133; 165 Mass. 146). That there was an appeal to other uneconomic instincts and fallacies which lowered the level of standards of trading was apparently not sufficient to warrant the outlawing of a practice which could not be brought under, any of the traditional categories of illegality. If this was the judicial attitude toward express legislation, it may be inferred that the practice would not be held to be affected by a mere general condemnation of unfair competition.

It is very likely that under the Trade Commission Act an attack will be made upon the practice of price-cutting, and a separate bill (the so-called Stevens Bill) was introduced in the Sixty-third Congress to permit under specified conditions an owner to prescribe the sole uniform price at which the articles manufactured or put on the market by him shall be resold to dealers or to the purchasing public. Legislation of this kind has a safer basis than ordinary restrictive regulation, for the restraint upon the right of the subvendor is not imposed by the law, but attaches to the property by virtue of a stipulation made by the original owner, the statute merely

[1] Freund, *Police Power*, sec. 293.   See, however, 240 U.S. 342 and 369.

lifting a common-law disability in connection with the disposition of property. Apart from legislation, the question would be whether what is ordinarily the exercise of a common-law right can be invested by the circumstances of the case with a tortious aspect. In certain cases the practice of price-cutting may serve the ulterior purpose of establishing a monopoly, but a prohibition confined to these cases would not afford adequate relief. In a somewhat exceptional case (163 Iowa 106, 143 N.W. 482) the advertisement of a cut price was even held to be a malicious attempt to injure and an actionable tort. This decision likewise can hardly be made to cover the ordinary cases. The effort has therefore recently been made to prove that what is designated as predatory price-cutting is an act in the nature of a direct and actionable injury. The manufacturer of an article by extensive advertising and by long-continued satisfactory service of the public associates in the minds of the public with the known and intrinsic qualities of the article a certain value expressed in a definite price. This is an achievement which constitutes something in the nature of a good-will, and at any rate is a vested interest. The person who advertises the article at a lower than the standard price as a "leader" creates the false impression that he generally gives standard value at less than standard prices, while if he wishes to make profits he must recoup on articles not standardized in value or price. In order to deceive the public, he robs the manufacturer of his vested interest, for the public is led to believe that the standard price is excessive; the producer's good-will is taken from him by fraud.[1]

This is a skilful and plausible presentation of a grievance which makes a strong appeal to equity. Its interest lies in the care with which the economic nature and effect of a practice is analyzed, which upon a superficial view appears to be a mere exercise of the right of ownership. One cannot help feeling that if the trading-stamp business were dissected with equal keenness it might likewise appear less legitimate than our courts have held it to be. If unfair-competition legislation—and the same is true of other advanced standards—is to be placed upon a safe basis, the ground must be prepared by an exhaustive and scientific analysis of the elements entering into the situation that will impress and convince the public mind and the courts.

5. *Oppression and exploitation.*—There is no common-law wrong corresponding to these terms, and both the right of property and the freedom of contract imply the legality of hard and even unconscionable acts and bargains. Usury is a canon-law and not a common-law concept, and the condemnation of usury means that the lending out of money at interest is intrinsically wrongful —an extreme and fallacious application of the idea of the exploitation of economic power, which, even while theoretically acknowledged, had to be evaded in many ways, and which is now universally dropped. The usury laws modeled upon the statute of Henry VIII in effect

[1] E. S. Rogers, "Predatory Price Cutting," 27 *Harvard Law Review* 139.

license and limit the taking of interest; the limitation is by a fixed rate which operates irrespective of particular circumstances. It is not confined to, although it tends to check, unconscionable practices, and it often fails to meet evasive devices. This type of usury law, common in the United States, was abolished in England in 1854 and the English example was followed in many other European states. But Germany in 1880 penalized the taking of excessive interest on loans under circumstances indicating exploitation, and in 1893 further generalized the penalties of the law of 1880 by extending them to any kind of transaction in which one party exploits the necessity, the improvidence, or the inexperience of another by stipulating or procuring for himself benefits which exceed the value of the consideration given to such an extent that, according to the circumstances of the case, there is a striking disproportion to the other party's disadvantage. The English Money Lender's Act of 1900 is confined to loans of money and affords relief against excessive interest or otherwise harsh and unconscionable terms. It has been suggested that the terms of the German law are wide enough to reach the evil of starvation wages, but, without going so far, it is clear that gross exploitation has been made a distinct offense.

From the socialistic point of view our entire industrial system might be made to appear as one of unconscionable exploitation, but it is obvious that such a view would be of no value for practical legislative or judicial purposes.

Given our capitalistic system as it is, exploitation or oppression as a subject of legislation must have reference to things not implied in the prevailing economic constitution.

All labor legislation that is not concerned with health, safety, and morals aims to check capitalistic exploitation, and judicial decisions reflect the difficulty of separating legitimate from illegitimate practices. The legislation for children is placed upon a clear and distinct title of protective power, and laws limiting hours of labor, particularly where they apply to women, can be supported as health and safety laws. But measures relating to the payment of wages must justify themselves upon wider grounds, and in studying advancing standards, truck or store-order and weekly-payment acts are therefore of particular interest. It is in connection with these laws that the doctrine of constitutional freedom of contract has grown up and has been most strongly asserted.

The keynote was struck by the brief and pointed denunciation of a store-order act which is found in the first case decided by the Supreme Court of Pennsylvania (*Godcharles* v. *Wigeman*, 113 Pa. St. 431). The act was declared to be an infringement alike of the right of the employer and of the employee:

More than this, it is an insulting attempt to put the laborer under a legislative tutelage which is not only degrading to his manhood, but subversive of his rights as a citizen of the United States. He may sell his labor for what he thinks best, whether money or goods, just as his employer may sell his iron or coal, and any and every law that proposes to prevent him from so doing is an infringement of his constitutional privileges and consequently vicious and void.

The cases in Illinois involving coal-weighing, store-order, and weekly-payment legislation were less pronounced (*Millett* v. *People*, 117 Ill. 294; *Frorer* v. *People*, 141 Ill. 171; *Braceville Coal Co.* v. *People*, 147 Ill. 66; *Ramsey* v. *People*, 142 Ill. 380; *Harding* v. *People*, 160 Ill. 459). In annulling the statutes in question the elements of discrimination which the court found in them were chiefly relied upon. The insistence upon the freedom of contract, however, which was at first subordinate, was gradually more emphasized, and finally the supreme court declared it to have been a controlling feature of those decisions (*Vogel* v. *Pekoc*, 157 Ill. 339). West Virginia and Indiana have been uncertain in their position and their decisions are difficult to reconcile with each other. In both states the later rulings are favorable to the legislation, but with qualifications (*State* v. *Fire Brick Co.*, 33 W.Va. 188; *Peel Splint Coal Co.* v. *State*, 36 W.Va. 802; *Hancock* v. *Yaden*, 121 Ind. 366; *Republic Iron & Steel Co.* v. *State*, 160 Ind. 379; *Seeleyville Coal & Mining Co.* v. *McGlosson*, 166 Ind. 561). Missouri in 1893 condemned a store-order act, likewise relying mainly upon unjustifiable discrimination (*State* v. *Loomis*, 115 Mo. 307). But it took the broader ground of constitutional liberty when the legislation was made general and was again contested (*State* v. *Missouri Tie & Timber Co.*, 181 Mo. 536). Decisions condemning the attempt to control the method or time of payment of wages are found, moreover, in Ohio (*Re Preston*, 63 Ohio St. 428), Kansas (*State* v. *Haun*, 61 Kans. 146), and Texas (*Jordan* v. *State*, 51 Tex. Cr. 531). Against these must be set the authority of the United States Supreme Court (*Knoxville Iron Co.* v. *Harbison*, 183 U.S. 13 [affirming 103 Tenn. 421]; *McLean* v. *Arkansas*, 211 U.S. 539), which in two decisions has strongly asserted the legislative power to protect the workman against methods of paying or computing his wages which may operate to his disadvantage. The same position is taken by a number of state courts (Opinions of Justices in Massachusetts, 163 Mass. 589; Colorado, 23 Col. 504; South Carolina, 47 S.E. 695; Washington, 88 Pac. 212; Vermont, 64 Atl. 1091). There are decisions sustaining the legislation with reference to corporations in Arkansas, Maryland, and Rhode Island. But it should be observed that Missouri maintained its ground after the decision of the Supreme Court of the United States had been rendered. We are not now concerned with preponderance of authority, but with the fact that so considerable a number of decisions have been adverse to this type of legislation.

It sounds almost like irony to attack store-order and wage-payment acts in the name of freedom of contract. To do so we have to regard the liberty to compete for employment upon unfavorable terms as a valuable right.

What, then, is the real basis of the adverse decisions? Surely it cannot be that the courts meant to deny the possibility of legislative relief against gross exploitation;

the explanation must be that they did not look upon the legislation from that point of view. When we inquire for information concerning the conditions against which this legislation was directed, we are struck by the scarcity of data. The report of the Industrial Commission of 1900 has something to say about the grievances in the Colorado mining industry, and from an official state report of 1890 we learn something of the conditions in the same industry in Illinois. There may be other similar accounts, but they are not readily accessible, and it does not appear that they were brought to the attention of the courts. Under these circumstances it is difficult to pass final judgment on the character and the effect of the practices which the statutes sought to abolish. The antiquity and universality of store-order or truck legislation, which in England reaches back to the middle of the fifteenth century, indicates indeed the existence of grievances and abuses so notorious that the courts ought to have taken judicial notice of them, and this position was strongly pressed in a dissenting opinion delivered in the first Missouri case. But with reference to the requirement of the weekly or bi-weekly payment of wages it must be observed that the customary practice of longer intervals between payments not only cannot in any proper sense be termed an abuse or form of oppression, but that the new requirement, where sustained by the courts, occasionally worked such hardship upon employers that its rigorous enforcement proved at first impracticable.[1]

[1] *New York Factory Inspector's Report*, 1890, pp. 102-3

If it be conceded or assumed that it was possible to look upon the alleged grievances as a matter of fair controversy, the conflict of decisions turns upon a very important issue, namely, whether at the discretion of the legislature any arrangement between employer and employee involving some disadvantage to the latter may be treated as a form of oppression amenable to compulsory relief.   It is easy to gather from the tone of some of the decisions that a number of courts thought it important that an emphatic denial should be given to this question.   On the other hand, the courts which sustain the statutes do so in a half-hearted way, without committing themselves to more than the particular provisions before them.   They do not repudiate the principle of freedom and do not indicate, except in the vaguest terms, the basis upon which it may be impaired. The failure to assign any limits to the legislative power of control may serve to explain the uncompromising stand taken against its recognition at the outset in so many jurisdictions.

The minimum-wage acts are the latest step in wage-payment legislation.   While sustained by one court,[1] they have not yet been passed upon by the federal Supreme Court.   They are confined to women, and this fact may perhaps be taken to indicate an entirely new departure in legislative policy.   But they are so framed that it may be claimed that they are sustainable as legislation against exploitation and perhaps even for the

[1] *Stettler* v. *O'Hara*, 69 Ore. 519, 1914.

protection of health and morals; at least there are recitals to that effect in some of the laws. The principle upon which the legislation is actually based is that of the living wage, which is variously defined, but in such a way as not to revolutionize the existing standards, and particularly (since the legislation is confined to women who are presumably not heads of households) without reference to the maintenance of a family. Minimum-wage acts also differ radically from other wage-payment acts in the method of their operation. Except in one state the wage is not fixed by the law, but by commissions acting under the law. This means that both the state of facts calling for relief and the measure of relief will in each case be determined upon investigation involving hearings and decisions. In fact, this type of legislation itself was in the first instance founded upon the careful investigation and report of a legislative commission of inquiry. One of the chief objections to the store-order and weekly-payment acts is thus avoided: it is not as easy to maintain that the legislation is simply an exercise of arbitrary and unwarranted control. A case is made in support of the position that there is, if not exploitation and oppression, at least a situation calling for redress or relief. Considering that no standard has as yet been discovered for fixing the just relation between service and return, exploitation and oppression shade quite insensibly into economic disparity, and if there were no further check, legislation based upon these heads would represent no tangible or controllable principle. But that principle is found if it is once established that some practice, even assuming the inevitableness of social injustice in a general way, has become an untenable grievance or carries with it evils disproportionate to the sacrifices that would be demanded in order to relieve it. Such a practice may be characterized as subnormal or antisocial; the determining factor in justifying legislation is that both defect and remedy have some basis of evidence and have ceased to be a matter of mere surmise and allegation.[1]

6. *Discrimination.*—Unjustifiable or arbitrary discrimination on the part of the lawmaking power or of other organs of the state violates the principle of the equal protection of the law which is incorporated in the Fourteenth Amendment; but discrimination, however arbitrary, when proceeding from individuals or corporations, is not within the purview of the fundamental clauses of the federal constitution (*Civil Rights cases*, 109 U.S. 1), and is not either a common-law offense or a common-law tort, and is dealt with by state legislation only in particular relations. A conspicuous legislative policy against one type of discrimination has found expression in the civil-rights acts of several northern states which have sought (in the nature of things, rather unsuccessfully) to secure to the members of the colored race the equal enjoyment of the accommodations of railroads, theaters, inns, and restaurants—a policy offset by the laws of southern states enforcing (with considerably greater success) separation in schools, on railroads, and above

[1] As to broader grounds of labor legislation, see chapter i.

all in marriage. The contention that a perfectly reciprocal segregation has no element of discrimination in it
would have greater force if there could be perfect reci-
procity in such matters; however, the race problem is so
peculiar that statutory attempts at its solution are likely
to strain principles of legislation to the utmost.

Apart from race relations, discrimination has engaged
legislative attention in connection with railroads and,
more recently, with trusts and monopolies. When we
speak of the common carrier's common-law duty of
equal service, we do not necessarily mean more than that
he may not refuse to anyone willing to pay for it transportation within the scope of his business, according
to his available resources, and on reasonable terms.
Whether he may, while performing that obligation,
discriminate by granting to favored parties special rates
or accommodations is a question that has been much
controverted. The English House of Lords has held
that such favors are not forbidden by the common law,
while the Supreme Court of the United States has
intimated the contrary (*Great Western R. Co.* v. *Sutton*,
L.R. 4 H.L. 226, 237; *Western Union Tel. Co.* v. *Call.
Pub. Co.*, 181 U.S. 92).

That in the case of railroads a right to grant favors
involves possibilities of great abuse, and an undesirable
power of controlling industrial developments, was recognized at an early period. In England it became customary to insert in the special acts incorporating railroad companies clauses forbidding them to discriminate

in their terms, and these clauses were made part of the general railroad acts of 1845 and 1854, from which they were later on taken into the federal Interstate Commerce Act of 1887. In Prussia, likewise, the earliest railroad act, that of 1838, prohibited discrimination for or against parties in interest.

In America, railroad legislation was slower to enforce the general principle of non-discrimination. It was ignored by the general railroad act of New York of 1848, the first of its kind, and was not explicitly laid down in that state until the Public Service Commission Law of 1907. Massachusetts formulated the principle in somewhat ambiguous form in 1869 (ch. 252, leaving it doubtful whether the duty was not confined to freight tendered by other carriers; the revision of 1882 removed the doubt); in 1870 it appeared in the constitution of Illinois, in 1873 in the constitution of Pennsylvania; as before stated, Congress adopted it for interstate commerce in 1887, and specifically prohibited a very considerable number of discriminating practices or colorable evasions of the principle by the Rate Act of 1906. At present the public service commissions of various states are vested with comprehensive powers to deal with discriminatory practices.

Discrimination has a double connection with the economic problem of monopoly. A monopoly even if legalized is tolerable only upon condition of equal service to all and no favors; this has become almost a commonplace of the law of privileged utilities. But discrimination is also one of the practices upon which monopolies grow up and develop. The case in which the Supreme Court of Ohio laid down the rule that discrimination on the part of a railroad company was contrary to the common law (*Scofield* v. *R. Co.*, 43 Ohio St. 571, 1885) was a case in which the favored shipper was the Standard Oil Company. While here a monopoly was built up by seeking and receiving preferential treatment, it is also possible to crush competition by granting favorable terms where the competition is to be met, recouping for the loss elsewhere or after the competitor has been removed.

Recent economic history has shown that this latter phase of discrimination is by no means a practice confined to common carriers; while, however, its prohibition is a relatively simple matter when applied to legalized monopolies, it is an undertaking as yet practically untried to compel equal treatment when there is no obligation to serve in the first instance. The constitution of Oklahoma (art. 9, sec. 46) contains a curiously lame attempt to deal with the matter. The provision is that no person engaged in the production or sale of any commodity of general use shall for the purpose of destroying competition in trade discriminate between different persons, associations, or corporations, or sections, communities, or cities, by selling the commodity at a lower rate in one section, community, or city than another, after making due allowance for difference in grade and quality and in actual cost of transportation. It will be noted that the

specification of the latter part of the clause virtually
nullifies the reference in the first part to persons in
addition to localities, and leaves only a prohibition of
local discrimination. The so-called Clayton Anti-trust
Act of 1914 covers personal as well as local discrimination,
but in its qualifying clauses it goes beyond the Oklahoma
provision, for it saves, in addition to differences based on
the cost of marketing the product, the right to discriminate in order to meet competition, and concedes the
right exercised in good faith of selecting customers.
Time alone can show what a prohibition thus qualified
will accomplish.

Even in the case of railroads an unqualified prohibition
of discrimination would be meaningless. The outright
prohibition can apply only to differences made between
persons requiring precisely the same service, and the
Interstate Commerce Act recognized this by adding to its
prohibition the qualifying words: "under substantially
similar circumstances and conditions."   These words were
found both in the clause (sec. 2) dealing with personal
discrimination and in the clause known as the long-and-
short-haul clause (sec. 4) dealing with local discrimination. It is significant that the Supreme Court took
a much more liberal view of the dispensation in the latter
case, permitting competitive conditions to be taken into
account as between localities, but not as between persons
(compare *Interstate Com. Commission* v. *B. & O. R. Co.*,
145 U.S. 263, and *East Tenn. R. Co.* v. *Interstate Com.
Commission*, 181 U.S. 1). Since the railroad company

exercised the primary judgment as to what competitive conditions required, its power of discrimination was not seriously impaired; the city of Danville in Virginia, which was generally understood to be particularly prejudiced as compared with rival cities, was unable to obtain relief in the courts (122 Fed. 800, 195 U.S. 639).

A further step was therefore taken in 1910 when Congress removed the qualifying reference to similarity of conditions from the long-and-short-haul clause and made the prohibition against charging more for a shorter than for a longer distance absolute, subject only to a dispensing power of the Interstate Commerce Commission, and to a temporary continuance of existing rates. Apparently the purpose of the change in the law was to shift the primary judgment as to the exigencies of competition from the railroad company to the Commission. As the Supreme Court has pointed out in the Intermountain Rate cases (234 U.S. 476), the considerations here coming into play are matters of "public concern," i.e., affect economic policies nation-wide in their operation, and this fact justifies the transfer of the power to give effect to these considerations from the private corporation to a governmental authority.   It is recognized that the principle of non-discrimination may be overcome by some other principle, which the act does not define. The Supreme Court says that this lack of definition is not fatal to the act, since the judgment of the railroad company likewise was not controlled by any definite principle.   This argument implies that the railroad company in making discriminations had been exercising in reality governmental functions. This can hardly be conceded, for the railroad company was guided by considerations of "sound business," and if sound business undoubtedly includes a regard for the development of the country and for the equities of vested interests, it also implies a residual factor of discretion which is more appropriate to the control of the railroad by the owner than to the control of the owner by the government. Upon what basis will the government sanction a departure from the principle of non-discrimination? The law apparently leaves it to the Commission to evolve policies for which there are neither precedents nor standards. The situation would be intolerably perplexing were it not for the fact that practically the conditions already established by railroad management must be respected, and that as long as railroads remain in private ownership their initiative must in the nature of things be always an important and often a controlling factor in the ultimate decision.

7. *New standards and ascertained facts.*—From the point of view of constitutional law it is clear that the new standards are debatable ground. The rule of non-discrimination is conspicuous for having escaped attack as being in violation of fundamental principles; practically all the other new restrictions or requirements have been declared by some courts to be inconsistent with constitutional rights. At best there is in the decisions a note of hesitation and uncertainty, and we are com-

pelled to consider whether the judicial attitude of skepticism or resistance is not in some degree justified or at least explained by legislative shortcomings.

The very category of contested or unmatured standards is likely to carry with it the same weakness as that of remote and conjectural dangers, namely, that the new legislation has neglected to substantiate itself by a foundation of demonstrated facts. Legislative activity is in most cases responsive to some grievance. In rare cases, as in some conspicuous instances of rate discrimination, the grievance may be fancied rather than real; generally it is a genuine one. But that it is genuine does not necessarily mean that either its nature or its remedy is understood; still less, that all has been done that is necessary to convince public opinion of an injustice done and suffered. The student of the history of legislation has constant occasion to wonder, not merely at the absence of impartial and authoritative statements of facts and conclusions, but at the entire failure on the part of those demanding legislative interference to make an impressive or plausible, or, for that matter, any kind of a presentation of their case.

The commission inquiries preceding the enactment of workmen's compensation and minimum-wage legislation serve to mark the contrast; had store-order, weekly-payment, or coal-weighing acts been prepared in a similar manner, it is hardly conceivable that they would have fared so ill at the hands of the courts. The action of the Supreme Court in sustaining the new Ohio coal-weighing statute tends to prove this (*Rail & River Coal Co.* v. *Yaple*, 236 U.S. 338). In California an act is passed forbidding the resale of theater tickets at an enhanced price. The legislature is vaguely aware that in connection with the sale of tickets at hotels and similar places some abuses exist. What precisely are these abuses? Is there a legitimate demand for sale elsewhere than at the box office? If so, does the new legislation meet it? How does it affect existing arrangements? Who is sponsor for the new law? If an answer to these questions exists, if they have ever been asked, the information is certainly not found anywhere on record. The consequence is that the court remains unconvinced; it finds in the forbidden practice no tendency to injure the public, and nothing in it more immoral than in the sale of any other commodity at a profit, and it declares the act invalid. (*Re Quarg*, 149 Cal. 79). The case is altogether typical. The judicial reasoning is not very satisfactory; neither, however, is the fact of such a decision unintelligible. The court simply refuses to accept the mere enactment of the statute as an explanation or as the expression of mature judgment. Had the court sustained the statute, the objection to it would be the same; indeed, the lack of substantiation does not insure judicial condemnation, just as the careful substantiation of the workmen's compensation act of New York did not insure its approval. But there can be no doubt that a statute is strengthened or weakened according to the degree of care with which its foundation is laid.

8. *Corrective and discretionary regulation.*—Another possible factor of weakness in the legislative establishment of new standards involves the difference between two degreees of regulation which may be designated respectively as corrective (abuse-correcting) and discretionary (standard-creating). The difference is perhaps best illustrated by the problem of aesthetic standards. The entire case for billboard legislation is prejudiced if extravagant claims are put forward on behalf of a legislative power to impose new canons of taste, for the advance from the protection of health, safety, morals, or even comfort, to the protection of refined sensibilities is too great to be taken otherwise than very gradually. The law should, for the present at least, go no farther than to deal with obvious disfigurement or the impairment of places already lifted to an exceptional plane of beauty, and thus mark distinctly its conserving function; and such is the character of European legislation upon the subject, which recognizes the difference between establishing a new norm and saving a norm already established.

The difference is of importance in other fields of legislation. The state as an employer of labor may set model terms of employment, although unfortunately it does not always do so; we concede to the state the same power over the employment of labor by municipalities, and—more reluctantly—by public contractors; but when the law deals with mere private employment, the view as yet prevalent is that its interference should be justified by some danger that calls for prevention, or by some abuse that calls for redress: protection, not reconstruction. The difference between a ten-hour day and an eight-hour day, between a one-day rest in seven and a Saturday half-holiday, between a minimum wage and a standard wage, between usury laws and other price regulations, while in one sense differences of degree, may in this light be also looked upon as differences of principle.

It is the difference between the eight-hour and the ten-hour maximum day, that the latter already represents a norm while the former does not, so that an excess over ten hours may legitimately be dealt with as an abuse, while the same is hardly true of a nine-hour day. So, also, to take away the employer's right to discharge the employee would mean an entire reconstruction of industrial labor, and would go far beyond the scope of corrective legislation, while, as before pointed out, the English legislation prohibiting with regard to agricultural holdings unreasonable notices to quit merely legalized existing social restraints and obligations.

It might be tempting to make this difference controlling for constitutional purposes, particularly in the matter of economic labor legislation. Freedom of contract is at best a vague concept; but some content might be given to it by insisting that in a free government the function of legislation is not to mold human relations, but merely to maintain them safe from harm or abuse. Perhaps the courts that enunciated the doctrine of a constitutional freedom of contract had something like this idea in mind.

If so, they not merely failed to formulate it clearly, but did not even apply it in any intelligible manner. For by the entire experience of industrial history truck or store-order legislation was abuse-correcting and not standard-creating in character; the abuses in connection with coal-weighing methods were patent and notorious, and long intervals between wage payments placed work-men in a state of undesirable dependence. Generally speaking, indeed, the demands of labor have been confined to the correction of evils and abuses, and the most conspicu-ous exceptions from this rule, the establishment by law of an eight-hour day in the mining and smelting industry of several western states, seems to have been considered as sanitary legislation and was sustained as such by the Supreme Court. If then labor legislation has been of the corrective and not of the standard-creating type, no con-stitutional issue on this basis was presented to the court.

The recent minimum-wage acts illustrate the same conservative spirit of legislation. The substantive pro-visions of some of these acts are perhaps somewhat liberal in their phrasing of the standard-wage require-ment, but these substantive clauses are inoperative without the machinery of administrative hearings and findings, by which they are consequently controlled. The constitution of the wage boards and their procedure is such that the wage established can hardly rise above that minimum, short of which the amount paid is acknowl-edged to be underpayment, the result being again cor-rective rather than discretionary action.

It is not always easy to determine whether legislative action belongs to the one type or to the other. The constitutional doctrine of the Granger cases subjected business affected with a public interest to a power of discretionary regulation, and such a power was exercised in the two-cent-passenger-fare legislation of 1907, a legislation not only not amenable to the ordinary canons of the police power, but entirely indefensible upon any principle. Congress, in undertaking rate regulation in 1887, adopted the corrective type by leaving the primary fixing of rates with the carrier, and requiring for Commission action some well-founded complaint, which is not made out by merely showing that the rate is higher than might constitutionally be fixed by legislation (*Interstate Com. Commission* v. *Stickney*, 215 U.S. 98; *Southern Pac. R. Co.* v. *Interstate Com. Commission*, 219 U.S. 433).

The long-and-short-haul clause was likewise conceived as corrective legislation, for the discrimination against which it was directed was considered as wrong in principle. If that assumption was not true, its outright prohibition would have been discretionary and not corrective legislation. No such outright prohibition was attempted in 1887, but the Act of 1910 did at least in terms attempt to create a prohibition absolute but for an uncircumscribed dispensing power vested in the Commission. Such a provision might develop into a type of discretionary regulation. If it is true that competitive conditions make local discrimination an economic necessity, then that discrimination is an essential part of the primary function of rate-making and cannot be transferred from the carrier to the government without changing the character of rate regulation. The administration of section 4 of the Commerce Act as amended in 1910 will determine this important issue.

Corrective legislation may be said to be the characteristic form of exercise of the police power. When acting in a proprietary capacity, in making expenditures, undertaking public works, managing public institutions and property, providing revenue by taxation or otherwise, the state must necessarily set its own norms, because there is no primary private discretion to act upon. The state's action is also likely to be discretionary where it operates by way of license, particularly in determining the form and scope of corporate organization and action, but such discretionary control is generally understood not to extend to the management of the corporate business within the scope of its charter powers.

In dealing with private relations the law will find it easier to impose entirely new norms where rights cannot be enjoyed otherwise than through invoking the aid and power of the law; it is, in other words, simpler to control remedies than primary rights, and simpler to control newly created than old-established remedies. In creating a cause of action for negligence resulting in death, a limitation of the amount to be recovered was readily imposed in many states, while until recently no such limitation was imposed in the case of non-fatal injuries which are actionable at common law. If the married women's legislation of the nineteenth century assumed the form of an entire reconstruction of a civil relation, this was possible because the law simply refused for the future the bestowal of benefits that depended upon its positive sanction; an equally incisive regulation in the opposite direction trying to re-establish the old régime of coverture would be so manifestly an impossibility that its constitutional aspects need not even be discussed. Any attempt to transform by law the distribution of property would naturally begin with controlling the transmission of decedents' estates, because here again rights depend upon the positive sanction of the law; only in a purely theoretical sense is this true of transfers by gift, and to control these in a similar manner would prove to be a very different undertaking. That restrictive legislation should be corrective legislation is a limitation of legislative power which depends upon actual conditions rather than upon abstract distinctions, and which is in consequence more powerful than constitutional guaranties; and a system of principles of legislation which should ignore the difference between the conservative and creative function of law because it is not expressed in the constitution would be fundamentally defective. Very little, indeed, would be gained, and considerable confusion might be caused by an attempt to formulate the difference as a rule of constitutional law. It carries its only possible and adequate sanction in the living constitution of society and the state. Conditions will arise under which radical steps may have to be taken by legislation; the history of the nineteenth century has seen fundamental changes, more perhaps in the law of personal status, in the relation of husband and wife and parent and child, than in the law of property; but, generally speaking, such changes have not been precipitated upon a society not fully prepared for them. Past experience does not indicate that in the matter of the establishment of new standards our legislatures are very much less conservative than the courts.

CHAPTER IV

CONSTITUTIONAL PROVISIONS

The advance of legislation to new fields of control is accompanied and sometimes checked by the constant recurrence of doubts concerning the constitutional validity of measures. We have for a considerable time been accustomed to express limitations in separate instruments which we designate as constitutions, and these have constantly grown in bulk and in variety of content. It is natural to inquire what relation the ever-growing mass of constitutional provisions bears to the problem of principles in legislation.

In approaching this inquiry we are struck by the attitude of indifference and neglect revealed in the teaching and writing of law toward the positive content of American state constitutions. The juristic treatment of constitutional law is almost exclusively concerned with the checks upon governmental power worked out by the courts upon the basis of very general clauses without very definite meaning. Only in the adjustment between state and national powers does the positive or conventional side of the subject claim equal attention, so that federal constitutional law has a very different character from constitutional law in general. No adequate systematic account of the development of state constitutions with reference to their place in our public law is to be found in any constitutional treatise. Yet without a clear view of the main currents of state constitutional provisions it is impossible to determine to what extent and with what success our constitutional law performs the function of controlling statutory legislation.

Even a cursory examination of state constitutions naturally leads to a differentiation of their provisions into several principal groups, the most important dividing line being between governmental organization and governmental action.

From the beginning the former group has occupied more space than the latter and, notwithstanding the relatively greater development of the latter, has retained its preponderance.

This is due to a considerable extent to the well-known tendency to fix more and more in detail the organization and jurisdiction of courts, left in the older constitutions entirely or nearly so to the legislature, while under the more recent instruments legislative action touching the courts is impeded at every step; and to the growing habit of giving a number of administrative officers (the selection being somewhat haphazard) a constitutional status.

This excess of detail forms one of the least defensible features of American constitutions. The line between province of constitution and province of statute is drawn on no discoverable principle. Important or distinctive policies regarding status, structure, or mutual relations of constitutionally recognized offices are either entirely absent, or are traceable only with difficulty in a mass of comparatively irrelevant detail. There is hardly any provision that makes for high quality or efficiency of administration, the tendency being, on the contrary, toward unwise decentralization and dissipation of power. Distrust of the legislature and the fear that its power over organization might be abused for partisan purposes was obviously the ruling motive when the tendency first asserted itself, and found some justification in the then widespread mischievous practice of special and local legislation. Today the danger of legislative impairment of the legitimate province of either judicial or executive action is extremely remote, and the constitutional status of courts and officers, without serving any valuable purpose, blocks the legitimate functions of legislation at points unforeseen or unforeseeable by the framers of the constitution.

Thus the constitution, in organizing an office, incidentally says that the head of the office shall appoint his subordinates; a subsequently enacted civil-service law is thereby made inapplicable to that office (*People* v. *Angle* 109 N.Y. 564). Or the constitution, in authorizing the establishment of probate courts, provides that such courts shall have original jurisdiction of all probate matters and the settlement of estates of deceased persons. This phraseology is held to exclude power over testamentary trusts, and an extension of jurisdiction, universally acknowledged to be beneficial and which on account of a slightly different wording may be given to county courts, must be withheld from probate courts (248 Ill. 520; 249 Ill. 30). Obviously governmental effectiveness is lost without corresponding gain.

It is the overloading of constitutions with unessential matter that makes them impediments in the path of needed progress after a relatively short time; a new constitution re-creates the same conditions, necessitating revision after a few decades. The constitution of Illinois, which dates from 1870, is said to be antiquated, but the features that make it antiquated will be multiplied and aggravated in a new instrument. The first constitution of the state, enacted a hundred years ago (1818), would need only two changes to be more serviceable at the present day than the constitution of 1870: in the provision for election of judges and treasurer by the legislature and the provision for constitutional amendment without resort to a referendum. The suffrage clause limiting the franchise to whites is superseded by the Fifteenth Amendment, and the word "male" is also in the constitution of 1870. The absence of the various clauses prohibiting legislation of various sorts would place Illinois simply in the condition in which Massachusetts is today; and in Massachusetts the chief demand is not for new limitations on the legislative power.

PROVISIONS TO INCREASE POPULAR CONTROL

If this phase of constitution-making is conspicuous for lack of definite purpose, the same cannot be said of another tendency which has likewise helped to swell the

bulk of constitutions on their structural side.   This is the
tendency to democratize state government.   For over a
hundred years the American people have experimented
upon the problem of how to give correct and adequate
expression to that elusive political factor, the popular will.
An abiding faith in popular government has been accompanied by an ever-renewed dissatisfaction with the forms
and organs through which it was sought to be realized.
Suffrage and the ballot, basis of representation, tenure of
office, and direct legislation are the instrumentalities and
methods through which the object of an enlarged popular
control has been sought to be attained, and it was legitimate and natural to fix as far as possible these points in
the constitution itself.   Leaving aside the race question,
the principle of suffrage had seemed to be settled until the
demand for the enfranchisement of women made it
again a political issue.   The problem of the most effectual
method of exercising the suffrage involved a machinery
of controlling nominations and guarding the secrecy and
honesty of the ballot too complex to be dealt with
adequately in the constitutions which, notwithstanding
some elaborate provisions regarding registration,[1] do not
fully reflect this movement.   The principle of elective
office had its most notable triumph when the New York
constitutional convention of 1846 accepted it, apparently
without serious opposition, for the reorganized judiciary
of the state.[2]   While up to that time appointment by

---

[1] Notably in Alabama, secs. 186, 187.

[2] The debates of the New York constitutional convention of 1846 are
meager upon the subject of the change to an elective judiciary.   There was

the executive or election by the legislation had been the almost unbroken rule (Georgia, 1798, 1808, and Mississippi, 1832, formed exceptions),[1] popular election of judges appears with increasing frequency after 1846 (Wisconsin and Illinois, 1848; California, 1849; Michigan and Kentucky, 1850; Iowa, Oregon, and Minnesota, 1857). Constitutional enactment was practically always necessary to effect the change.

The principle of direct legislation first expressed itself in sporadic provisions for periodical constitutional conventions (New Hampshire, 1792) and did not (except in the form of local option) become an important factor until the very end of the nineteenth century, when referendum and initiative started on their rapid career.[2]

This phase of constitution-making is evidence of the persistent desire to establish direct popular control in some way: if representative assemblies prove unsatisfactory, then through the organs of administration; if that method, too, proves disappointing, then through a

some opposition, and it was stated that sentiment was divided. It appears that with regard to the highest court the fact counted that it had been partly elective in the past, the Senate having formed part of the Court of Errors, while with regard to inferior courts there was a feeling that appointment had degenerated to a mere ratification of caucus nominations.

[1] Both states subsequently abandoned the method of popular election; Mississippi, however, returned to it in 1912 for the judges of the circuit and chancery courts, and Georgia somewhat earlier by a series of constitutional amendments.

[2] South Dakota adopted a constitutional amendment looking toward initiative and referendum in 1898. Utah followed in 1900. A self-executing amendment was adopted in Oregon in 1902. The following other states have since committed themselves to the new movement: Arizona, Arkansas, California, Colorado, Maine, Massachusetts, Michigan, Missouri, Montana, Nebraska, Nevada, North Dakota, Ohio, Oklahoma, and Washington. New Mexico and Maryland have adopted the referendum only.

direct voice in the adoption or rejection of measures. In either case the possession of the power is more highly prized than its exercise: the relatively slight vote on initiative propositions is even more striking than the indifference often manifested in elections for minor offices.

The genuinely popular desire for potential control is, however, a sufficient basis to support the demand of the relatively small group of those possessed of political skill and ambition for an active share in the government, and it has been found necessary and probably wise to give an outlet to their aspirations. Hence first the chance to obtain office, next the chance to become a candidate for office, and finally a direct voice in the determination, and even a hand in the shaping, of policies. Since the entire movement makes for dissipation of power and responsibility, the huge apparatus of popular control has always been disappointing in its results to those who favor it, and has not realized the alarms of those who fear it. From time to time a slight reaction is noticeable, as in the present "short-ballot" movement, but, generally speaking, the forward movement has been maintained with great constancy. Referendum and initiative have certainly not run their full course, and in really important matters the principle of popular election is advancing and not receding; witness the diminution of the number of states which retain the appointive judiciary, and the adoption of the Seventeenth Amendment of the Federal Constitution.

PROVISIONS RELATING TO LEGISLATIVE POLICY
OR ACTION

Turning to the second main group of constitutional provisions, relating to legislative or governmental policy or action, there has likewise been much addition and expansion. Not only, however, has the development been less homogeneous in spirit, but there has been an almost complete reversal from the tendencies originally manifested. To demonstrate this it will be helpful to differentiate provisions according to their historical relations.

The first place belongs to the inheritances of former centuries: to achievements and the results of struggles of English and Colonial constitutional history (bills of attainder, habeas corpus, subordination of military to civil authority, searches and seizures, free speech, press, religion, and assembly, the various procedural guaranties in criminal cases and jury trial, and due process or the law of the land) or to philosophical doctrines of natural right (*ex post facto* laws, taking of private property for public use, hereditary privileges and honors, titles of nobility, standing laws, reasonable laws, declarations reserving powers to the people or referring to the people as the source of political power).

Many of these clauses were not in the first instance directed against abuses of legislative power, but rather against the executive; in a small number of cases, indeed (taxation, standing army, suspension of laws), legislative action is relied upon as the sole security of constitutional rights.

It is noteworthy that the constitutional experiences of the two most critical periods of American history, the Revolution and its aftermath and Civil War and Reconstruction, left their impress primarily upon the Federal Constitution. The prohibition of laws impairing the obligation of contracts and the guaranty of the equal protection of the laws first appeared as national restraints upon state action, and, where adopted by the states, have been borrowed from the Federal Constitution.

The numerous additional restraints which the nineteenth century brought were all directed against the legislative power, for the executive had practically ceased to be an independent source of authority. Being, moreover, the fruit of experiences derived from the legislative history of the states, they were no longer dictated by a fear of suppression of popular liberties. Political danger now meant the danger of practical politics: waste, improvidence, fraud, local or special interests. Popular right was no longer identified with individual right, but rather with common public interests. The restrictions look to everyday concerns of government and not to critical periods of constitutional struggle.

Restraints on the formal side of legislation.—The restraints relating to the purely formal side of legislation are either procedural or style requirements. The following are the most common or the most conspicuous of the procedural requirements:

That bills shall be read three times; first found in North Carolina, 1776; qualified so that readings must be on separate days (first, South Carolina, 1780) or, in addition, so that reading shall be at large or at length (so in Illinois).

That bills shall be referred to committees and be reported by them.

That bills shall not be introduced after a stated period.

That rejected measures shall not be reintroduced at the same session; that a motion to reconsider shall not be entertained on the day of the passing of the motion.

That bills and all amendments shall be printed.

That bills shall be on the desks of members in their final form three days before their passage.

That the majority of all the members is required for the passage of a bill; that the vote must be by yeas and nays and entered on the journal.

That the signature of the presiding officer shall be affixed in open session under suspension of business.

Some of these provisions are salutary, and their fulfilment can be very readily verified; so particularly the one regarding the final vote. Others, on the other hand, are quite impracticable; e.g., that a bill be read at large three times. In the case of long bills this must be ignored, and the clerk will simply read the first and last few words, and the necessary fraud will be covered up by a false entry in the journal. Some can be reduced to unmeaning and perfunctory forms, so that really nothing is gained by the requirement; e.g., the requirement to report on bills, or the recitals indicating an emergency. Some give rise to difficult questions of construction, as, e.g., whether an amendment alters the subject-matter of the bill, or still more, whether it alters it substantially.

The sound policy of constitution-making is to impose procedural requirements only under the following conditions: (1) that they serve an object of vital importance; (2) that they can be complied with without unduly impeding business; (3) that they are not susceptible of evasion by purely formal compliance or by false journal entries; (4) that they do not raise difficult questions of construction; (5) that the fact of compliance or non-compliance can be readily ascertained by an inspection of the journal. The application of these tests would lead to the discarding of most of the existing provisions without any detriment to legislation, as is proved by the experience of the states which never adopted them.

As regards requirements of style, the constitutions, in addition to prescribing an enacting clause, deal with title and unity of subject-matter and with amendatory acts; very exceptionally also with referential legislation. The provision concerning the title of acts is usually coupled with the other provision that the act shall not embrace more than one subject.

In the state constitutions the provision regarding title seems to appear first in the constitution of Georgia of 1798: "Nor shall any law or ordinance pass containing any matter different from what is expressed in the title thereof" (art. 1, sec. 17). The conjunction of the requirement of title with that of unity of subject-matter appears for the first time in the constitution of New Jersey of 1844 (IV, 7, 4): "To avoid improper influences which may result from intermixing in one and the same act such things as have no proper relation to each other, every law shall embrace but one object, and that shall be expressed in the title." Such a provision is found now in about two-thirds of the state constitutions.

The provision forbidding amendments of statutes by mere reference to title, but requiring the section as amended to be re-enacted, appears first about the middle of the nineteenth century.[1] In 1835 it is found in no constitution. It is at present found in about twenty state constitutions.

The requirements regarding title and subject-matter undoubtedly inculcate a sound legislative practice, and in the great majority of cases amendment by re-enacting a section is preferable to the amending of words or passages torn from their context. If the requirement to amend in the form of re-enacting sections were generally construed, as it has been in Illinois and Nebraska, as forbidding or throwing doubt on supplemental acts altering the effect of existing sections, its inconvenience would be much greater than its benefit; but the Illinois and Nebraska decisions are anomalous and indefensible.

Conceding that these requirements of style have had on the whole a beneficial effect upon legislative practice

[1] Louisiana, 1845, seems to be the first.

and the clearness of statutes, they have a reverse side which must not be ignored. They have given rise to an enormous amount of litigation; they have led to the nullification of beneficial statutes; they embarrass draftsmen, and through an excess of caution they induce undesirable practices, especially in the prolixity of titles, the latter again multiplying the risks of defect. While the courts lean to a liberal construction, they have in a minority of cases been indefensibly and even preposterously technical, and it is that minority which produces doubt, litigation, and undesirable cumbrousness to avoid doubt and litigation.

The requirements were introduced to protect legislatures from fraud or surprise and to stop the practice of logrolling. The experience of those states which have not adopted the provisions would probably show that they are less necessary now than seventy-five years ago, that better practices have been compelled by public opinion, and that the benefits of the improvement may be enjoyed without the attendant risks and evils.

These risks might be greatly reduced by limiting to a very brief period after the enactment of a statute the right to question it in court by reason of the alleged violation of any of these provisions, and a like limitation should be applied to procedural requirements. The dangers against which the constitution desires to guard in formal and procedural requirements are necessarily of a transitory or ephemeral nature, which by the lapse of time become substanceless. If interests are prejudiced by precipitate haste, surprise, or logrolling, a reasonable chance should be given them to attack the law. After that chance has been given and no one has availed himself of it, the violated constitutional provision becomes merely a technical loophole of escape from the law, and the constitution makes it possible, not to protect legitimate interests, but to defeat the legislative will.

Substantive limitations.—Restrictions upon local indebtedness are commonly found and are sound in substance, but they have been framed without sufficient flexibility and have had to be aided by judicial construction; those upon state indebtedness have given rise to no difficulty. The common policy of a hard-and-fast constitutional rule of equal and uniform taxation of property, conceived in the dominant spirit of democratic equality, has proved a hindrance to the development of sound revenue policies.

Unqualified praise, on the other hand, may be given to the practical abrogation of private and special legislation, and although the attempt to secure absolute uniformity of local legislation has not proved equally successful (as the experience of Ohio and Illinois has shown), the benefit of these restrictions, has greatly outweighed their occasional inconveniences, caused in the main by the problem of the metropolitan city, which modern constitutions attempt to deal with by a policy of constitutional home rule.[1]

[1] California, Minnesota, Missouri, Oklahoma, Washington, Ohio.

Even those of the nineteenth-century constitutional limitations which have outlived their usefulness, or which in the light of later experience should be revised, formed at the time when they were first enacted valuable correctives of notorious legislative abuses. While differing from the more fundamental guaranties that originated in an earlier period, they had this in common with them, that in either case the danger aimed at was the misuse of governmental power and the remedy applied a mere inhibition of governmental action.

Humanitarian provisions.—A more constructive tendency, however, makes itself felt as constitution-making progresses. This divides itself somewhat unequally between two classes of provisions: those which represent advanced human or social standards, and those which reflect a popular apprehension of dangers that lurk in the abuse of private action, and which consequently seek primarily to curb social and economic tendencies and not an excess of governmental power.

Education, penal reform, the abolition of imprisonment for debt, the emancipation of married women, and, latterly, the rights of labor, are the chief topics of the "humanitarian" provisions. With regard to the first two, the constitutions are hardly in a position to give more than expressions of policy. The provisions against imprisonment for debt are generally self-executing, and in a few cases the constitution has by its own force done away with the disabilities of the marriage status. The provisions on behalf of labor are relatively meager and would make a very poor charter or program of labor legislation; there is not even a happily worded phrase that would, as in the case of education, emphasize the leading thought that should guide legislative policy. The significant thing about these humanitarian provisions is not their achievement, but the fact that new impulses and aspirations demanded and found recognition, though of the most perfunctory kind, in the organic law of the state.

Social and economic policies.—It is instructive to compare with them in this respect the restrictive provisions of a social or economic character. Of the social policies, those against lotteries and intoxicating liquors are the most conspicuous; of the economic polices, those concerning corporations, and particularly banks and railroads.

Since lotteries were operated only by specific legislative authority, it was only natural that they should have been combated by constitutional limitations upon legislative action, and from 1821 on, when it first appears in New York, the constitutional prohibition of lottery charters and lotteries is common. Liquor clauses in the constitutions are few, and they also present the exceptional instance of the organic law being used to place a controverted policy beyond the reach of shifting majorities in the legislature. Ohio and Michigan undertook to place a constitutional ban on licenses without suppressing the business entirely; in Michigan the provision was abrogated in 1875; and while in Ohio it lingered until 1912, it was evaded by ingenious legislative devices, and there can be no doubt that in both states the undertaking to formulate in the constitution a policy falling short of absolute prohibition was recognized as a failure.

The practice of special legislative authorization of important financial or industrial enterprises to be carried on in corporate form was also (as in the case of lotteries) originally responsible for the attempt to frame economic policies in the form of constitutional limitations. As objects of popular distrust or animosity banks in the earlier part of the nineteenth century held the position now occupied by railroads, although then as now the solicitude of constitutional conventions extended to corporations in general. The problem to be solved was not, however, the simple one presented by the abuse of lottery charters.

When banks became the object of constitutional provisions—first in Indiana in 1816—the initial policy was likewise one of prohibition pure and simple; but this policy did not stand the test of practical experience, and courts construed the prohibition to refer to banks of issue only.[1] Even with this restricted interpretation, the prohibition proved inconvenient, and ten years' experience with this régime led in Iowa to a demand for a constitutional revision,[2] while in other states the pro-

---

[1] With regard to the apparent prohibition in the constitution of Oregon, see 8 Ore. 396; California: 52 Cal. 196; 105 Cal. 376.

[2] See *Clayton* v. *Allen*, 63 Iowa 11. A member of the constitutional convention of 1857 remarked: "There are but few gentlemen on the floor who will not admit that we were sent here for the purpose of removing from our constitution the prohibition against banking."

hibition gave a monopoly to already established banks (so in Florida). Eventually the federal tax on bank notes rendered further prohibitions of banks of issue superfluous and those previously enacted objectless.

With regard to railroads, a policy of prohibition was of course out of the question. Both the universal desire for railroad expansion and the difficulties of railroad control kept the subject practically out of the constitutions until Illinois in 1870 established a new precedent in this field.

If the simple negatives of bills of rights were not available in dealing with capitalistic undertakings that performed essential economic functions which the state was unwilling to assume or incapable of carrying out, how did the constitutions adjust themselves to the more complex demands of regulative policies? Lawmaking through the constitution here encountered a new test.

There were in the first place the limitations upon the manner of granting corporate charters, particularly the prohibition of special legislation for that purpose. This indirect method of control was of considerable value in removing abuses and even in compelling improvements in the substance of legislation. It is found in some of the foremost states: in New York, where the prohibition was not made absolute except with regard to banks (special charters being allowed for other corporations where, in the judgment of the legislature, the objects of the corporation cannot be obtained under general laws), this qualified constitutional injunction was sufficient to secure the enactment of the first important general railroad incorporation law, which has since served as a model for other states. No state, having once adopted the policy of forbidding special charters for private corporations, has found it necessary to recede from it, whereas experience has shown that a faithful adherence to a similar policy in the organization of municipalities or in the grant of municipal powers is almost impossible.

Banks.—The strong feeling aroused by "wild cat" banking was responsible for another procedural limitation peculiar to banking laws, namely, the requirement of their submission to popular vote. The states of Illinois, Wisconsin, Michigan, Ohio, Iowa, Kansas, and Missouri placed this supposed safeguard in their constitution. In Iowa (103 Iowa 549), Kansas (20 Kan. 440), Illinois (under the constitution of 1848, 93 Ill. 191), and Ohio (42 Ohio St. 196) the requirement was construed to apply to banks of issue only; in Ohio, Michigan, and Wisconsin it has been removed by constitutional amendment. It is true that in Illinois the constitution of 1870 made the requirement explicitly applicable to all banks, whether of issue, deposit, or discount. Notwithstanding this isolated case of extension, it is clear that the referendum on banking laws has been found, not merely not to serve any valuable purpose, but to produce considerable inconvenience; since 1875 no constitution has adopted it, and public opinion would at the present time be unfriendly to it everywhere—one of the instances in which a constitutional experiment has proved a mistake and the mistake has been recognized.

Of much greater interest are the constitutional provisions specifying the conditions to be observed in the exercise of banking powers, for here we find the first attempt to formulate positive and definite principles of legislation through the constitution.

The general banking law of New York—the model for all subsequent American banking legislation—was enacted in April, 1838; in December of the same year a constitutional convention met in Florida, which framed and adopted a constitution that became effective when the state was admitted in 1845.

This constitution has an elaborate article on banking. Since it confines banks to the business of exchange, discount, and deposit, the safeguards prescribed by the law of New York for the issue of bank notes were naturally omitted; otherwise, however, the article contains every important provision of a banking law and constitutes a tolerably complete code of sound banking principles as understood at that time: the requirement of a specific sum in specie as capital; the prohibition of certain kinds of business and transactions regarded as unsafe; limitation on liabilities to be incurred; limitation on dividends; provision for inspection and reports.

The practice of making the constitution perform the office of a statute is here and at this early date perhaps more strikingly exemplified than in any other American constitution, not excepting the corporation article of the constitution of Oklahoma; indeed, Florida seems to have regarded the constitutional article quite adequate as a banking law, for the early session laws show no other banking legislation.[1]

Although perhaps not quite in so pronounced a statutory form, the banking articles of nearly all the constitutions from about 1840 for a considerable period onward lay down principles of banking legislation: forbidding the suspension of specie payments by banks of issue; prescribing the registration of circulating bills or notes, and the method of securing their redemption; creating a special individual liability of shareholders, making billholders preferred creditors, and requiring the registration of stockholders and their holdings and of the transfer of stock. With one exception these principles, even if not expressed in mandatory language (the more recent constitutions are more careful in this respect; see, e.g., Alabama, 1901, sec. 248), have been readily acquiesced in; the one exception is the special shareholder's liability. Though subsequently adopted for national banks, and in New York extended by the constitution of 1894 (art. 8, sec. 7) from banks of issue to other banks, this provision appears to have encountered much opposition: in Kansas (61 Kan. 869) and California (24 Cal. 518) it was held inoperative without appropriate legislation (Thompson on *Corporations*, secs. 3000–3007);

[1] A banking law was enacted, however, in 1852 purporting to give power to issue notes to circulate as money—on what theory, in view of the constitutional restriction of banking charters, it is impossible to say. As far as the reports show, the act was not passed upon judicially.

in Iowa (63 Iowa 11) it was by construction limited to banks of issue, and in Missouri it has been abrogated by constitutional amendment.

Railroads.—As pointed out before, railroads as such did not become conspicuous subjects of constitutional enactment until 1870. Earlier constitutions in throwing restrictions around the grant of public subsidies to private corporations did not mention railroad companies specifically, nor did these prohibitions become absolute until the same year. In 1870 Illinois made railroads (in conjunction with warehouses) the subject of a separate article in her new constitution, and from that time on they nearly always figure prominently in constitutional revisions or in new constitutions (see, e.g., West Virginia, 1872; Pennsylvania, 1873; Texas, 1876; California, 1879).

Leaving aside restraints on special charter legislation and on public grants in aid, which are not confined to railroad companies, the constitutional provisions relate to certain facilities for public control (maintenance of public office, registry of shareholders, annual reports of railroad or corporation commissions), to reciprocal relations between roads (right to physical connections and to connecting business, non-discrimination in relation to other lines, prohibition of consolidation between parallel or competing lines), to service of public (power or duty to regulate rates, non-discrimination, liability of common carriers), to certain abusive or corrupt practices (free passes, contracts with directors), and in more recent times to rights of employees (fellow-servant doctrine, etc.). The most important of these appeared in the constitution of Illinois of 1870, and Pennsylvania in 1873 covered practically all the points except the power to fix rates, which that state did not until 1913 assume to exercise by general legislation. Almost from the beginning, therefore, the constitutional provisions in the matter of railroads had attained their full development. The most conspicuous phases of public control and restraint which they recognized had been previously established in New York and in Massachusetts by legislation (right to connections, New York, 1847, 1867; non-consolidation of competing lines, New York, 1869; non-discrimination, Massachusetts, 1869). These two states never found it necessary to resort to the constitution to fix their policy of railroad regulation, while in Pennsylvania not even the constitution succeeded in introducing the policy of rate regulation, which in New York (1848) and Illinois (1849) had received formal statutory recognition before 1850. The most effectual weapon of state control—the establishment of railroad commissions—not only likewise originated in legislation (Massachusetts, 1869; Illinois, 1872), but has found its way into relatively few constitutions (California, 1879; Kentucky, 1891; Louisiana, 1898; South Carolina, 1895; Virginia, 1902; Oklahoma, 1907).

The important subjects of railroad finance, safety, and liability to users and to the public figure slightly, if at all, in the constitutions, although they are prominent subjects of legislation; vague phrases, such as that railroads are highways and the companies common carriers, have to serve in lieu of more definite principles. The constitutions vary, and apparently pursue no clear policy, whether to make their provisions self-executing, or depending upon legislation; the directory formulation is as common as the mandatory. Where the constitutional provision merely expressed a generally recognized policy, the readiness of legislatures to comply with constitutional mandates made the difference rather irrelevant; where, on the other hand, the carrying out of a policy encountered great practical difficulty, as in the regulation of freight rates, it was of no avail that a constitutional direction was added to ineffective statutory clauses, as was done in Illinois in 1870.

Altogether, the very considerable bulk of railroad legislation in the constitutions carries public control very little beyond the point reached by uncoerced statutory legislation, and the slight impress left by the constitutional provisions upon judicial decisions shows how little occasion there has been to rely upon the superior sanction of the constitutional prohibition or command. The railroad provisions in the constitutions apparently represented less of controverted "issues" than did those regarding banks.

Corporations in general.—The first constitution of Ohio, of 1802, contained a somewhat remarkable provision (VIII, 27), that every association of persons should on application to the legislature be entitled to receive letters of incorporation, separate legislative action for each particular case being apparently regarded as indispensable. The idea of general incorporation laws did not become familiar until later on, and it was not until the end of the thirties (Florida, 1838) that the prohibition of special charter grants was introduced into the constitutions. Florida added to her elaborate article on banks one that was also exceptionally full on corporations, requiring for incorporation laws public notice[1] and a two-thirds vote, limiting the duration of special privileges to twenty years, fixing causes of forfeiture and authorizing a summary process of revocation, forbidding the restoration of forfeited charters, and prohibiting the state from pledging its credit for a corporation. The provision for a two-thirds vote on charter bills had even before that time been incorporated in the constitution of Michigan (1835).

Florida's example was not at once followed by other states; the constitutions confine themselves for a considerable time to the prohibition of special charter grants and of state participation in private corporate enterprise (so Iowa, 1846). Otherwise the constitutions of the period concern themselves only with banking corporations, and these occupy the principal place in the articles headed "Corporations" which begin to appear about the middle of the century.

[1] Rhode Island, 1842, required a bill for a corporate charter to be continued to the next legislature.

Gradually the provisions regarding corporations expand, and at present a separate article dealing with the subject is the rule.

The primary object of constitutional provisions seems to be to guard the fulness of state control over corporations: the right to alter and amend charters is reserved; in order to extend the power to previously granted charters, corporations are required to accept the constitution before they receive the benefit of any amendments to their charters; charters are invalidated unless acted upon within a specified time, and corporations are declared to be subject to the police power of the state.[1] The provisions regarding foreign corporations, and particularly the requirement that the corporation keep an office or agents in the state, serve the same end. The "last word" in asserting state control is of course the creation of a corporation commission by the constitution itself, which we find in Virginia and Oklahoma—another illustration of the tendency to lay the main stress upon the machinery of state control rather than upon giving a particular direction to its policy.

As regards corporate organization, powers, relations, and liabilities, it is not easy to discover uniformity or definite lines of policy in constitutional provisions. Most common is the injunction restraining corporations to the business specified in their charters; the correlative

---

[1] Some of these provisions render it impossible to secure to a corporation the right to charge fixed rates on a contractual basis.

and equally important prohibition against accomplishing the forbidden object by holding stock in other corporations is found only in Georgia and Oklahoma; and the scarcity of provisions regarding real estate holdings by corporations seems to show that mortmain policies have at any rate not made a very strong appeal to popular sentiment or imagination.

A number of state constitutions undertake to guard against the issue of fictitious stock or the fraudulent creation of indebtedness; the requirements as to payment for stock are, however, of the most perfunctory kind, and in the absence of supplementary legislation have accomplished little.

A great many state constitutions have something to say on shareholders' liability, some (Oregon, Nevada, Nebraska, West Virginia, Ohio,) expressly excluding individual liability, some, on the contrary, extending from banks to other corporations the personal liability to the amount of and in addition to the stock held, or (California) establishing a rule of proportionate liability, while still others leave the matters expressly to legislation. In California (24 Cal. 587), Kansas (61 Kan. 569), and Missouri (79 Mo. 148) these provisions were, however, held by the courts to be inoperative without legislation, and in Minnesota, Ohio, and Kansas the additional shareholders' liability was abrogated by constitutional amendment altogether or for certain classes of corporations. It is obviously impossible here to speak of clear or uniform policies.

In those of the recent constitutions which reflect most strongly the demand for a direct expression of the popular will, the public-service corporation appears as the object of special solicitude and the corporation commission as the instrument to enforce the constitutional policies. In Oklahoma, not merely is the article on corporations twice as long as that on the legislature, but there are separate articles on banking, insurance, manufactures and commerce, corporate ownership of land, and a number of provisions protecting the interests of labor. The statutory character of many of the rules is indicated by the fact that they are made subject to change by ordinary legislation—a new form of compromise between constitutional and statutory lawmaking. The most interesting addition to constitutionally fixed policies is that against local price discriminations in the sale of articles of general use (Okla. IX, 46).

Effect of constitutional policies.—If we accept the articles on corporations, banks, and railroads as representing the most persistent attempt to assert popular control over economic factors directly through the fundamental law, we are naturally led to inquire what measure of success has attended the undertaking.

Is there any evidence to show that constitutions have thwarted or resisted legislative tendencies or policies unduly favorable to powerful capitalistic interests, or that they have inaugurated new policies that had to be forced upon the legislatures by a direct popular mandate?

If such was the purpose and effect of the movement, it is not susceptible of demonstration. The nature of the source material in constitutional and statutory history is such that as a rule no record evidence is available to trace causes and factors.[1] It is safest to draw conclusions from the internal evidence afforded by the constitutions themselves, the statutes, and the judicial decisions.

A number of points strongly impress themselves upon the mind.

The constitutions as a rule do not inaugurate, but merely register previously established, legislative policies; the exceptions prove the rule. Such an exception may perhaps be found in the railroad-control policy formulated in the Pennsylvania constitution of 1873, but the novelty lay in such minor points as free passes and semi-corrupt directors' contracts, while the fundamental principle of rate-regulating power was kept out of the constitution as it was kept out of the statute book.

The constitutions evince no particular care in the choice of the language which controls the operation of a provision, whether self-executing or dependent on legis-

[1] Mr. Thorpe, in his *Constitutional History of the American People, 1776–1850* (New York, 1898, 2 vols.), has analyzed with considerable care the debates upon a number of important issues in the constitutional conventions of Louisiana, 1845 (I, 400–486), of Kentucky, 1849 (II, 1–182), of Michigan, 1850 (II, 183–286), and of California, 1849 (II, 287–394). Every reader must be impressed with the desultory and frequently superficial character of argument and discussion. The same impression is created by a perusal of the debates of the New York constitutional convention of 1846, or of the account of other debates in Lincoln's *Constitutional History of New York*. Committee debates may have been more thorough and instructive, but we have no records of these.

lation; but since the legislatures were as a rule quite ready to carry out the constitutional mandate, this indifference did little harm. It has been said that courts have been unduly inclined to treat provisions as not self-executing;[1] but the reason has generally been that the constitutional provision was too vague to afford a definite rule of decision; and where the legislature contented itself with reproducing the clause of the constitution in statutory form, difficult questions of construction were sure to arise (see as to fictitious stock issues 96 Ala. 238, 250; 168 Mo. 316, 330; 206 Pa. 488).

Where constitutional conventions have been confronted by legislative abuses or unfortunate results of legislative experiments, the reaction not uncommonly transcended the bonds of statesmanlike circumspection and foresight. A number of states undertook apparently to prohibit banking corporations absolutely; the courts had to construe this as applying to banks of issue only; even in that restriction the policy proved unworkable in some states, and was saved in others only by the appearance of national bank legislation.

Similarly, the absolute limitation of corporate charters to a relatively short period of years was an untenable measure: as soon as the Supreme Court of Michigan decided that the prohibition covered extensions of charters, the clause in question was amended (art. XII, sec. 10, of constitution; decision 73 Mich. 303, 310, 1889; amendment same year).

[2] Thompson on *Corporations*, secs. 3000–3007.

The relative scarcity of judicial decisions on the constitutional articles in question is characteristic. It indicates to a certain extent the entire agreement between legislative and constitutional policy; to some extent it is also due to the general, if not ambiguous, form of some of the provisions which left the legislature a very free hand. In a few cases judicial interpretation has solved apparent conflict between legislation and constitutional provision, while in others judicial enforcement led to constitutional amendment. The judicial history of this phase of our constitutional law is meager and singularly unilluminating.

Only two of the clauses stand out as important additions to the principles of our public law: the prohibition of special legislation and the prohibition of public aid to private corporate enterprise.[1] In both these matters the constitutions performed their legitimate function of checking strong legislative tendencies with which statute law was unable to cope, and the policies thus enforced have been unqualifiedly beneficial and probably constitute the most important achievements of American public policy in dealing with private enterprise.

It would, however, be a mistake to measure the significance of the other corporation clauses of the

[1] At least three-fourths of the states have constitutional provisions designed to prohibit or check the practice. No state that has once adopted the policy of prohibiting such aid has abandoned it; in Michigan the constitutional convention of 1867 by a small majority adopted a provision allowing public aid to railroad companies, which was much desired by the Northern Peninsula; the proposed constitution was rejected, however, by the people, largely, it is said, on account of this provision (Utley, *History of Michigan*, II, 36).

constitutions by what they have actually achieved. Irrespective of success and failure, the mere fact of activity and the bulk of the product must arrest the attention of every student of constitutional history. From the second third of the nineteenth century on there has hardly been a constitutional convention that has not attempted to formulate economic policies and to deal directly through the organic law with some of the conspicuous factors of this economic life of the people.[1] And while there has been much perfunctory and thoughtless borrowing and reiteration, there has also been considerable change, and above all constant addition and a slow advance in the range of interests subjected to the constitution and in the methods of handling them. Experience may show that the constitution by its very nature cannot be made to serve as an adequate instrument of fixing means and methods of checking and curbing abuses and transgressions of corporate enterprise. There can be little doubt of the popular desire to utilize it for that purpose to its utmost capacity.

CONSTITUTIONS AND FUNDAMENTAL RIGHTS

Having thus traced the growth and development of the constitutional provisions directed against the danger threatening from the abuse of private and particularly

[1] New York, 1894, constitutes a striking exception. There are only two new provisions concerning or affecting industrial corporations: the abrogation of the limitation of amount recoverable for wrongful death, and the extension of shareholders' liability to other banking corporations than banks of issue.

of corporate action, it is instructive to turn back to the original stock of clauses to which we look for the recognition of the claims of private right in the ordering of civil relations. Does the formulation of checks and limitations keep even pace with the enlargement of public activities and of public control?

Undeniably there has been enlargement at some points. Thus the guaranties of freedom of religion and separation of church and state have been strengthened in the course of the nineteenth century. Pennsylvania in 1776 required of members of the legislature a declaration of the belief in God and the inspiration of the Scriptures; South Carolina in 1778 declared the Christian Protestant religion to be the established religion of the state; Mississippi in 1817 and Arkansas in 1834 debarred from office those who denied God or a future state, and Connecticut in 1818 recognized equality only for all denominations of Christians; these clauses have disappeared. And the First Amendment to the federal Constitution, forbidding Congress to establish a religion or to prohibit the free exercise thereof, falls short of the full declaration of the constitution of Illinois of 1870 proclaiming, in addition to freedom, also equality, the independence of civil rights from religious belief, and the principle of non-compulsion in the matter of church attendance and support.

The freedom of speech and of the press has been somewhat extended by cutting off the qualifications under which alone the earlier constitutions made the truth admissible in defense to a prosecution for libel.[1] Mississippi in 1817 and Connecticut in 1818 seems to have first omitted this qualification. It was only by the constitution of Pennsylvania of 1873 that the defense of the qualified privilege of good faith in the criticism of public officials was given constitutional recognition for criminal prosecutions, irrespective of the truth of the publication.

In some respects the right to compensation in the case of an appropriation to public use has been made more secure: in Indiana we find it extended to services; and from 1870 on the damaging of property is coupled with the taking of it in guaranteeing the right to compensation. Although these guaranties operate now perhaps more frequently against corporations exercising the power of eminent domain than against the state, they constituted in their inception a concession made by public power to private right.

Certain other enlargements of private right—the right to recover unlimited damages in case of wrongfully inflicted death, the abrogation of the fellow-servant doctrine, and the protection against "contracting out" of strict rules of employers' liability—operated from the beginning chiefly against the corporations which are the great employers of labor.

The most noteworthy addition to fundamental guaranties is to be found in the equal-protection clause of the Fourteenth Amendment; the principle of equality, so

---

[1] As to this see Schofield, "Freedom of the Press in the United States," *Publications of the American Sociological Society*, IX, 67, 79, 95.

prominent in France, had been theretofore conspicuous rather by its absence in American constitutions, or had found merely an indirect and incomplete recognition in the prohibition of privileges and monopolies.

On the other hand, the enormous growth of the exercise of the police power, the entirely new problems arising out of corporate personality and out of the relatively new concept of the public-service calling, have hardly called forth a single new guaranty of private right against the possible abuse of public power; it is exceptional that the reservation of the power to revoke corporate charters is qualified by a direction that no injustice be done to the shareholders (Mississippi, sec. 178).

In some cases concessions made to the defense of private right are subsequently taken back or qualified: in 1898 Louisiana relieves from the penalties of disobedience to the orders of the Railroad Commission pending a contest of the validity of the order (sec. 286); in 1908 this is amended by providing for a daily penalty of from ten to fifty dollars.

In the constitutional conventions the bill of rights is never a prominent subject of discussion, and only now and then some provision is considered with a view to its possible effect upon some "live issue." Thus in Iowa in 1857 it was proposed to add to the prohibition of laws impairing the obligation of contracts that of laws impairing rights of property. A debate arose on the effect of such prohibition upon liquor legislation, and the proposition was rejected. In the same convention the clause regarding the security against unreasonable searches and seizures was amended by adding to papers "persons," the change being due to a desire to counteract the Fugitive Slave Law. At one stage of the proceedings it was sought to make all privileges and immunities revocable; thereupon it was proposed to amend by giving a right to damages in case a corporate charter should be taken away; but it was feared that this would authorize suits against the state, and finally all these propositions were rejected. The phrase "all men are by nature free and independent" was changed to "free and equal," the proposed change being first defeated by a large vote, but finally incorporated in the report of the final special committee, it does not appear why. The lack of the common clause against self-crimination was supplied on the first reading, but omitted in the report of the final committee, which was adopted without debate.[1]

Doubtless the examination of the proceedings of other constitutional conventions would reveal similar haphazard and half-considered actions; and caution is clearly necessary in drawing inferences from the mere fact of change. This would apply, for instance, to the slight changes in the guaranty of jury trial in the constitutions of Illinois. The constitutional convention of Ohio of 1912 proposed to give a jury trial to persons charged with the violation of an injunction in labor disputes which was to be granted only for the preservation

[1] I am indebted for these notes on the Iowa constitutional convention of 1857 to an essay written by Mr. Worcester Warren, one of my former students.

of property. This was the only "labor provision" that was defeated at the polls. The anomaly is explained by the fact that another popular provision allowed a three-fourths verdict in civil cases, and that the labor interests did not hope for more than three labor men on any jury. No amount of conjectural reasoning would work out this explanation. It is also reasonably clear that the enlargement of the right to jury trial demanded in connection with the exercise of contempt jurisdiction is not demanded as an additional guaranty of private right and justice, but as a measure of protection to class interests.

Bills of rights have become stationary and, relatively speaking, retrogressive parts of our constitutions. Phrases have been taken over from historic documents without very particular attention to their meaning or significance. The term "due process of law" is not found in the earliest constitutions, but rather the terms "law of the land," "standing laws" (taken from Locke); in New York it was held (20 Wendell 365) that its introduction into the constitution of 1821 enlarged the protection of private right, but there is no evidence that that was the purpose of the convention. The opinions written by the Supreme Court of the United States in the Slaughter House cases (16 Wallace 36) in 1872 show very clearly that the members of that court did not realize the far-reaching effect of the due-process and equal-protection clause of the Fourteenth Amendment, and while a few individuals at the time of the adoption of the amendment may have foreseen its larger implications, the general opinion was undoubtedly that a security had been created mainly to prevent oppression of a particular race.

In fulness and variety of provisions the earliest of the bills of rights, the Body of Liberties of Massachusetts, of 1641, has never since been equaled; it is the only one which extends the guaranty of due process to family rights,[1] and the principle of equality before the law is likewise more adequately expressed than in most of the present constitutions.[2] Special provisions regarding liberties of women, liberties of children, liberties of servants, liberties of foreigners and strangers, winding up with an article "of the brute creature," give evidence of the universal range of its thought, and there is nothing perfunctory or stereotyped about its ninety-eight clauses. The "laws agreed upon in England for Pennsylvania"[3] likewise evince a solicitude for individual rights unrivaled at the present day.

Some of the earlier guaranties (right of migration in the charter of Rhode Island, right of emigration in Pennsylvania) have been dropped, and such an essential political right as that of association, such an important economic right as that of freedom of vocation, has uniformly been left without recognition, with the result that the enumeration of fundamental rights is more complete in Switzerland than it is in the United States.

---

[1] "No man shall be deprived of his wife and children."

[2] "Every person within this jurisdiction, whether inhabitant or foreigner, shall enjoy the same justice and law that is general for the plantation, which we constitute and execute one towards another without partiality or delay."

[3] Thorpe, *American Constitutions*, p. 3059.

Not only is there no attempt to express the individualistic concept of society or the permanence of the institution of property with its essential correlative of the right of testamentary transmission, but not even the idea of vested rights has been formulated or developed.[1] And while there have been at least rudimentary attempts to lay down general principles of criminal legislation, as, e.g., that penalties shall be proportionate to the offense, or that the penal code shall be based on principles of reformation and not of vindictive justice (Indiana, 1816, IX, 4), no constitution has ever undertaken to formulate any principle of justice or reasonableness for civil or public welfare legislation, although the enormous development of the police power calls urgently for some authoritative adjustment of its claims to the claims of vested rights. Even with regard to such historic rights as freedom of speech and of the press, the bills of rights have not kept pace with the advance of public opinion as expressed in legislation or the administration of justice; the law of libel is more liberal than the constitutional guaranty; Pennsylvania even now restricts the constitutional right to hold office to those acknowledging the being of God, and New Hampshire retains to the present day a clause according to the Protestant church a privileged status. A proposed amendment failed in 1912 through popular indifference. Indifference is, indeed, the dominating attitude toward guaranties of individual right; there is much greater interest in cutting them down where they

[1] It appears in the constitution of Louisiana of 1845.

are inconvenient obstacles in the enforcement of popular policies (so with regard to the protection against self-crimination) than in preserving them unimpaired.

This does not mean that there is not sufficient sentimental attachment to the bills of rights to muster ample support in their defense if they should be seriously attacked. This sentimental attachment also has a very real political value; for the belief in the ideals of liberty is one of the chief elements in the stability of American institutions, and creates a fundamental political contentment under governmental imperfections which is hardly rivaled in countries where a technically more perfect government is provided by less popular authority.

In estimating the practical importance of bills of rights, it should also be remembered that, while we place a greater faith in charter documents than the British people, in America, too, the written law represents the living constitution but imperfectly. Absence of militarism, absence of official caste, decentralized administration, popularized education, great vocational mobility, absence of sharp sectional or denominational antagonism, a very pronounced consciousness of national achievement and promise—these are the things that impress American institutions with their distinctive character, and there is neither any possibility nor any need of giving all of them constitutional formulation.

Confining, however, our view to the written constitutions, and contrasting our bills of rights with the tendencies shown in dealing through the organic law with economic policies, it is safe to conclude that guaranties of right and justice are not the deliberate creation of a constitution-making democracy, or its chief or even serious concern.

CHAPTER V

JUDICIAL DOCTRINES

As the formal expression of the prevailing economic constitution of society, private law has necessarily a strong individualistic cast. The two systems which have exerted the most powerful influence on legal history, the law of Rome and the law of England, have also been the most individualistic, while German jurists of the school whose foremost representative is Professor von Gierke take considerable satisfaction in pointing to the manifestations of a superior social spirit which they find in Germanic private law, and which they desire to strengthen against the influences of a Romanizing jurisprudence.

The individualistic spirit of the private law is epitomized in the right of ownership, the *jus utendi abutendi consumendi*, a right divorced from any obligation, intolerant of restraints upon alienation, and suffering the servitude of easements only within narrow bounds. In recognizing a free power of testamentary disposition, unrestrained by duty portions, an executor's administration practically exempt from official control, and a marital property right of the husband unqualified by community claims of the wife, the common law has carried the right of ownership to extremes from which in part at least it has been found necessary to recede, but the modifications are slight as compared with the power that remains.

The law of contracts breathes a similar spirit. It has been pointed out before how chary the common law is in implying obligations in connection with the principal contractual relations: seller and purchaser, landlord and tenant, master and servant, creditor and debtor. The principle *caveat emptor*, the paucity of tenant's rights, the rules of employer's liability, testify to the reluctance of the common law to carry obligations beyond what has been stipulated and assumed explicitly. Expressed in procedural terms in which the older law reveals itself most clearly, individualism means the favored position of the defendant who relies upon his possession or upon the letter of his bond.

In the promises of the Great Charter the procedural principles of the common law assumed the character of guaranties, and the thirty-ninth clause, the main precursor of our fundamental rights, is a defendant's charter. To transform a right into a guaranty means to protect it, not merely against invasion by private third partes, but against official invasion under the guise of authority. Procedural guaranties could be thus created because they were conceived as guaranties against royal action. That is to say, the administration of justice was part of the royal prerogative. Parliament, when it became a powerful organ of government, was content to leave it on the whole to custom and tradition, and was supposed to be watchful only that the royal power should not create dangerous innovations. Hence the early remonstrances against the jurisdiction of the Chancellor; and while eventually this jurisdiction was acquiesced in as a necessary complement to the common law, the abrogation of the Star Chamber by act of Parliament may justly be regarded as an insistence upon the carrying out of the promise of the Great Charter that the Crown would not exercise punitive powers except in accordance with the law of the land.

The idea that private right should be protected, not merely against private wrong, but against public and authoritative encroachment, was not confined to the province of procedure, but extended wherever authority was conceived as subject to law. Thus royal power was again met by common-law liberty when the attempt was made to exercise the prerogative by the grant of monopolies, and the struggle for freedom of private action terminated successfully in the beginning of the seventeenth century, first by the judicial and then by the legislative declaration of the illegality of monopolies under the principles of the common law.

The general civil liberty of the individual to enter into legal relations with other individuals, which underlies all private law, is perhaps the vaguest of all rights; like the air around us, it is so abundant and so little likely to be disputed or invaded by others that it does not normally stand in need of protection, and until the advent of constitutional limitations it had hardly any recognized legal status. It is all the more instructive that we can construe a common-law theory even with reference to this general liberty.

For from times immemorial this liberty was subject to local regulation by corporate by-laws which extended, not only to the preservation of local order, but to the enforcement of standards of honesty and quality in manufacture and trade. Since, in the absence of special custom, no corporation could make any by-law contrary to the common law or common right and yet was allowed to regulate the exercise of rights, it follows that the common-law concept of civil liberty was by no means repugnant to regulation in the public interest, but recognized such regulation as a proper and ordinary incident and qualification. It was regulation imposed by royal authority which Parliament in course of time came to consider as a violation of its own legislative prerogative; but this is far from saying that regulation in itself was considered as contrary to the common law.

However, the common law admitted of regulation only within certain limits: a corporate by-law transcending those limits was treated as void. This was particularly true of by-laws in restraint of trade, which created trade monopolies or restrictions not looking solely to "the good of the commodity" (*Tailors of Ipswich*, 11 Reports 53*a*). They were said to be against common right. Put in other words, the common law treated a certain quantum of liberty as protected from corporate regualtion. Here, then, we have realized the idea of economic liberty secured against governmental action, a common-law right of civil liberty as against unreasonable regulation.

From the fifteenth century on subordinate powers of regulation declined in England; the making of corporate by-laws was in important respects restricted,[1] and the function of trade regulation was assumed by Parliament; and the royal power to regulate by ordinance or proclamation gradually came to be considered as unconstitutional. Regulation and restraint of individual liberty henceforward proceeded from the legislative power of Parliament exclusively. It is true that toward the end of the seventeenth century a long period set in during which economic and social regulation was sparingly used (except so far as external "commerce" was concerned), and incisive interference with the conduct of private business revived only with the new factory legislation at the beginning of the nineteenth century.

The transfer of practically all regulative power to Parliament had the effect of removing from the English law the concept of a sphere of individual immunity from regulation as a legal right. That happened at the very time when Continental jurists began to claim for natural law a positive force and status. They not only now developed the theory of vested rights, which has remained foreign to the technical terminology of the English law, but contended that laws violating the natural limitations of sovereign power were null and void, and in Germany territorial statutes were questioned on that ground in

[1] Kyd on *Corporations*, II, 107-9.

the imperial court as denials of justice, just as they are attacked in America as violating due process of law.

It is true that in England Locke argued for the inviolability of property and a consequent limitation of sovereign power;[1] but he appears to have thought of natural as contrasted with legal rights, and he conceived of a power superior to the legislative only by way of revolution;[2] there is nothing comparable in English literature to the full elaboration of a doctrine of vested rights by German and Dutch jurists, and it is characteristic that Mr. Thayer, in introducing his chapter on "Eminent Domain" in his *Cases on Constitutional Law*, quotes from the writings of these jurists exclusively.

The English state of mind is easily understood. The great revolutions—religious and political—of the sixteenth and seventeenth centuries had assumed the forms of acts of Parliament; it was therefore natural that English lawyers should believe in parliamentary omnipotence. If there was a common right against corporate or royal regulation, and in this sense a common-law guaranty of individual liberty, a similar guaranty against parliamentary regulation was unthinkable. The subjection to the laws, i.e., to acts of Parliament, is assumed as a necessary qualification of every right, not merely of political or civil liberty, but also of the vested right of property. The compensation paid in the exercise of eminent domain is treated by Blackstone as a firmly established parlia-

---

[1] *Second Treatise concerning Government*, sec. 138.

[2] *Ibid.*, Sec. 149.

mentary practice, not as a legal right. The idea of rights which the state is bound to respect, with which German writers not uncommonly operate, is foreign to English jurisprudence. Strong as is or was the conviction in England that the male adult person should not be interfered with in his economic arrangements, even the most individualistic of English thinkers do not hint at possible limitations of a legal character upon Parliament; the idea of a legal right to freedom from economic of social regulation has disappeared.

The American state of mind was different from the beginning. The circumstances of the settlement of the colonies made it natural and almost inevitable that political and legal ideas which in England after the seventeenth century were relegated to the domain or philosophical speculation should appear as having practical effect and operation. The establishment of self-government on a new soil realized the idea of the people as the source of political power as it had not been realized in historic times; the primitive conditions of life and the opportunities afforded by a virgin continent justified a belief in natural rights; the distinction between fundamental and non-fundamental laws found expression at once in a number of colonies (Connecticut, Massachusetts, Pennsylvania), and thus was carried into American public law the habit of laying down abstract principles, where English constitutional tradition had stated concrete rights. And while English legal thought acknowledged limitations on the royal prerogative, but regarded parliamentary omnipotence as axiomatic, the eighteenth-century controversies over the power of taxation produced the curious result that the colonists, while protesting their loyalty to the king, denied the power of Parliament to bind them, since they could not be represented in it, and free people could be bound only through their representatives.

Thus the experiences of the colonies prepared the way for the advent of the American constitutional system. There was a theory of popular supremacy, a theory of natural rights, a theory of paramount laws, a theory of limited legislative power, but it does not follow that there was also a theory of inherent or implied limitations upon the power of the legislature. Where it was intended to secure a right against legislation it was specifically expressed, as had been the custom in the earlier colonial fundamental orders and bodies of liberties; very general declarations in favor of popular supremacy and reserved and natural rights were thrown in for good measure, and a check of a legal nature was hardly contemplated by these declarations.

It is true that even with regard to the specific clauses there was no explicit method pointed out of giving them legal effect; but the judicial power to annul unconstitutional laws was foreshadowed and established itself quickly and firmly.

The history of this phase of American constitutional law has been frequently set forth, and it is sufficient to say that by the beginning of the nineteenth century it was fully recognized, and that the power has never since been seriously shaken. But the present scope of the power was a matter of slower development, and it is controversial to what extent the courts recognized from the beginning general limitations as judicially enforceable. A brief review of the decisions will therefore be useful, and for the sake of simplicity this will be given in form of a chronological enumeration of cases in which general clauses as distinguished from specific guaranties were discussed.

DEVELOPMENT OF THE JUDICIAL ENFORCEMENT OF CONSTITUTIONAL LIMITATIONS ON THE BASIS OF GENERAL CLAUSES·

1789. South Carolina, *Ham* v. *McClaws*, 1 Bay 93. An act forfeiting imported slaves; retroactive effect said to be against common reason, but avoided by giving the act a non-retroactive construction.

1789. South Carolina, *Bowman* v. *Middleton*, 1 Bay 252. Act of 1712 changing the course of descent after the death of the owner. Held to be against common right and against Magna Charta, and therefore *ipso facto* void.

1800. U.S. Supreme Court, *Cooper* v. *Telfair*, 4 Dall. 14. Act of attainder and confiscation, passed by Georgia in 1782, sustained. Chase: "The general principles contained in the constitution are not to be regarded as rules to fetter and control, but as matter merely declaratory and directory." Paterson: "I consider it a sound proposition, that wherever the legislative power of a government is undefined, it includes the judicial and executive attributes."

Cushing: "The right to confiscate and banish, in the case of an offending citizen, must belong to every government."

1805. North Carolina, *Trustees of University* v. *Foy*, 1 Murphy 58. Act divesting lands previously given to State University, held unconstitutional. The constitutional clause protesting against deprivation of life, liberty, and property would be idle, if the legislature can make the "law of the land."

1811. New York, *Dash* v. *Van Kleek*, 7 Johns. 477. Act allowing a new defense to a right of action; retroactive effect upon a pending action avoided by construction; judges rather incline in favor of the legislative power.

1814. Massachusetts, *Holden* v. *James*, 11 Mass. 396. Act allowing a suit to be brought after the statute of limitations has run against the right of action; held void; no power to suspend laws in favor of an individual; reliance on civil liberty, natural justice, and standing laws.[1]

1818. New Hampshire, *Merrill* v. *Sherburne*, 1 N.H. 204. Act granting new trial unconstitutional; relying on unprinted precedents.

1822. Connecticut, *Goshen* v. *Stonington*, 4 Conn. 209. Act curing an invalid marriage sustained; dictum that a direct invasion of a vested right would be a violation of the social compact and within the control of the judiciary.

1825. Vermont, *Ward* v. *Barnard*, 1 Aikens 121. A special act of the legislature releasing an imprisoned debtor held void. So far as an act of the legislature is retrospective, or *ex post facto*, it is not a prescribed rule of conduct. An act conferring upon any one citizen privileges to the prejudice of another and which is not applicable to others in like circumstances, does not enter into the idea of municipal law, having no relation to the community in general.

[1] See two articles, 13 *American Jurist*, 72; 14 *ibid.*, 83, 1835, commenting on this decision.

1826. Kent's *Commentaries*, I, 455: "A retrospective statute affecting and changing vested rights is very generally considered in this country as founded on unconstitutional principles and consequently inoperative and void."

1829. United States Supreme Court, *Wilkinson* v. *Leland*, 2 Pet. 627. Act of Rhode Island confirming an executor's sale sustained. Webster as counsel relies on inherent principles of liberty and on the principle of the separation of powers as inherent in a republican government, no matter whether there is a written constitution or not (Rhode Island had at the time only the old colonial charter without express limitations). Giving property of A to B must be done judicially and not legislatively, though it may perhaps be done by the legislature. He concedes that the former practice has been to the contrary. Judge Story agrees to the general principle, but the act in question does not violate it.

1830. Federal District Court, *Bennet* v. *Boggs*, 1 Baldwin 60, 74. Judge Baldwin: "We are not the guardians of the rights of the people of a state unless they are secured by some constitutional provision which comes within our cognizance."

1830. Tennessee, *Marr* v. *Enloe*, 1 Yerg. 452. The taxing power cannot be delegated to the justices of the county courts, holding permanent offices and wholly irresponsible to the people. The court also relies upon an article of the constitution requiring equal taxation of all lands, which the legislation in question sought to evade.

1831–36. Tennessee. A number of special acts declared unconstitutional as usurpations of the judicial power by the legislature, or as violating the "law of the land," which must be a general and equal law. The cases are reviewed in *Jones* v. *Pary*, 10 Yerg. 59; a discussion of the "law of the land" is found in 2 Yerg. 599, 605, 1831.

1833. Kentucky, *Gaines* v. *Buford*, 1 Dana 481. Act forfeiting lands for failure to improve them held void. P. 501:

"The idea of a sovereign power is incompatible with the existence and permanent foundation of civil liberty or the rights of property." This is the first judicial reference to civil liberty as an inviolable right; but the decision relates to a vested right of property.

1834. New York, *Matter of Albany Street*, 11 Wend. 148. Taking by eminent domain more of a lot than is needed for public use held unconstitutional. It is a violation of natural right, and if it is not in violation of the letter of the constitution it is in violation of its spirit and cannot be supported.

1838. New York, *Cochran* v. *Van Surley*, 20 Wend. 365. Act directing sale of infant's real estate sustained. Walworth says that to transfer property from one to another would be void as being against the spirit of our constitution and not within the powers delegated to the legislature by the people. Verplanck says that he can find no authority for a court to vacate or repeal a statute on that ground alone; he would require an express constitutional sanction, but finds in the fact that the constitution of New York of 1821 added to the "law-of-the-land" clause a "due-process" clause, a protection against mere arbitrary legislation under whatever pretext of private or public good; at the same time deprecates a broad, loose, and vague interpretation of a constitutional provision; very significant dicta, particularly the reliance upon the due-process clause.

1838. Alabama, *Ex parte Dorsey*, 7 Porter 293. Act requiring of an attorney an oath that he has not engaged in a duel held void, partly on the ground of the violation of procedural guaranties, since the offense must be ascertained by due course of law, but also relying upon an extremely strong article (30) of the Bill of Rights retaining rights non-enumerated for the people, and excepting the Bill of Rights out of the general powers of government, and declaring all contrary laws to be null and void. This is the first decision declaring a statute invalid without vested rights being involved.

1843. New York, *Taylor* v. *Porter*, 4 Hill 140. Act permitting property to be taken for a private road, on payment of compensation, held void, as exceeding the scope of true legislative power, as violating the "law of the land" and "due process." The practical effect of the decision was nullified by constitutional amendment.

1844. Arkansas, *Riggs* v. *Martin*, 5 Ark. 506. An act requiring a plaintiff to support his claim by oath in open court; held unconstitutional as a practical denial of justice, since it prevents an absent plaintiff from recovering.

1847. Pennsylvania, *Parker* v. *Commonwealth*, 6 Pa. 507. 1848. Delaware, *Rice* v. *Foster*, 4 Harr. 479. County local-option law held void as unconstitutional delegation of legislative power to the people.

Having thus arrived at the middle of the century, we find that while there have been far-reaching dicta spread over the entire period, the actual decisions annulling laws on the basis of non-specific clauses have been few, and have either involved a violation of vested rights of property or of principles of procedure or a delegation of legislative power. Civil liberty is mentioned once as a constitutional right, but no law restraining the exercise of civil rights prospectively has been declared unconstitutional. This issue is not presented until the following decade.

1852 TO 1858. LIQUOR PROHIBITION CASES

1852. Illinois, *Jones* v. *People*, 14 Ill. 196. Prohibition law sustained; "a government that did not possess the power to protect itself against such and similar evils would scarcely be worth preserving."

1852. New Hampshire, Opinion of Justices, 25 N.H. 537. So long as liquor is property it would be unconstitutional to take away all remedies to recover its possession.

1853. Massachusetts, *Com.* v. *Kendall*, 12 Cush. 414. Prohibition law sustained; it violates no principle of the constitution; brief four-line opinion.

1854. Michigan, *People* v. *Hawley*, 3 Mich. 330. Prohibition law sustained; objectors rely on vested rights and contracts; the objection is briefly disposed of.

1855. Iowa, *Santo* v. *State*, 2 Iowa 167. Prohibition law sustained; relies on the license cases decided by United States Supreme Court.

1855. Vermont, *Lincoln* v. *Smith*, 27 Vt. 335. Prohibition law sustained, "certainly not contrary to the social compact"; conflicting views as to limitations of legislative power.

1855. Indiana, *Beebe* v. *State*, 6 Ind. 504. Prohibition law declared unconstitutional, chiefly because destroying vested rights of property; strong dicta on limitation of legislative power in general; court has power to inquire whether the traffic is harmful. This decision appears to be ignored in later Indiana cases.

1856. Michigan, *People* v. *Gallagher*, 4 Mich. 244. Prohibition law sustained; a very full discussion reviewing the decisions on the power to declare laws unconstitutional, chiefly dicta; a large discretionary power is indispensable; should it be in the courts rather than in the legislature? A dissenting opinion insists strongly on inherent limitations and on the protection of vested interests; the judicial department is a conservative body designed to stand between the legislature and the people.

1856. New York, *People* v. *Wynehamer*, 13 N.Y. 378. An absolute prohibition law is unconstitutional so far as its acts on liquor owned at the time of the passage of the act; the power of prospective prohibition is recognized.

1856. Connecticut, *State* v. *Wheeler*, 25 Conn. 290. Prohibition law sustained; power purely legislative in character.

1856. Delaware, *State* v. *Allmond*, 2 Houst. 612. Prohibition law sustained; better presume the impossibility of an abuse of legislative power than predicate upon its assumption the right to review legislative action on any other than specific grounds.

1858. Rhode Island, *State* v. *Paul*, 5 R.I. 185. Prohibition law sustained; does not violate any specific provision (obligation of contracts, *ex post facto*); far within the legislative competence to enact.

We thus find only two cases in which prohibition is declared unconstitutional, mainly or exclusively in reliance upon the protection due to vested rights; there is no constitutional recognition of a right of reasonable exercise of civil liberty, except perhaps in Indiana and in a dissenting opinion in Michigan. The general judicial acquiescence in an unprecedented exercise of legislative power is all the more noteworthy, as the legislation in question was for the time almost unenforceable and in most states short-lived.

1857. California, *Billings* v. *Hall*, 7 Cal. 1. A betterment act operating in favor of tresspassers held unconstitutional as depriving of a vested right.

1858. California, *Ex parte Newman*, 9 Cal. 502. A Sunday law held unconstitutional with strong expressions against legislative omnipotence, Judge Field dissenting. The first decision squarely enforcing civil liberty against legislative regulation. Overruled in 1861, *Ex parte Andrews*, 18 Cal. 678.

1858. Pennsylvania, *Mott* v. *Pa. R. Co.*, 30 Pa. 9. Act discharging Railroad Company forever from certain state taxes in consideration of a payment, held unconstitutional as a surrender of delegated power.   An entirely novel inherent limitation.

1862. Iowa, *State* v. *County of Wapello*, 13 Iowa 388. Act authorizing railroad-aid bonds held unconstitutional, citing no authority, but relying in part on retention of non-enumerated rights by people; followed in Michigan, *People* v. *Salem*, 20 Mich. 452, 1870, but contrary to weight of authority, which is supported by United States Supreme Court. Subsequently settled by express constitutional prohibitions.

1865. New York, *Powers* v. *Shepard*, 54 Barb. 524 (court of first instance).   An act prescribing the amount that may be paid for substitutes in the army held unconstitutional; if valid, same decision of case by construction; sweeping statements as to limitation of legislative power to legal sphere; moral, religious, and economic interests being out of that sphere; such legislation inconsistent with constitutional republican government. The first decision maintaining the freedom of contract against legislative regulation; no authority cited.

The period from 1850 to 1870 is thus marked by the first decisions opposing general constitutional limitations to the legislative regulation of civil liberty, but of the two decisions one was three years later overruled, and the other came from a single judge and was rather inconclusive.   The decisions against the surrender of the taxing power and against its unlawful exercise in aiding private enterprise are, on the other hand, significant as recognizing limitations not operating directly in favor of an individual right of liberty or property, but inherent in the nature and purpose of governmental functions and particularly of the taxing power.

Surveying the period of approximately one hundred years from the establishment of independent government, we find a thin but continuous stream of dicta in favor of the judicial power to control the exercise of a plain abuse of legislative power, the clauses relied upon being: separation of powers; law of the land and due process; retention of non-enumerated rights by the people and the non-delegation of power to the legislature; and as additional principles not specifically expressed the inherent limitations of republican government and the incapacity further to delegate delegated power. But not until 1857 do we get actual decisions declaring laws unconstitutional except for violating vested rights or the separation of powers, and until 1870 decisions involving other principles are so isolated and so contrary to the general trend as to be almost negligible.

From 1870 on we have to take account of the Fourteenth Amendment, but apart from that courts begin to declare with greater frequency and confidence legislation to be unconstitutional because it appears unreasonable either in degree or in kind. In the seventies this new development is illustrated by three decisions from Illinois: the first, 1873 (*Toledo* v. *Jacksonville*, 67 Ill. 37), holding certain safeguards required of railroads unreasonable;[1] the second, 1875 (*O. & M. R. Co.* v. *Lackey*, 78 Ill. 55), holding an act requiring railroad companies to take care of and bear the expense of burial of the bodies of

---

[1] A case of an ordinance, but the court said that it would treat the question as if the measure had direct legislative sanction.

persons dying on their cars arbitrary and void; and 1878 (*Gridley* v. *Bloomington*, 88 Ill. 554), holding that there is no constitutional power to require owners to clean sidewalks—upon a principle not theretofore intimated that liabilities may not be imposed without some intelligible justification.

The Fourteenth Amendment gave an express sanction, hitherto lacking, to the principle of equality; on the other hand, the due-process clause merely added the federal guaranty to a principle already familiar under state constitutions; the privileges and immunities of United States citizenship were so narrowly construed in the Slaughter House cases that they have become a negligible quantity.

The decision in the Slaughter House cases in 1872, sustaining the grant of a monopoly charter (16 Wall. 36), in a sense marks a new departure: the conservative construction of the Fourteenth Amendment looks backward; but the emphatic dissent of four justices out of nine foreshadows an enlarged view of constitutional guaranties. This view was presented by Justice Field, while the prevailing opinion was written by Justice Miller, who subsequently wrote the prevailing opinion in *Loan Association* v. *Topeka*.

The decision in *Loan Association* v. *Topeka* in 1875 (20 Wall. 653) recognized with regard to municipal bonds issued in favor of a manufacturing company the principle, asserted first in Iowa with reference to railroad-aid bonds, that the taxing power may not be exercised for private benefit. In protecting private property against the most insidious source of attack—the abuse of taxation—this decision, based, not on the Fourteenth Amendment, but purely on inherent limitations, gave to the individualistic conception of government a strong support and evinced a disposition to scrutinize loose governmental practices more closely than had been done in the past.

In 1877 came the Granger cases (*Munn* v. *Illinois*, 94 U.S. 113). It is well to observe that the leading opinion was not written in a railroad case, but with reference to the state regulation of grain-elevator charges, the elevator business, unlike the railroad business, never having sought public privileges on the plea that it was public in character. It was nevertheless declared to be affected with a public interest on the basis of the obscure public or common calling of the common law, and the reliance upon certain monopolistic features which distinguished the business as carried on in Chicago was tacitly dropped in a later case coming from North Dakota (*Brass* v. *North Dakota*, 153 U.S. 391). The business affected with a public interest was declared to be subject to regulation in the economic interest of the public—a phase of state power which had long lain dormant.

In estimating the importance of the Granger decisions the following points should be borne in mind:

First, the decision did not overturn previously established judicial doctrines. This appears from the fact that Justice Field, who, in his dissenting opinion contended for a general limitation upon legislative power upon the basis of the due-process clause, was not in a position to cite a single authority in favor of his view. He himself had dissented from the early California decision denying on equally general grounds the validity of Sunday legislation.

Secondly, the practical effect of the decision was confined to railroads and public utilities, which almost from the very beginning by universal consent had been treated as subject to an extraordinary legislative control.

Thirdly, the coming judicial view of a constitutional right of economic liberty was foreshadowed in the significant observation which came from Chief Justice Waite to the effect that the constitution does not confer power upon the whole people to control rights which are purely and exclusively private.

From the middle of the eighties the main interest in the problem of constitutional liberty shifts to labor legislation.

Before that time there had been too little of that legislation, and the enforcement of what there was had been too lax to raise serious questions.

In 1874 the governor of Massachusetts, in recommending a ten-hour law for males as well as females, adverted to no constitutional question; and in 1876 the Supreme Court of Massachusetts, in sustaining the law which had been enacted for women only, was obviously a good deal puzzled to understand the grounds upon which the measure was contested (*Com.* v. *Hamilton Mfg. Co.*, 120 Mass. 383).

The New York tenement labor decision of 1885 (*Ex parte Jacobs*, 98 N.Y. 98) was the first to take a decided stand against the power of the state to control the conditions of labor; the relation between employer and employee, however, was not involved or discussed.

The new doctrine of freedom of contract between capital and labor was inaugurated in 1886 by two decisions (*Godcharles* v. *Wigeman*, 113 P. St. 431; *Millet* v. *People*, 117 Ill. 294).

Since then probably about half a hundred cases have come before the courts involving legislation dealing with hours of labor, methods of wage payment, and the protection of union labor. The decisions have greatly varied, but the trend adverse to the validity of legislative control of the labor contract has been strong enough to make a profound impression upon public opinion. The decision of the Supreme Court in the New York Bakers' case in 1905 (*Lochner* v. *New York*, 198 U.S. 45) adopted the extreme view on that side; but the case of the Oregon ten-hour law for women in 1908 (*Muller* v. *Oregon*, 208 U.S. 412) indicated the setting in of the receding tide.

The New York decision of 1911 against the validity of the new type of workmen's compensation (*Ives* v. *South Buffalo R. Co.*, 201 N.Y. 271), while involving a different problem of a more technically juristic character, again asserted the judicial authority to enforce inherent and general limitations. The doctrine there pronounced has, even in the brief period which has elapsed since the decision was written, been shown to have very much less vitality than the doctrine of freedom of contract. It is true that the latter doctrine, too, as applied to capital and labor, strongly supported as it was for about twenty years by professional opinion, will, in the light of a longer history, probably appear as a merely transitory phase of legal and judicial thought. But to measure correctly the strength of the doctrine that the power to regulate economic freedom is constitutionally limited, we must take into account other decisions invalidating legislation relating to business or property which is less affected by the present trend toward social reform. Acts have been held unconstitutional creating mechanics' liens in favor of subcontractors (*Spry Lumber Co.* v. *Trust Co.*, 77 Mich. 199, 1889), prohibiting gift sales or the issue of trading stamps (*People* v. *Gillson*, 109 N.Y. 389, 1888), making ticket scalping illegal (*People* v. *Caldwell*, 168 N.Y. 671, 1901), forbidding the sale of merchandise in bulk (*Block* v. *Schwartz*, 27 Utah 387, 1904), prohibiting the manufacture of oleomargarine (*People* v. *Marx*, 99 N.Y. 377, 1885), requiring a license as a condition for permission to engage in the business of a horseshoer (*Re Ambrey*, 36 Wash. 308, 1904), plumber (*State v. Smith*, 42 Wash. 237, 1906), undertaker (*People* v. *Ringe*, 197 N.Y. 143, 1910), or dancing master (*People* v. *Wilber*, 198 N.Y. 1, 1910), and attempting to restrict outdoor advertising (*Com.* v. *Boston Advertising Co.*, 188 Mass. 348, 1905).

In none of these cases was any specific clause of the constitution applicable, but the doubts which the courts felt were regarding the applicability, and not regarding the existence, of general and inherent limitations.

From the point of view of constitutional history the decisions in the labor cases will retain their significance as the most conspicuous expressions of the theory—at the present accepted in no other system, and repudiated particularly in the other English-speaking jurisdictions and in foreign democracies—that it is not only on the ground of specific clauses, or on the ground of vested rights, or on the ground of a violation of the separation of powers, but upon the basis of a general right of liberty, of a certain degree of freedom from legislative regulation and control, that statutes can be declared unconstitutional.

We now associate the exercise of this judicial power with the due-process clause. The Supreme Court has refused to define the meaning of due process, but its underlying philosophical concept is not likely to be disputed: it stands for the idea that it is not the mere enactment of a statute in constitutional form that produces law, but the conformity of that enactment to those essentials of order and justice which in our minds are indispensable to the nature of law. Viewed in the light of history, these essentials are few, and the legislature is not likely to violate them except through inadvertence or in the heat of political passion. There consequently appeared to the original framers of the American constitutions as little need of insuring by express constitutional mandate the general conformity of statute to law as is now felt in Great Britain or in her colonies. Indeed, they seemed willing to concede that public exigency might now and then demand arbitrary action: thus Massachusetts, while guaranteeing in her bill of rights the application of the "law of the land" and of "standing laws," yet recognized the possibility of the suspension of laws, only requiring that it be done by the legislature or by its authority; only bills of attainder and *ex post facto* laws, sometimes also retrospective laws, were specifically and absolutely forbidden and reasonable compensation was assured in case private property should be appropriated to public uses. Massachusetts in this respect is typical; the term "due process" does not even occur in the first constitutions of the original states. The specific clauses of the bills of rights practically all dealt with issues that at one time or another had been the subject of political and constitutional controversy, and they were by no means looked upon as merely circumscribing the idea of government by law; thus in guaranteeing trial by jury it was well understood that certain phases of law could and would be duly administered without it.

But the judicial power to declare laws unconstitutional gradually and perhaps inevitably introduced a new concept of due process by expanding the inherent limitations upon the legislative power. Practically all the early applications of that idea turned upon the protection of vested rights, which had for over one hundred years been treated as the cardinal principle of natural law wherever natural law had been systematized. Thus far, then, inherent limitation merely enforced an almost universal dictate of justice. It was a very different matter to insist in the name of the idea of due process upon a demarcation of spheres of government and liberty, upon an immunity of individual action from legislative control. Until the middle of the nineteenth century no such idea was suggested by lawyers, courts, or text-writers. The prohibition legislation of the fifties gave the first opportunity of asserting such a liberty, but the slight attempts made in that direction found practically no judicial response. The second opportunity was given by the Granger legislation of the seventies, the first great attempt to control the traditional economic freedom; and now the Supreme Court, while sustaining the legislative power over railroads and warehouses, spoke in approving terms of the immunity of private business from legislative control. This idea then grew and established itself in connection with the attacks upon labor legislation from about the middle of the eighties and produced the doctrine of a constitutional right of freedom of contract. The true nature of this judicial control revealed itself in the decision of the New York Court of Appeals which annulled the first American workmen's compensation law. The point at issue was a rule of liability, a subject closely interwoven with the very elements of the concept of law; yet the court suggested an appeal to the people to sanction the principle which it declared violative of the guaranty of due process. It is well known that the appeal has been successfully made and that the Court of Appeals has bowed to the popular verdict (*Jensen* v. *So. Pac. R. Co.*, 215 N.Y. 514).

Obviously, the Court of Appeals believed that the people of the state of New York in adopting their constitutions had intended to place certain fundamental notions of right and justice beyond the reach of the legislative power, and that the due-process clause served that purpose, but that in the hands of the people themselves these notions were legitimate subjects of change with the progress of social and economic thought. This view also explains the apparent paradox that the same words bear a different construction in the state and in the federal Constitution. The situation is best understood when we say that the court in the name of due process enforced fundamental policies and not merely what the United States Supreme Court had designated as cardinal and immutable principles of justice.

For nearly a century economic freedom had reigned almost unquestioned. Labor legislation was the most conspicuous manifestation of a new era of regulation of private business. The new legislation was in many respects experimental and badly worked out; some of it was premature. Legislative methods failed to command that degree of popular confidence which would be willing to dispense with further control if such control was available, and in America it was. The conservative sense of the community demanded a judicial check which had to operate under the guise of legal and not of political control. The idea of a constitutional policy and corresponding rights and limitations was thus readily entertained, not only by the courts, but by the great preponderance of public and professional opinion, and to a very considerable extent this opinion prevails today.

This point of view should control the interpretation of much that goes in America under the name of constitutional law. The decisions enforcing so-called inherent limitations are among the most loosely reasoned in our entire case law. There is much talk about inalienable rights on the one side and about the police power on the other; as the case may be, either denunciation of the arbitrary will of the legislature, or disclaimer of judicial superiority of judgment or power of control; practically the only criterion that is suggested is that of reasonableness. From the point of view of legal science it would be difficult to conceive of anything more unsatisfactory.

Extreme indefiniteness, however, appears in the light of a wise avoidance of irrevocable conclusions, if we apply to this phase of constitutional law as a whole the test of political performance. The greatest defects of the decisions from a legal standpoint constitute their saving grace. No constitutional right is asserted without placing in convenient juxtaposition a saving on behalf of the public welfare. No rule has been formulated in such a manner as to embarrass an honorable retreat, and if an inconvenient precedent is encountered there is little hesitation in overruling it. Even the brief period of thirty years, during which the courts have enforced constitutional policies, has been sufficient to demonstrate that any apprehension of a permanent hindrance on their part to any phase of legislative progress is groundless.

Indeed, there is rather reason to fear that the courts will exercise the guardianship committed to them with less confidence and boldness than is desirable. A legislative body, in pursuing some particular social or economic policy demanded by popular clamor for the attainment of tangible and immediate objects, will easily be inclined to underestimate and neglect the larger policy of individual right and liberty which at one time was believed to be safest in its hands. For the protection of these larger and more permanent interests, so essential to the maintenance of our institutions, we naturally look to the courts which by constitution and habit are best qualified to appreciate the claims of individual right. There is a constant demand for restricting the entrance to callings and professions by license requirements. Plausible grounds are usually not wanting, and the valuable policy of freedom of vocation, slowly won in a long struggle for industrial emancipation, is very likely to be overlooked. Such a policy must look to the courts for support. A similar situation arises with regard to the tendency toward the creation of large discretionary administrative powers. In many cases the courts have only been too willing to relinquish that guardianship which they have claimed so freely when it was a question of resisting labor legislation. Yet on the whole our main reliance for the perpetuation of ideals of individual liberty must be in the continued exercise of the judicial prerogative.

Upon a larger view, then, of our constitutional history we are impressed with the fact that in assigning a controlling function to the courts we have after all not altered the universal character of constitutional issues: in America as well as in other countries they are, in the main, issues of power and policy. Compared with these issues the question of the conformity of legislation to fundamental principles of law has engaged the attention of the courts only to a relatively slight extent, and their decisions offer little in the way of enlightening discussion of canons of justice applicable to legislation.

This is after all what a true appreciation of the constitutional functions of courts should lead us to expect. It is unlikely that a legislature will otherwise than through inadvertence violate the most obvious and cardinal dictates of justice; gross miscarriages of justice are probably less frequent in legislation than they are in the judicial determination of controversies. The courts have therefore had little, if any, occasion to set up elementary canons of justice in opposition to legislation. Nor have they had occasion to elaborate those higher standards of greater refinement and complication in which imperfectly considered legislation is not unlikely to be deficient. For the constitutional power of courts over statutes is exercised only by annulling them altogether; and to attempt to apply this power by reason of mere imperfection would play havoc with legislation. No merely negative power will ever perform a standardizing function.

Perhaps a somewhat more constructive influence upon legislation might be exercised by the courts through their function of constitutional and statutory interpretation, and it will be necessary to dwell in its proper place upon that aspect of judicial power.

But above all it is necessary to realize, not only that constitutional law as represented by judicial decisions does not furnish us with a body of principles of legislation, but that it does not even indicate fully and clearly the nature and scope of these principles. It is indeed from the combined legislative, administrative, and judicial experiences that we gather the problems of legislation and their solution, but the solution does not proceed from or rest upon judicial authority, but must be worked out upon the basis of a discipline hardly recognized either in England or in this country—an independent science of jurisprudence.

CHAPTER VI

THE MEANING OF PRINCIPLE IN LEGISLATION

By contrast with the common law, every proposition of which claims to be a dictate of reason and logic, statute law is conventional in the sense that in many cases it merely represents the legislator's free choice between a number of different possible and perhaps equally reasonable provisions. The natural desire to avoid the charge of arbitrariness in legislation produces a strong tendency to follow precedents, and, in consequence, a certain uniformity of provision with regard to relatively indifferent matters which has nothing to do with principle, and which is yet likely to impose itself upon legislation with more than the force of principle. In every jurisdiction it is possible to cite instances of this kind in which the mere force of habit supports practices which have nothing else to recommend them; witness the usual clause at the end of a New York statute: "this act shall take effect immediately," or the requirement which is common in Illinois that the governor approve vouchers for expenses which are charges against appropriations. Such practices offer little general interest.

So long as legislation claims to produce law it must also strive to realize in its product that conformity to principle from which law derives its main sanction and authority. The difference between common law and statute law in this respect, however, is that while the data of the common law are fixed and beyond conscious and deliberate transmutation, those of legislation vary with varying purposes and conditions. While principle in common law simply stands for logic, reason, and established policy, its meaning in legislation is far more complex. We can hardly say more to begin with than that it means a settled point of view, and any closer analysis requires careful differentiation.

At the opposite ends of the various classes of considerations that move the legislator we should place constitutional requirement and policy. The constitutional rule must be obeyed no matter what opinion may be entertained of its wisdom, and is thus withdrawn from argument except for the purpose of interpretation. It may be absolutely conventional, as, e.g., in the requirement and wording of an enacting clause, or convention and principle may be mixed, as in specifying brief terms of office, or it may state a principle pure and simple, as in the rule against *ex post facto* laws or against double jeopardy. The mandatory character of the rule is affected by these differences only in the varying latitude of constitutional construction.

Policy, on the other hand, represents the freedom of legislative discretion. No matter what array of facts and arguments we may bring to bear upon certain problems, we must recognize that in the present state of human thought and knowledge their determination is controlled by considerations which lie beyond the forum of compelling reason, and depends upon fundamental differences in habits and ideals. Strict or liberal divorce laws, high license or prohibition, free trade or protection, free or regulated business, the limits of combination and of competition, form or informality in legal acts—these constitute issues with regard to which opinions of men will continue to differ, and which for the present must therefore be left to the domain of policy.

Contrast with these the legislative attitude toward polygamy, toward monopoly, toward gambling, or toward vice, and we shall find these latter policies as firmly established as any common-law principle. The common law embodies, in addition to reason and logic, also a great deal of policy, as, e.g., the pronounced favor to the accused in criminal procedure. That policy has in America been transformed into a constitutional rule, as has been the more modern policy of freedom of thought and of religion; there are even instances in which highly controversial policies have been enacted into constitutional provisions in order to withdraw them from legislative change; witness the prohibition clauses in the constitutions of Kansas and Oklahoma.

Where this is done, it is not inaccurate to say that policy has been changed into principle; we then simply attribute to principle the meaning of settled policy. In this sense any policy adopted by the legislature becomes the principle of the statute enacted to effectuate that policy—principle to the extent that it controls or should control the details of provisions and their application and interpretation. Considering the statute without reference to these details, we should of course realize that we deal with legislative policies and not with principles of legislation in the more specific sense. The legislative determination of policies is generally, and in a sense justly, regarded as a matter of free discretion; in any event the considerations guiding that discretion are ordinarily not counted as falling within the province of jurisprudence.

Principle as applied to legislation, in the jurisprudential sense of the term, thus does not form a sharp contrast to either constitutional requirement or policy, for it may be found in both; but it rises above both as being an ideal attribute demanded by the claim of statute law to be respected as a rational ordering of human affairs; it may be a proposition of logic, of justice, or of compelling expediency; in any event it is something that in the long run will tend to enforce itself by reason of its inherent fitness, or, if ignored, will produce irritation, disturbance, and failure of policy. It cannot, in other words, be violated with impunity, which does not mean that it cannot be or never is violated in fact. Perhaps the best criterion of principle is that reasonable persons can be brought to agree upon the correctness of a proposition, though when they are called upon to apply it their inclinations or prejudices may be stronger than their reason.

The question is whether our legal science has developed an adequate system of principles of legislation in this sense.

Now and then our constitutions specifically express a principle, so particularly with regard to criminal legislation, the rule against double jeopardy, and the rule against retroactive operation (*ex post facto* laws); but the bulk of constitutional provisions crystallize historic or modern policies and not permanent principles.

Where legislation is attacked in court as violating fundamental principle, reliance is always placed upon the Fourteenth Amendment, less commonly upon the equal-protection clause than upon the due-process clause. So far as equality means absence of arbitrary discrimination, it is almost undistinguishable from due process. So far as it is opposed to class legislation, a distinction should be made: equal justice between classes is of the essence of justice, and if in practice justice is not the same for rich and poor this is merely an inevitable effect of economic conditions which it is beyond the power of the law to remedy; equal legislation for all classes, however, so far as a definite meaning can be attached to the idea, is more in the nature of a policy than of a principle, and cannot be said to be firmly established. There remains, then, due process of law as the main, if not the sole, guaranty of principle in legislation.

Due process is so general a phrase that for its content we turn to judicial interpretation. The Supreme Court refers us to a gradual process of judicial inclusion and exclusion (*Davidson* v. *New Orleans*, 96 U.S. 97), and declines a compendious definition, which, indeed, if it were to claim authoritative value, would be worse than no definition at all. In the enormous number of decisions, however, that have applied the test of due process to legislation we might justly expect, after a lapse of forty years, some beginning in the working out of a system of principles. Unfortunately, opinions in constitutional cases rarely go beyond rhetoric and generalities; and quotations from similarly elusive pronouncements take the place of searching analysis. We are referred to reasonableness as a criterion of validity, as if "reasonable" were not the very negation of scientific precision. Whatever may be the merit or demerit of the actual decisions upon the validity of legislation, the theory of constitutional law as found in the opinions interpreting due process of law is perhaps the least satisfactory department of American jurisprudence. We ought to know to what extent due process means definite principles, and to that extent these principles should be judicially stated; and we ought to know, on the other hand, to what extent principles are beyond judicial enforcement and must be left to legislative method and practice.

If in the following an attempt will be made to give to the idea of principle in legislation a more definite content than it has hitherto received, it can of course be only by way of outline and illustration. But this will be sufficient, if it be possible at all, for the purpose of demonstrating the defects of present doctrine and the possibilities of scientific legislation. Much of what has been said before in the course of this essay was intended to bring out and illustrate what are believed to be true principles of legislation, and consequently the following outline will, in part at least, be merely in the nature of a recapitulation of previous statements and conclusions.

Prohibition.—The previous discussion of this subject[1] should have made it clear that it is a true principle of legislation that a remote or conjectural danger, or the danger of fraud or abuse, does not justify the entire suppression of a legitimate and valuable interest. That interests of no intrinsic economic utility may be sacrificed in the exercise of the police power is demonstrated by the course of prohibition legislation; the consumption of intoxicating liquor represents normally only pleasure, indulgence, and license, which are not generally counted as assets of positive value. Where intoxicating liquor serves mechanical, medicinal, or sacramental purposes, it represents an essential interest which is respected in legislative practice.

The force of the principle of conserving genuine values is demonstrated by the history of oleomargarine legislation and of legislation prohibiting dealings in futures and options as set forth in another connection. It will be remembered that the Supreme Court of the United States recognized the validity of prohibitions which the better sense of the community finally repudiated as untenable. Only a theory of judicial infallibility can continue to treat prohibitions thus discredited as legitimate forms of exercise of legislative power. Against judicial opinions which fail to state clear issues, which are hesitating in

[1] Pp. 84–95.

their expressions, and which are qualified in subsequent cases, we set the striking consensus of widely separated jurisdictions in abandoning policies which were imprudently adopted and which experience proved to be intolerable, and we cannot doubt on which side we should find the true principle of legislation.

The principle is, indeed, one which commends itself by its good sense, and which any *a priori* theory of legislation would readily accept. It needs to be emphasized merely because it failed to receive the supreme judicial sanction. And while it is in a sense obvious and commonplace, it may still be claimed for the principle that it has a more tangible content than mere phrases about liberty and property, reasonableness and the public welfare.

Indefinite penal provisions.—The history of the criminal enforcement of the Sherman Anti-trust Act should prove another principle, namely, that penal legislation ought to avoid elastic prohibitions where the difference between the exercise of a valuable right and the commission of a proposed criminal offense is entirely one of degree and effect. As interpreted in the Standard Oil and the Tobacco cases, the Act of 1890 creates a crime of monopolizing an industry which no one as yet has been capable of defining. Whether an organization like the Harvester Company is a contribution to the economic efficiency of the nation or is a violation of the law of the land is a question which the Supreme Court takes years to make up its mind on, and the erroneous private decision of which subjects to the risk of fine and imprisonment.

The United States Supreme Court says that the act is, notwithstanding this, constitutional (*Nash* v. *U.S.*, 229 U.S. 373); again, however, it must be permitted to vouch history as a witness. The criminal enforcement of the Sherman Act has been an absolute failure; a few fines have been imposed and one imprisonment of four hours' duration in the custody of the sheriff has been suffered; in its strongest case—that of the National Cash Register Company—the government has been defeated; and what success it has had in enforcing the act has been through the power of proceeding in equity, which was an afterthought and, as it were, an accident in the history of the preparation and enactment of the law. And even this phase of the law is likely to be superseded by the more specific methods provided for by the legislation of 1914. The draconic penalties of state anti-trust laws have remained dead letters.

Yet in deciding the Nash case the Supreme Court was confronted with the fact that the Sherman Act after all expressed merely in statutory form the vague prohibitions of the common law of conspiracy. It may be that nothing that the common law sanctions can be a denial of due process; if so, it follows that the constitution is not an adequate safeguard of the observance of true principles of legislation. The indefinite crimes of the common law clearly violate these principles. An unspecified crime is entirely inconsistent with the requirement of specific charges in indictments, the principle being the same in both cases. The strong demand for a codification of the criminal law both in America and on the continent of Europe was largely inspired by the horror of undefined offenses which also found expression in the Fourth Article of the French Declaration of Rights of 1789. And practical experience shows that except in cases of strong popular prejudice the sense of the injustice of the law will lead both juries and courts to minimize or neutralize its effect, so that it will operate, if at all, only in cases where constitutional protection would be most urgently needed.

It has been said that the strength of a statute lies in its general phrases and terms, and there is truth in the statement if properly understood and applied. That is to say, a general phrase leaves to court or jury, as the case may be, a much greater latitude of interpretation than a specific term does.

A pure enabling act of a civil character, like the grant of a charter power, is more desirable to the grantee of the power if it is couched in general terms. The same is true of an act granting a civil remedy, if the plaintiff can count on the sympathy of court and jury; thus in Illinois the miners objected to the specification of safeguards in the mining law because it diminished their chances of recovery. And it will be observed that while the criminal clauses of the Sherman Act have remained unenforced, no contrivance has succeeded in escaping condemnation under the civil proceedings brought in equity by the government. However, what in civil proceedings is an advantage to the plaintiff is a disadvantage to the defendant, and vague and undefined statutory rights which burden a third party, while they may be desirable from the point of view of the party to whom the right is given, be it private party or government, remain objectionable from the point of view of general justice.   In the long run this objection may be likewise fatal, and it is very probable that the more specific provisions of the legislation of 1914 will practically put the Sherman Act out of operation.   In a criminal statute, however, the generality of the prohibition is not only unjust to the defendant, but disadvantageous to the prosecuting government, not only because it will make convictions difficult, but because it will diminish the vigor and confidence of official enforcement.   In this latter respect the history of the Sherman Act affords no fair example, considering the enormous special efforts that have been made through large appropriations and political pressure to initiate prosecutions.   The experience of factory legislation is more typical, and here the testimony of administrative experience is strong that general requirements cannot be criminally enforced.

THE CORRELATION OF PROVISIONS

The correlation of distinct and separable provisions makes a system out of a conglomerate of rules, while the correlation of necessarily interdependent provisions is an imperative requirement of logic, the violation of which must nullify the offending statute in whole or in part. The legendary Irish act which provided that the material of an existing prison should be used in the erection of a new one, and that the prisoners should continue to be confined in the old prison until the new one should be completed, illustrates the fatal inconsistency against which even the omnipotence of Parliament cannot prevail.

If the constitution of Oklahoma (IX, 46) prohibits discrimination between persons or sections for the purpose of destroying competition by forbidding sales of commodities at a lower rate in one section than in another, it clearly fails to deal effectually with discrimination between persons in the same section, for the restricted specification of means necessarily qualifies the wider substantive provision. If the statute of wills of Illinois permits the signing of a will by another for the testator only if it be done by direction and in the presence of the testator, and yet permits probate of the will upon proof of the attesting witnesses that the testator acknowledged the signature as his, it allows the requirement that the vicarious signing be done in the presence of the testator to be neutralized or nullified by a misstatement of the latter. Inconsistencies like these are not fatal to the entire statute, but merely to one of the two inconsistent provisions. They need no further comment.

It is the lack of correlation which does not amount to direct and fatal inconsistency of terms that constitutes a problem in jurisprudence. The common law, indeed, is necessarily free from verbal inconsistency, since, being unwritten, its rules are not formulated in authoritative terms. The common law is, however, also relatively free from the inconsistency of separable provisions, since it is built up by reason and analogy, and disharmony is a legitimate ground for rejecting a rule as unsound. This does not mean that the demonstration of disharmony in spirit in the widest sense can be relied upon to defeat settled rules of common law. It is inconsistent that the state should hold corporations to the rule respondeat superior and claim immunity from liability for the wrongful acts of its own servants, yet there is no inconsistency of operation, and conceivably a disharmony of this kind might be justified on special grounds of policy. Perhaps the grossest common-law instance of lack of correlation is to be found in the husband's right to appropriate the entire personalty of his wife, coupled with his power to will that same personalty to strangers and leave her penniless. This can be explained only by the fact that the adjustment of property rights between husband and wife belonged to the three distinct jurisdictions of the courts of common law, the court of equity, and the ecclesiastical courts, no one of which had entire control or responsibility, and that in the seventeenth century, when the free power of testamentary disposition came to be recognized, the common law had entered upon a period of stagnation, which prevented the necessary readjustments called for by this innovation. The operation of the rule of correlation may, however, be illustrated from the law of parent and child. If the father has the right to appropriate the earnings of the minor child, it must necessarily follow that he is under legal duty to support the child; a doctrine that would deny the father's liability must also deny his right to earnings. It is mere thoughtlessness if the duty of support is sometimes discussed without reference to the right to earnings, and the actual state of the law is in accordance with this principle of correlation. Similarly, the common law places upon the husband at least the duty to support his wife, in return for his right to appropriate her property or income.

When the legislature made the wife the mistress of her own property or income, it should have placed upon her a correlative obligation to contribute to the support of household and family. This has been done by the German Civil Code, but not by American or English married women's acts. We have thus the anomaly that a rich wife may obtain a divorce from a poor husband for non-support where that is a ground for divorce. Similar results may happen in other cases in which a statute changes one common-law rule without dealing with related rules; the generally accepted principles of statutory construction are not liberal enough to supply the defect, and a disharmony results.

The lack of correlation may be due to the fact that the various provisions of statutes do not harmonize with one another, or to the fact that the legislature has failed to supplement the provisions of a statute by others which are necessary for their satisfactory or just operation. The former defect is more obvious and easier to avoid than the latter. The one as well as the other may in appropriate cases be remedied by statutory construction,

and the extent to which this remedy will be applied will
depend upon the degree to which the courts realize and
are impressed with the existence, the soundness, and the
importance of the principle of correlation.

The entire problem is well illustrated by a number of
cases decided in recent years by the Supreme Court of the
United States and other American courts.

1. *The doctrine of the Abilene case (Texas & P. R. Co.* v.
Abilene Cotton Oil Co., 204 U.S. 426, 1907).—The Interstate Commerce Act of 1887 establishes two important
principles: that of reasonableness of rates and that of
non-discrimination, i.e., of equality of rates under similar
conditions. Carriers are required to publish schedules of
rates. The Interstate Commerce Commission is authorized to grant relief against unreasonable rates, and the
act expressly provides that a person claiming to be
damaged by a common carrier may either make complaint to the Commission or may bring suit for recovery
of damages for which the carrier may be liable under the
provisions of the act (sec. 9); and again (sec. 22), that
nothing contained in the act shall in any way abridge or
alter remedies now existing at common law or by statute,
but that the provisions of the act are in addition to such
remedies. When in the above case a shipper claiming to
be overcharged brought an action at common law against
the carrier to recover the amount paid in excess of a
reasonable rate, the Supreme Court held, notwithstanding
the very explicit provision just cited of the statute, that
no common-law action could be brought before application

made to the Commission to establish the extent of over-
charge. The same rule was subsequently applied to a
criminal prosecution instituted by the government prior
to administrative action by the Commission (*U.S.* v.
Pacific, etc., Co., 228 U.S. 106, 1913). The court found
two equally dominant principles in the act, that of equal
rates and that of reasonable rates, and both had as far as
possible to be maintained. If shippers were at liberty to
sue at common law, the question of reasonableness would
as a question of fact go to a jury, and different juries
might find different rates, with the result that the rule of
equality might be destroyed and published rates, perhaps through verdicts reached by collusion, be departed
from, whereas administrative correction would act upon
all cases in like manner. In this case, then, the various
purposes of the act are correlated to each other by a
judicial construction which has to override the apparently
plain provision of the act in favor of the common-law
remedy; the principle of correlation, in other words,
controls the construction of the act entirely. In no
other case is the principle so emphatically recognized.
Great interest also attaches to the plain implication that
the operation of the common-law remedy negatives the
idea of equal operation—a remarkable reflection upon
the idea of equal justice under the régime of jury verdicts.

2. *The traffic agreement cases.*—The Supreme Court of
the United States has not always been so amenable
to arguments urging correlation and consistency. The
Interstate Commerce Act preceded the Sherman Anti-

trust Act by three years. The former act was believed
to have brought a temporary and tentative solution of
the railroad-rate problem, and in 1890 no disposition to
reopen it had been manifested. If the Commerce Act
had not dealt specifically with railroad monopolization, it
was partly because the monopolistic nature of railroad
transportation was to a certain extent inevitable, and
because state laws on the whole sufficiently prevented
the consolidation of competing roads. The "Northern
Securities" problem was a thing not thought of. The
Sherman Act was understood to be directed against
monopolistic practices and enterprises in the sale of
commodities, i.e., in the domain of trade and commerce
apart from railroad transportation. The act did not in
terms refer to railroads; it is true, however, that its
terms were wide enough to cover transportation as well
as any other form of commerce. Agreements restrictive
of competition had long been customary among railroad
companies and had commonly assumed the form of
pooling agreements. These were specifically forbidden
by the Interstate Commerce Act, which was silent with
regard to other agreements. The forbidden pools having
been discontinued, the Trans-Missouri Freight Association
was formed for the purpose of establishing and maintaining rates and otherwise securing joint action in matters
affecting common interests in traffic and rate-making.
In January, 1892, the government instituted proceedings
in equity to have this association restrained from continuing its operation. The Circuit Court and the Circuit

Court of Appeals held that the agreement was not covered by the Anti-trust Act, but the Supreme Court in March, 1897, by a bare majority held that the Sherman Act applied to railroad transportation and that any agreement for the common establishment and maintenance of rates, however beneficial its economic purpose or effect, was in restraint of competition and therefore forbidden and unlawful. The decision was reiterated in the following year in the case of the Joint Traffic Association (171 U.S. 505).

The dissenting opinion written by Justice, now Chief Justice, White relied upon the inconsistency between the Anti-trust Act and the Commerce Act. The Commerce Act had superseded the principle of the competitive rate by the principle of the reasonable rate. Rates were to be published, not to be departed from, and not to be raised or reduced until after notice. Effective competition was thereby rendered impossible, and if competition as a regulating factor was displaced, how could a reasonable rate be established except by common understanding? As Senator Root put it in 1910: "Not the mere law of competition obtains, but the law of conformity; how is that to be reached but by bringing the railroads together either with a voluntary agreement or by force?"

The dissenting opinion, in other words, contends for what is here called the principle of correlation, and demands that it shall control the inexplicit, if not ambiguous, provisions of the Anti-trust Act; the majority decision gives effect to what it conceives to be the intrinsically correct construction of the Anti-trust Act.

Let us again test the principle which the majority rejects or denies to be applicable, by the criterion of experience. The two associations which the court declared illegal were, or had already been, dissolved, but it should be observed that even before the dissolution, before the judicial decision, before the passage of the Sherman Act, the associations were powerless to enforce stipulations for maintenance of rates, for these being void at common law, nothing short of positive statutory sanction would make them actionable, and such a sanction the Interstate Commerce Act failed to provide. Anti-trust legislation in America has not been enacted to nullify agreements in restraint of competition—that would have been a work of supererogation—but to penalize the entering into agreements that might be voluntarily observed, though unenforceable by legal process. To determine the success of the Freight Association cases we must therefore ask whether they caused joint action and understanding in the matter of rates to be considered and to become as a matter of fact illegal. President Roosevelt in his message of December 2, 1906, quoted from the *Report* of the Interstate Commerce Commission as follows: "The decisions of the United States Supreme Court in the Trans-Missouri case and the Joint Traffic case have produced no practical effect upon the railway operations of the country. Such associations in fact exist now as they did exist before those decisions and with the same general effect. In justice to all parties we ought probably to add that it is difficult to see how our interstate railways could be operated with due regard to the interest of the shipper and the railway without concerted action of the kind afforded through these associations." In other reports the Commission says: "To one familiar with actual conditions it seems practically out of the question to establish rates that are relatively just without conference and agreement. But when rates have once been established the act itself requires that they shall be observed until changes are announced in the manner provided Certainly it ought not to be unlawful for carriers to confer and agree for the purpose of doing what the law enjoins."[1] "If carriers are to make public their rates and to charge all shippers the same rate they must as a practical matter agree to some extent with respect to these rates."[2]

President Roosevelt and President Taft repeatedly urged the legalization of rate agreements. The bill for the Act of 1910 creating the Commerce Court contained a section to that effect, which, however, did not become law. The prejudice against dropping legal inhibitions affecting corporations is well known, and the attitude of Congress is of a piece with the unimpaired maintenance of the Sherman Act, notwithstanding the legislation of 1914. The legalization of rate agreements would render them legally enforceable and hence more effectual. At

---

[1] *12th Report*, 1898, pp. 15, 16.   [2] *14th Report*, 1900, p. 9.

present they are not merely not enforceable, but they are supposed to be illegal; yet everyone knows that all recent important railroad action in the matter of rates has been joint sectional action, and that in the nature of things it could not be otherwise. In declaring such joint action to be illegal the Supreme Court has created what Senator Root characterized as an anomaly, an abuse, a discredit to our system of law. Surely another instance where a principle of legislation has proved stronger than a decision of the Supreme Court.

3. *The Pipe Line cases* (*U.S.* v. *Ohio Oil Co.*, 234 U.S. 548).—Probably in consequence of a report made in May, 1906, by the Commissioner of Corporations upon the conditions existing with regard to the transportation of petroleum, Congress, in the Act of June 29, 1906, amending the Interstate Commerce Act, provided that the provisions of the act should apply to corporations or persons engaged in the transportation of oil by means of pipe lines, who should be held to be common carriers within the meaning of the act. Various pipe-line companies were in consequence ordered by the Interstate Commerce Commission to file schedules of rates, and they contested the validity of the requirement. It had been the practice of these companies not to accept oil produced by other companies than the company owning the pipe line, except upon condition that the oil should first be sold to them, so that technically they were transporting only their own oil, and one of the companies had never carried any oil but that which the owner of

the line had produced. Under these circumstances the companies contended that Congress had no power to force them into a business which they had never voluntarily undertaken. This contention found favor with the Commerce Court, but was rejected by the Supreme Court as against the companies which had carried oil produced by others, the court holding that they had engaged in the transportation of oil, and that the preliminary purchase of the oil was only a form of doing business, so that Congress merely imposed upon carriers in fact the obligation of common carriers. As regards the company that had carried only its own oil, the court held that it could not be said to be engaged in the transportation of oil, and that the act therefore did not apply to it. Chief Justice White was of the opinion that the act could not be constitutionally made to apply to this latter company. Justice McKenna thought that Congress had no power to make those companies common carriers that were not so before the act.

The decision has a negative bearing upon the principle of correlation. It did not apparently occur to any of the judges that the construction of this provision might be legitimately affected by other provisions of the same act. The Act of 1906 contained what is known as the commodity clause, the clause forbidding railroad companies to carry any products or commodities (with certain exceptions) produced or owned by them. With great deliberation Congress inaugurated the policy that the common carrier should be exclusively the servant of others, in order that there might be no temptation to use his position as carrier to favor himself as producer or owner to the disadvantage of competing shippers. This is an important and fundamental policy in the regulation of public-service business. And yet the government contended that Congress in the same act forced this inconsistent relation upon those who never theretofore had sustained it. Even if special conditions made it desirable to permit and require producers of oil who had theretofore carried for others, to continue to do so, and to submit them to control and regulation, the court was justified in refusing to impute to Congress the inconsistency of creating a relation which in another part of the act it condemned. The court as a matter of fact avoided that inconsistency, but without realizing this phase of the problem. Nothing could show more clearly how little, as yet, the value of correlation is appreciated as a controlling principle of legislation.

4. *Illinois warehouse legislation.*—A striking instance, on the other hand, of the judicial enforcement of the principle of correlation as a principle controlling not merely the construction but the validity of legislation is presented in connection with the regulation of grain elevators in Illinois. The constitution of that state has an article containing full provisions regarding the storing of grain, declaring elevators to be public warehouses, requiring weekly statements, giving owners of grain full liberty of examination, and making it the duty of the General Assembly to prevent the issue of fraudulent

warehouse receipts, to give full effect to the article of the constitution, and to provide for the inspection of grain and for the protection of producers, shippers, and receivers.

The legislature gave statutory effect to the specific requirements of the constitution, but did not expressly impose additional restrictions or prohibitions of an essential character upon the business. As a matter of fact, a large proportion of the grain-elevator business in Chicago was in the hands of grain dealers and owners. This practice was attacked by the Attorney-General, and the Supreme Court held (*Central Elevator Co.* v. *People*, 174 Ill. 203, 1898) that it was inconsistent with the fiduciary position of warehousemen that they should store grain of their own, because this would give them an undue advantage over other grain dealers. Before the decision of the lower court was affirmed, the enactment of a statute was procured relieving warehouse owners from the disability thus pronounced, subject to provisions for special inspection and to regulations to be framed by the warehouse commissioners to prevent fraud, discrimination, or any advantage to the owner over other depositors (Act of May 26, 1897). This statute the Supreme Court declared to be contrary to the constitutional policy and therefore void (*Hannah* v. *People*, 198 Ill. 77), partly perhaps because the act delegated the function of reconciling the inconsistencies of the dual position to the warehouse commissioners, while the constitution enjoined the duty of giving adequate protection

upon the legislature itself.   In any event the correlation
of privilege and duty or restraint in the conduct of public-
service business was here recognized before Congress
adopted the same policy by the commodity clause
of 1906.

It is much easier to avoid placing in the same statute
several provisions that do not harmonize with each other
(which would reveal the defect of the statute on its face)
than to succeed in making adequate provision for all
correlative rights and obligations needed to insure a just
and harmonious operation of the act.   It is the difference
between positive error and imperfection due to omission.
The latter defect can in some cases be remedied by allowing
the statute to be controlled or supplemented by common-
law principles.   The famous controversy whether the
statute of descent or of wills should or can be construed
so as to prevent the murderer from inheriting from the
person he has murdered is complicated by the difficulty
of finding a common-law rule exactly in point.   The
possibilities of construction are better illustrated by a
statute of Texas which required a corporation discharging
an employee to furnish him on demand a true statement
in writing of the cause of his discharge.   The court held
that in the absence of an express provision a statement
untrue in fact cannot in an action for libel be held to be a
privileged statement (*St. L. & S.W. R. Co.* v. *Griffin,* 154
S.W. 583)—plainly an inequitable result.   Had the express provisions of the statute been qualified by the
application of common-law principles, the new obligation

would have been offset by a correlative privilege, and better justice would have been accomplished.

In many cases, however, the common law has no principle that fits a new statutory situation, but on the contrary the rules of the common law, being harmonious with each other, disharmonize with the new statutory provision. To do perfect justice it would therefore be necessary to supplement the provisions of the statute in accordance with its spirit and purpose, and the prevailing canons of statutory construction will not as a rule permit this to be done. If a married woman is given by statute the control of her own property, it does not follow as a matter of construction that she is now jointly or ratably liable for family or household expenses; the preponderance of authority leans even against relieving the husband from liability for her torts.

Correlation in labor legislation.—It is this failure to perform the difficult task of adequately surveying and covering the entire aggregate of rights and obligations involved in new legislation which accounts for much of the alleged unreasonableness of modern statutes, and has been particularly conspicuous in labor legislation. Reciprocal obligation is of the essence of employment. A statute enacted at the request of labor interests generally seeks to redress some injustice or grievance, but very often the practice which employers are forbidden to continue has some element of justification in the shortcomings of labor; and a mere one-sided prohibition without corresponding readjustments leaves the relation defective, with the balance of inconvenience merely shifted from one side to the other. Under such circumstances the courts are much inclined to assent to the claim that there has been an arbitrary interference with liberty or a violation of due process, and there is a sufficient falling short of sound principles of legislation to make adverse judicial decisions intelligible. It may be well to illustrate this by conspicuous examples.

Coal-weighing legislation.—The value of coal depends in part upon the size of the pieces mined, and this in turn depends upon the skill and care of the miner. A practice had grown up in the coal-mining industry of paying the miner for the coal mined by him by weight; but in order to eliminate the inferior coal, the coal before being weighed was sifted by passing the rejected pieces through a screen. The obvious result was that the miner received no pay for part of the coal mined by him which yet had a certain market value and which was appropriated by the mine-owner. The miners, feeling this to be an injustice, procured the enactment of statutes which required the weighing of the coal without passing the same through a screen. In Ohio and Illinois these statutes were declared unconstitutional, the court of Illinois relying chiefly upon the constitutional right of freedom of contract (*Millet* v. *People*, 117 Ill. 294). Since the practice sought to be forbidden involved an injustice, it was perhaps unfortunate to emphasize the constitutional right of the miner to submit to it. The Ohio court adopted a wiser line of argument when it pointed out that one injustice was simply superseded by another, the mine-owner now being compelled by law to pay the miner irrespective of the quality of his work and product (*Re Preston*, 63 Ohio St. 428). It is interesting to note the subsequent development in Ohio, which appears in the case of *Rail & River Coal Co.* v. *Yaple* (236 U.S. 338), decided by the Supreme Court in February, 1915. The amended constitution of Ohio expressly authorized the legislature to provide for the regulation of methods of mining, weighing, measuring, and marketing coal and other minerals (II, sec. 36). It is needless to inquire whether the old law would have been sustained under this express provision; the important thing is that the legislature did not undertake to re-enact it. What it did was to refer the controversy to a coal-mining commission, which recommended a law which was enacted and which in substance provides that the coal as mined and weighed shall contain no greater percentage of slate than ascertained and determined by the Industrial Commission of Ohio, and that miners and operators shall agree for stipulated periods upon the percentage of fine coal and slack coal allowable in the output of the mine. We are not concerned with the details of the measure, which are technical; sufficient that there was, as the Supreme Court says, "an earnest attempt to eliminate the objections to the 'run of mine' basis of payment to the miners (sought to be compelled by the old coal-weighing law), and to enact a system fair alike to employer and miner." Obviously the difference between the new law (sustained

by the Supreme Court) and the old one is that the
present law seeks to correlate rights and obligations
while the old law undertook to cure one anomaly by
substituting another.

Membership in labor unions and the right of discharge.—
With great, if not entire, unanimity American courts have
held that a statute cannot make it unlawful for an
employer to require of an employee, as a condition of
employing him or retaining him in his employment, an
agreement that he will not during the time of the employment become or remain a member of a labor organization,
or to discharge or to threaten to discharge him by reason
of such membership.   Decisions to that effect have been
rendered in New York, Illinois, Missouri, Wisconsin,
Minnesota, Kansas, and by the federal Supreme Court
with reference to an act of Congress, and a later decision
of Kansas sustaining such a law was reversed by the
Supreme Court of the United States (*Coppage* v. *Kansas*,
236 U.S. 1, January, 1915).   The argument against the
validity of the statute seems to be as follows: A laborer
has the right to quit his employment, subject to a liability
to damages for breach of contract, since the spceific or
penal enforcement of personal service would violate the
Thirteenth Amendment, resulting in a condition equivalent to involuntary servitude.   But the relation being
reciprocal, the employer must have a like right to discharge the employee, subject to a liability for breach of
contract.   The right to discharge being absolute, it cannot logically be qualified by specifying certain causes for

which it may not be exercised; he may therefore discharge because the employee belongs to a labor union. And if he may discharge, does not that involve the minor right to inform the employee in advance that he will be discharged if he joins a labor organization or continues in it? Superficially considered, this chain of reasoning seems plausible; and the first part of it seems a recognition of the principle of correlation. More closely scrutinized, the argument shows weakness. I have contended elsewhere,[1] and still believe it to be true, that the right to discharge implies neither the right to make threats of discharge nor the right to make any or all exactions as a condition of non-discharge, and the dissenting opinion of the Supreme Court in the Coppage case expresses itself to the same effect (236 U.S. 32, 36). The reasoning of the present decisions would lead to the nullification of all the statutes which forbid the threat of discharge by way of influencing the exercise of political rights[2]—statutes which do not appear to have been questioned, and which are eminently sound in principle. It is also impossible to believe that the last word has been spoken upon the constitutional right to quit service and to discharge an employee; some day the relation of involuntary servitude and breach of contract will have to be reconsidered.

Again, however, as in the coal-weighing legislation, if the decisions are unsatisfactory, the legislation is no less so, and the defect of the statute may account for the decision.

[1] *Police Power*, sec. 326.   [2] *Ibid.*, sec. 325.

The true principle of correlation requires, not that a right to quit service arbitrarily should be offset by an arbitrary right to discharge, but that the employer should not be deprived of a legitimate weapon of defense without being given some assurance that his defenselessness will not be abused.   Put in other words, if some particular union is actively hostile to some employer, it is unjust to require him to retain the members of that union in his employ.   A statute that deals with the matter at all ought to weigh carefully the possible effects of altering common-law rights and offset privilege by obligation.   It affords no solution of the problem to give legitimate protection to the employee by taking the means of legitimate protection from the employer.

It is quite futile to argue, as is the present fashion, the question of abstract power, and it does not take much gift of prophecy to see that a bare denial of legislative power by the courts can under our institutions prevail only for a short time.   What is needed is to point out the defects of legislation as measured by sound principles, for these must ultimately prevail unless we are to despair of our system of government.   Liberty does not furnish an intelligible principle of legislation, because all police legislation is necessarily, as far as it goes, a negation of liberty;   and reasonableness means nothing without a more definite content, while the correlation of rights and obligations at least suggests a way to constructive justice.

Absolute correlation is, of course, a counsel of perfection.   It may be impossible for the present to work out a formula which measures out precisely equal protection to employer and employee in the matter of organization; it may be necessary to operate with such general ideas as privilege, interference, abuse, intimidation, coercion, etc., and leave their further development to courts and juries, so that, as in the development of the common law, the principle would be gradually elaborated by adjusting rights and obligations in particular cases and allowing these to operate as precedents.

The uncompromising logic of correlation may also lead to demands that at present are obviously beyond realization. Thus it may be pointed out that it is inconsistent to impose upon public utilities the obligation to serve the public without giving them the power to command the services of employees. In answer it can only be said that such a power is at present beyond the reach of the attainable, and that therefore it is necessary to be illogical. The anomalies of political, economic, and social conditions will inevitably now and then counteract the operation of principle. The claim is not that legislation shall be perfect, but that it shall approximate perfection so far as actual conditions will permit. Only to this extent is the principle of correlation contended for.

It is easily demonstrated that much legislation falls short even of the attainable standard. An improvement of legislative methods will regularly lead to a greater approximation to the standard. It is interesting to compare recent English with American legislation in that respect. Our minimum-wage acts are silent as to the corresponding duty of service, whereas the English Act of 1912 relating to coal mines provides for rules with respect to the regularity and the efficiency of the work to be performed.

Our statutes making railroad companies liable for fire caused to adjacent property by sparks from locomotives are much older than that of England; in England a statute was first enacted in 1905 (5 Ed. VII, ch. 11); but this statute contains a provision found in no American act, giving the railroad company the right to have its servants go on the land for the purpose of clearing it from underbrush or other worthless inflammable material, a right to control in part at least the conditions that give rise to the liability.

The principle of correlation is indeed most fruitful in the law of liability. The shortcomings of legislation in that respect can best be studied in the history of the mechanics' lien acts, the constitutional status of which has become uncertain by reason of the failure to work out adequately the complex relations between owner and subcontractor. The most careful elaboration of the principle, on the other hand, is found in the workmen's compensation acts of recent years. In connection with these the general reflection suggests itself that statutory liability is likely to represent a higher type of law than common-law liability, for the reason that the common law is less capable, if capable at all, of producing positive and measured duties. The requirement of notice to the person sought to be charged, so essential to his protection against fraudulent claims, is thus regularly found in liability acts (not, however, in the wrongful-death acts copied from Lord Campbell's Act), while in the nature of things common-law liability is not qualified in this way.

Altogether the principle of correlation means the interdependence of right and obligation. In so far as it is recognized it compels the legislator to examine a relation, if the term may be used, from the debit as well as the credit side, and it works against the assertion of absolute and unqualified right. It complicates the simplicity of the common law, but for that very reason indicates an advanced stage of jurisprudence.

THE PRINCIPLE OF STANDARDIZATION

If correlation means more carefully measured justice, standardization serves to advance the other main objects of law, namely, certainty, objectivity, stability, and uniformity. Common-law rules carry their justification in the reasoning upon which they are based, but legislation generally involves a choice between a number of rules of equal or of equally doubtful equity, and thus presents the problem of avoiding the appearance of arbitrariness in fixing upon some particular provision. It is therefore desirable that conclusions be reached as far as possible upon an objective and intelligible basis, and that this basis be not needlessly varied from statute to statute. Standardization thus represents a definite, if comprehensive and far-reaching, ideal in legislation, and while it enters into every other principle, it does so as a distinct and additional attribute.   If liability needs correlation, any system of correlation will gain by being standardized, and so with regard to classification, the protection of vested rights, and so forth.

The principle of standardization has four main applications or phases in the making of statute law: conformity to undisputed scientific data and conclusions, the working out of juristic principles, the observance of an intelligible method in making determinations, and the avoidance of excessive or purposeless instability of policy.

1. *Conformity to scientific laws.*—The bulk of modern legislation deals with social, economic, or political problems.   These problems are not amenable to the same methods of treatment as the problems of physical science, and few of the conclusions offered in the name of the social sciences can claim finality or acceptance as absolute truths.   Those who insist that the legislature is bound to defer to experts do well to remember that, of the great social measures of the nineteenth century, the factory acts were carried against the protests of economists, while the public-health laws were largely based on theories of the spread of disease which are now rejected. So far as undisputed conclusions are available, they ought to be accepted as a basis for legislation, but even this modest demand represents an ideal rather than an actuality, for even if skepticism, prejudice, and selfish interest did not count as factors, the limitation of available resources must often stand in the way of the realization of policies conceded to rest on an indisputable

foundation. It is sufficient to refer to laws concerning taxation, financial administration, and charity and correction, which admittedly at best approximate the recognized scientific standards. Where legislation involves the operation of the physical sciences (health, safety), there is a greater readiness to submit to authority, and a failure in this respect will usually be due to inadequate means.

These are commonplaces; no one speaking of scientific legislation could possibly ignore standardization in this sense. In mapping out a science of legislation, however, it would hardly do to claim as belonging to its province all the social any more than all the physical sciences that have to be considered in carrying out legislative policies. It is true that legislation in a sense controls and fashions the former, while it merely applies the latter, and the legislator is therefore likely to feel with regard to the former a responsibility which easily translates itself into a sense of duty to form independent opinions, while in matters of sanitation or engineering he would defer to expert authority.

Nevertheless, a science of legislation desirous of establishing a status of its own would treat the data of the social sciences as lying outside of its own sphere and consider that its task begins only when their conclusions have been reached and formulated. The task would then be the technical one of translating a policy into the terms of a statute and judging as a preliminary matter whether such translation is practicable. The first of the four phases of the principle of standardization would therefore mean chiefly a draft upon other sciences, and, as part of the science of legislation, would express itself only in methods of organization and operation calculated to make sure that legislation is not enacted in ignorance of relevant data that are capable of being authoritatively established. To illustrate: the valuable work which is being done at present to find rational and "scientific" bases for rate-making, for tax valuations, for public-service requirements, and generally for terms of franchise grants is not the work of legal experts, but of economists, accountants, and engineers; but the principle of standardization demands at the very least the adoption of legislative methods which give an opportunity for this kind of work and information and bring its results to the notice of the legislators.

2. *Standardization of juristic data.*—The division of sciences is a practical matter, and it is for practical purposes that we should refuse to encumber the science of legislation with the tasks of social, economic, or political science. The problems of jurisprudence are, however, so closely related to the technical problem of legislation that, in so far as legal science has established or is capable of establishing settled conclusions, they are properly treated as part of the science of legislation and should contribute to its standardization. Unfortunately, hardly any systematic thought has been given to problems of jurisprudence in their constructive aspect; the law of evidence furnishes perhaps the only conspicuous exception. Littleton's *Tenures* has been extravagantly praised

as the most perfect work written in any science; but in treating the law as purely static it has set a model to all subsequent legal literature. Where Blackstone wanders off into critical estimate he becomes absurd, as where he speaks of the woman laboring under the disabilities of coverture as a favorite of the laws of England. Professor Gray's *Rule against Perpetuities* has no superior, if any equal, among American legal writings, but his treatment of the problem of how to deal constructively with settled property is negligible and, so far as it goes, superficial; his condemnation of spendthrift trusts in his essay on *Restraints on Alienation* manifests a fine virility of legal philosophy, but is hardly an objective estimate of a difficult and delicate legislative problem. It is only in recent years that technical questions of land legislation have been discussed critically and constructively in English legal reviews and parliamentary papers or reports; the reforms of the nineteenth century passed almost without literary comment. In America the critical treatment of technical legislative problems is even more meager and unsystematic.

It must be conceded that some of the most fundamental problems of jurisprudence seem as yet incapable of any other than a purely empirical or conventional solution. Which is preferable in legal acts, form or informality? What should be the extent of the protection of bona fide purchasers? What limitations and restraints upon the freedom of property should be conceded? Should a consideration be required to make a promise binding? Should the right of corporate organization be conceded for all legal or only for specified purposes? No answer can be given to any of these questions that is "scientifically" or even empirically indisputable; in the construction of civil codes they are treated as questions of policy, determined by a mutual balancing of conflicting considerations.

On the other hand, practically undisputed conclusions have been reached with regard to other subjects, perhaps mainly on the adjective side of the law (penalties, methods of enforcement, etc.), wherever any serious thought has been given to these subjects. Thus informers' shares and multiple damages survive only where legislation is in amateur hands. The range of these settled conclusions will be greatly extended when once systematic study shall be devoted to the technique of statute law. In many cases it can be demonstrated that the preference of one formulation to another will without alteration of substance make a provision practically more available for its intended purposes. The acceptance of the better form should then be a matter of course.

In discussing the terms of a statute there can ordinarily be no difficulty in distinguishing juristic considerations from other considerations of expediency, which belong to political science rather than to jurisprudence. Suppose some legislative policy or object is accepted as intrinsically desirable, it is still necessary to take into account the operation of adverse factors: the likelihood of public resistance due to widespread hostile sentiment (class, sectional, religious, national sentiment), the likelihood of private resistance and consequent difficulties of enforcement (inquisitorial methods of tax assessment), the likelihood of administrative resistance, where there is a disharmony between legislative and administrative standards. It is also necessary to have a proper appreciation of the unintended reactions of the proposed legislation resulting either from its normal operation (housing legislation and increased rents), or from the conditions of enforcement (white-slave legislation and blackmailing; declaring common-law marriages void and thereby rendering issue illegitimate), or from attempts at lawful evasion (marriage or divorce outside of the state; factory laws increasing tenement labor), or from illegal evasion (prohibition leading to increased consumption of the more easily concealed but also more harmful kind of liquor; closing of houses of prostitution and scattering of vice; more stringent marriage laws and increase of illegitimate births).

Under careful methods of legislation these considerations are not likely to be overlooked, but it is not easy to standardize the weight which should be given to them respectively, and in any event they do not (except as they bear upon technical conditions of enforcement) fall within the province of the jurist. There is, however, one consideration which, while not technically juristic, has such an intimate relation to the entire nature and purpose of law that in discussing the principle of standardization it cannot be ignored: that is, the observance of a certain order of transition in advancing to new policies or standards.

American legislation has sometimes violated this principle, but the very violations have served to illustrate its correctness. In the fifties of the last century the country was not prepared to accept entire prohibition as a method of dealing with the evils of intoxicating liquor; its establishment by statute necessarily produced lawlessness. In 1893 a general eight-hour law for women (had it not been declared unconstitutional) would have been as unenforceable as an eight-hour law for all persons employed in any kind of service would be today. The status of unmatured and precocious standards in our legislation has been explained before, and it has been pointed out that it is, generally speaking, the function of legislation to remedy grievances and correct abuses, and not to reconstruct society *de novo* or to force standards for which the community is not prepared. In practice the observance of this principle is ordinarily a matter of course, but it should be emphasized that it is of the very essence of the idea of law that progress should be gradual and orderly, and that violent and extreme change, even if in the right direction, must produce disturbance and a sense of insecurity.

3. *The observance of a definite method in reaching determinations.*—In matters not susceptible of scientific demonstration, when either of two different solutions of a problem can equally claim to be reasonable, arbitrariness in reaching conclusions can be best avoided by adherence

to intelligible and settled methods which insure a reasonably constant relation between determinations on cognate matters, each of which taken by itself must be the result of compromise or of free choice. This satisfies at least the strong and universal demand for order and proportion; and the danger of overlooking this requirement would hardly arise were it not for the fact that the legislature deals with related problems by distinct and disconnected measures.

This latter phase of standardization is most conspicuous when legislation deals with figures, and it has therefore no place in the common law, which has practically no measured quantities. It applies chiefly to rates and charges, allowances and expenditures, penalties and time provisions. It would be almost impossible to conceive of a progressive tax rate otherwise than as following an orderly line of progression.[1]   Exact proportion, it is true, may yield to simplicity and uniformity, as when a flat rate is prescribed for street-car fares instead of one varying with distance; but otherwise a departure from an orderly relation would be regarded as prima facie arbitrary and unjust. That is the trouble with the greater charge for the shorter haul, as long as the economic law of competitive rates is not fully understood, and if the practice was strongly resented when coming from private owners of railroads, it is almost unthinkable that it should be imposed by legislative regulation except after first

---

[1] A mathematical formula will be found in *National Tax Association Bulletin No. 1*, p. 13, taken from the report of a commission on taxation presented to the legislature of Massachusetts in 1916.

demonstrating scientifically its economic justification. It is one of the intolerable features of the assessment of real property for purposes of taxation that it has so generally been absolutely unstandardized. The new devices for valuation proposed in recent years have all this in common, that they establish a definite relation between location and value; in the last analysis value may escape scientific definition, but these methods at least secure an orderly relativity of valuations.[1]

This kind of standardization comes naturally where a legislative plan is conceived and carried out as a unit, but will necessarily be deficient where measures are disconnected and proceed from many independent sources. American legislation, initiated by shifting bodies and often framed by unascertained and irresponsible persons is therefore inferior in this respect to European legislation, which is practically controlled by the executive government. Taking the matter of official salaries, a cursory examination of state statutes shows figures that have hardly any relation to each other; the *Report* of the Economy and Efficiency Committee of Illinois particularly points out the lack of system in that state.[2] In Prussia this matter is standardized to the extent of the differentiation of one hundred and eighty salary classes. A similar standardization arises in America as soon as the adjustment of salaries is left to be handled in accordance

[1] See discussion of the Somers system in *Proceedings of National Tax Association*, 1913, pp. 234–85.

[2] *Report*, p. 20.

with civil service rules.[1] In the federal government likewise, with its high administrative centralization, the standardization of salaries is better than in the states. But the lack of co-ordination of appropriations in general even in the federal system is shown by President Taft's Commission on Economy and Efficiency, and the strong movement for the European form of budget bears testimony to the need for reform. It is hardly conceivable that the appropriations for river and harbor improvements or for public buildings should not bear at least some degree of relation to population, wealth, or commerce, but no consistent or systematic plan has ever been presented to the public, and failure to make a system generally intelligible is almost as bad in such a matter as having no system at all.

It is not possible to measure penalties upon a strictly scientific basis, but if there is a science of penology it must be one of its cardinal principles that penalties should be proportioned to the offense. In fact, the principle is expressed in some American constitutions; and this again means that penalties should be proportioned to one another. In most jurisdictions the criminal law is codified; the codification covers all the common felonies which are consequently considered in relation to each other, with the effect that there is a tolerable proportionateness of penalties. The differentiation of each generic felony into its possible subspecies is, however,

[1] See "Standardization of Public Employments," *Municipal Research No. 67*, November, 1915.

only very imperfectly carried out in American codes, as compared, e.g., with the German Penal Code. The American system is to allow a liberal margin between minimum and maximum penalty, with the result that individual estimate is substituted for abstract differentiation. This may be intended to make for better justice, but it is likely to make for greater arbitrariness and chance. The indeterminate system tends toward uniform leniency and thus avoids at least undue hardship.

The great mass of misdeameanors is created by separate statutes, and the benefit of unity of plan which belongs to codification is lacking. We should therefore expect a lower degree of standardization of penalties; but, on the other hand, the range in the possible terms of imprisonment being small, the problem practically reduces itself to one of pecuniary fines, in which a large delegation of discretion is less serious. The serious grievance with regard to pecuniary penalties is not their disproportionateness as between different offenses, but objectionable bases of admeasurement (cumulation of offenses, multiple damages, etc.). It would, however, be an advance of justice if violations of statutory requirements or prohibitions (*mala prohibita*) were simply declared misdeameanors punishable by fine and imprisonment not exceeding a moderate term, and then a system were evolved of measuring the gravity of the offense by certain criteria relating to the offender, the value of the interest affected, and the circumstances of commission, and penalties were required to be scaled accordingly. But we are far from such a system.

4. *Stability of policy.*—Standardization should mean finally the avoidance of instability of policy. Where policies are really contentious, an abstractly undesirable degree of variability is perhaps an inevitable result of democratic institutions. Moreover, the American practice of introducing new legislative ideas in the form of tentative statutes which will be amended repeatedly until satisfaction is obtained leads to an appearance of unsteadiness and lack of purpose when in reality there is merely experimentation. But apart from this, European standards cannot be applied to American legislation so long as we deliberately prefer an unconcentrated system of legislative initiative to a practical government monopoly in that respect.

There is no particular reason why procedural regulation should be more unsettled in America than it is in Europe. Compare, however, the codes of New York (1877, 1880) and of the German Empire (1879), which date from about the same time. The German Code of Procedure has been changed only twice, first after the enactment of the Civil Code, which necessitated extensive alterations to conform procedure to the new substantive law, and again in 1909, when about one hundred sections were amended, mainly in relation to the courts of inferior jurisdiction. In New York amendments are of annual occurrence, and in some years number upward of fifty; in 1909, when the Board of Statutory Consolidation recommended about one hundred changes which were adopted, there were in addition twenty-three separate amendments. The number of amendments in the last ten years, not counting those recommended by the Consolidation Commissioners, is about three hundred and fifty. The contrast between the two codes needs no comment.

Equally unfavorable is a comparison of the code legislation of New York with the practice legislation, e.g., of Illinois; indeed, the differences in degree of permanence of legislation in general between the American states are sufficiently striking without pointing to foreign examples. The legislation of the state of New York exceeds in bulk by far that of any other state, perhaps that of any other known jurisdiction, and a reference to such a state as Illinois shows that the enormous disproportion cannot be due to greater magnitude or diversity of interests, but is chiefly a matter of loose practice. It is self-evident that with such a mass of legislation as we find in New York the degree of standardization must be low; for mass in legislation means variety, while standardization means uniformity. Permanence and uniformity are in themselves elements of strength and authority; and with all its defects the common law has never failed to command that respect which belongs to settled and consistent rule. Conversely, lack of standardization must weaken the authority of statutes. As a principle of legislation the consistent observance of standards in the exercise of discretion is therefore of the highest political value.

Assuming, however, that instability of controverted policies proves at least that there is no stagnation, and that there is a ready response to changing popular desire, that mitigating circumstance cannot be pleaded to excuse the lack of established policy in the technical detail of statute. However controversial the main object of a bill, there are always matters incidental to it, upon which there are no settled convictions, and about which the only legislative purpose is to do the right thing. Occasionally there may be a desire to make enforcement clauses particularly strong or even drastic, but since experience has frequently demonstrated the futility of excess in this direction, this desire is likely to yield to more conservative counsels on behalf of the greater efficiency of standard methods of enforcement.

Barring exceptional cases, it is not impossible to obtain agreement upon what is regarded as the technical detail of a statute, and there is every reason why subsidiary clauses should be standardized. The result would be both greater economy of legislative labor and more equal justice in administration.

The practice of English legislation recognizes the distinction between controversial policy and technical detail in an interesting manner. The government assumes responsibility for the policy and expects to carry it through Parliament. This policy is discussed on second reading and is then affirmed or rejected by a vote of the House. At this stage it is irregular to discuss detail. In the committee stage, however, questions of machinery and detail are properly brought up, and the members may propose amendments which, from whatever side they come, the government will consider and, if they make for better justice, is likely to adopt.   Such, at least, is the theory.   The long tradition of the House of Commons has evolved a method whereby the judgment of members of all parties may be utilized in the technical perfection of a measure, while the control of policies is reserved to the majority or to the government which speaks for it.

Equally important is the English practice of clauses' consolidation.   This serves to standardize private-bill legislation.   Experience shows that in authorizing railroads, waterworks, or other public improvements certain provisions of constant recurrence are the most efficient; these are finally codified and subsequently incorporated by reference into special bills.   A series of notable clauses' consolidation acts were enacted in the early part of the reign of Victoria.   These clauses embody the result of years of experimentation and of the fullest discussion and consideration.   Somewhat different, but serving the same general purpose, is the more recent English practice of incorporating into a statute by reference a clause of an earlier statute relating to a subsidiary matter common to both, where the clause in the earlier statute has proved particularly serviceable or effective.   So in the matter of the procedure for adopting administrative regulations.

It should be observed that even without reference to clauses' consolidation acts special or, as it is usually called, private-bill legislation is remarkably standardized in England, so much so that the introduction of a new principle is rejected as irregular except under quite special safeguards. A unique private-bill procedure almost automatically insures the observance of the accepted standards. In America special legislation flourished for a long time, and still exists in a number of states; but it conformed to no ascertainable principle, and in course of time became discredited to such an extent that in the majority of states it has been almost entirely suppressed by constitutional restrictions.

If French and German statutes are generally much briefer than American acts on similar subjects, the reason is that a comprehensive administrative machinery is provided once for all and is as a rule available for new legislation. A clause that the act shall be carried out by the Minister of the Interior, or of Commerce, or that the higher administrative authorities shall be competent, is all that is needed. A carefully elaborated administrative code (in Prussia particularly the Act of 1883) furnishes the detail which we place anew in each separate act. The result in Germany and France is greater uniformity, greater economy, and a more carefully thought-out type of administrative provision.

In America the federal system is in this respect closer to European arrangements than that prevailing in the states. The executive departments, and more recently the great commissions, are capable of taking care of at least some part of the new legislation. Even so complex and poorly drawn an act as the Income Tax Law of 1914 was somewhat simplified by utilizing the existing administrative powers of the internal revenue commissioner, at least so far as these powers were not sought to be amended. The customs tariff has been the game of parties and has undergone frequent changes; in the twenty-three years beginning in 1890 there have been five tariffs. But the Customs Administration Act of 1890 has been kept in force by all these tariffs except for a number of changes recommended by the administrative officials, and during the entire changeful history of tariff legislation its administrative law has been relatively permanent. In fact, in the beginning it was suggested that the administration might be left to the states, and for a long time the remedy for excess duties paid was state common law and not federal law. All this goes to show how separable subsidiary clauses are from the substance of a policy.

In the states it is customary for each important statute to provide its own administrative detail, since there is no comprehensive state administrative organization with anything like general or residuary powers. There is a sharp contrast in this respect to the machinery of judicial enforcement. The judiciary has that unity and comprehensiveness which the administration lacks; it is therefore possible to grant rights without providing the detail of remedial procedure which is standardized by common law and equity or by code provisions. So the exercise of powers of condemnation is generally regulated once for all by eminent-domain statutes. But general administrative statutes are rare. New York has a few such acts of general application, as, e.g., the Public Officers' Law. Civil-service acts may likewise be classed in this category. However, the only real parallel in American states to the European practice is to be found in municipal ordinances; these are generally confined to substantive provisions exclusively, the administrative machinery being provided by state statute. The municipality has sometimes a limited power to create offices, but practically never a power to create or regulate administrative processes. This shows the possibility of segregating the subsidiary clauses from the main provision. The practice might well be extended to such matters as the grant and revocation of licenses, the making of regulations, the furnishing of bonds, the giving of notices, the issue of certificates, the exercise of examining powers, the organization and mode of action of boards, etc. Such standing clauses would not be absolutely inflexible, but could of course be varied in any particular statute if deemed necessary. It should also be observed that the statutory interpretation or construction acts which exist in many states fulfil a precisely analogous function.

The great advantage of separately codifying subsidiary administrative provisions is that in that manner alone will they ever receive adequate consideration. As part of another statute they are ordinarily left to the draftsman and, compared to the main substantive parts of a bill, attract little attention. At the worst they lend themselves admirably to the perpetration of "jokers"; at the best they follow without much thought previous models. Occasionally the advocates of a policy, in their desire to overcome resistance to its enforcement, make the administrative clauses as drastic as they believe the constitution will permit.   In a number of states the violation of anti-trust laws was thus declared a felony, but it must be doubted whether in a single case the corresponding penalty was inflicted.

When Senator Sherman first introduced the bill which later on resulted in the anti-trust act known by his name, it provided for imprisonment in the penitentiary.   How much thought he had given to the matter appears from his statement a few months later that he was clearly of the opinion that it was not wise to include provisions for penalties in the bill at all.   Senator Reagan, of Texas, however, again recommended penitentiary sentences. The provision for civil proceedings by the government, which saved the act from utter failure, was not contained in the original bill, the equitable jurisdiction to enforce the act being apparently suggested by the decision of the Supreme Court sustaining the like jurisdiction under the Iowa liquor law, a decision which happened to be rendered while the bill was before the Finance Committee of the Senate.   The provision for triple damages seems to have been adopted without any discussion; it subsequently received its principal application in the Danbury Hatters' case, i.e., to the detriment of those labor interests which Congress in 1914 sought to exempt altogether from the operation of the act.   Equally little thought was probably given to the grotesque clause of forfeiture relating to property in course of transportation under any combination, which the government has never sought to enforce. It is impossible to imagine that a carefully considered administrative code would sanction a similarly loose system of enforcement provisions.

The trend of modern legislative opinion is against the practice of allowing private parties not injured by a violation of a law to recover penalties in whole or in part for their own benefit (informers' shares, *qui tam* actions). The practice is unworthy and demoralizing. It has practically disappeared from England, was abrogated in Prussia in 1868 and in the state of New Hampshire in 1899. It used to be common in the federal revenue legislation, but was abolished in the internal revenue in 1872 and in the customs revenue in 1874. These acts must be taken as the expression of a deliberate policy. Yet informers' shares appear again in the Immigration Act of 1907, and they are not uncommon in state statutes. It is safe to say that they do not represent matured and well-informed legislative opinion, and if the merits of the practice could be considered abstractly, apart from the prejudices engendered by particular measures, it would not be difficult to make a case for its entire suppression.

There ought to be a consistent policy applied to the system of penalties. In connection with rate legislation we find it urged at one time that the power to inflict prison sentences is necessary to make the law obeyed, at another time that the threat of imprisonment is futile

and should be abandoned. The history of liquor legislation illustrates the failure of drastic penalties to make a
law effective. In 1867 Maine added imprisonment to
fine as a punishment for the illegal sale of liquor, but in
the following year imprisonment was made discretionary.
The experience was repeated in 1891 when the illegal
transportation of liquor was sought to be checked by
adding imprisonment to fine, whereupon, we are informed
prosecution virtually ceased, and again in 1892 imprisonment was made discretionary.[1]

Conceding that experiences like these are not absolutely conclusive, the constant change is in itself clearly
undesirable and unfavorable to vigor of enforcement.
If policies regarding subsidiary clauses are determined
anew for each measure as a mere matter of habit or as a
consequence of the absence of a general rule, it means for
the legislature the waste and wear of responsibility for
new decisions, for the administration the inefficiency
which results from lack of consistent purpose, and for
the individual lack of uniformity and therefore something
that approaches the deprivation of the equal protection
of the land.

It is curious to observe that when we compare a
particular statute with its enforcement, the administrative
standard is more conservative than the legislative
standard, while, on the other hand, the legislative standard is more conservative when it is abstract than when it
is specific. This shows that considerations in favor of

[1] Koren and Wines, *Legislative Aspects of the Liquor Problem*, p. 55.

the individual as against the government will have the slightest chance when a particular policy is under discussion and the checking influence of its application to individual cases is not operative. Where individual right is weighed against policy on general principles, a fairer and more even balance will be struck. For it will then appear, just as it will appear when sentence is to be pronounced in a particular case, that the carrying out of a controverted policy is not the last and only consideration in a free state, but that excessive powers and exorbitant penalties are not only unwise, but unjust, and may violate a higher policy than the one that may be represented in a particular measure. That is why guaranties of individual right are placed in constitutions. The separate codification of administrative clauses will have a similar purpose and effect: it will constitute a statutory bill of rights.

CONSTITUTIONAL PRINCIPLES

The principles so far discussed are not recognized by our constitutions, except that legislation grossly violating them may, in extreme cases, be held to fall short of due process of law. On the other hand, our constitutions do recognize two other fundamental principles of legislation: the protection of vested rights and equality. The constitutional protection of vested rights has not been adjusted in a satisfactory manner to the supposed overriding claims of the police power, but is generally respected in legislative practice. The principle of equality has, on the other hand, to contend against the unceasing demand for legislation confined to special classes and subjects.

Where peculiar conditions demand specific remedies, or where the public interest is involved in varying degrees, or where there are special problems of administration and enforcement, discrimination or differentiation may more nearly approximate the demands of justice than a mere mechanical equality, and class legislation may then be in perfect harmony with the equal protection of the law. Very often, however, the restriction of legislation to a particular group merely means the following of the line of least resistance: there is a strong demand for relief on the part of, or with reference to, one particular calling, industry, or business, and while the same measure is capable of more general application, it has not sufficient strength or support to carry as a general policy, or the general policy meets determined opposition on the part of one or more groups claiming exemption, which is granted. It is this kind of class legislation which is opposed to the spirit of constitutional equality and against which some American courts, particularly the Supreme Court of Illinois, have set themselves. The attitude of these courts has put some check upon loose practices of special legislation which are liable to great abuse. At the same time it makes the framing of legislation a difficult and hazardous undertaking. The standardization of all relevant elements of differentiation would afford an ideal solution of the difficulty; but neither legislative practice nor judicial control has been so far able to standardize.

And it is safe to say that no scientific standard could maintain itself against the strong political pressure for special legislation which will always find a plausible plea for which it may hope to gain judicial approval. The tendency will be encouraged by the tolerant attitude of the Federal Supreme Court: the solitary condemnation of the anti-trust law of Illinois, by reason of its exemptions (184 U.S. 540), has been followed by an unvarying deference to superior local knowledge of local conditions. Such recent measures, on the other hand, as the workmen's compensation acts, the minimum-wage laws, and the latest types of factory and child-labor laws show a careful survey of the entire field and correspondingly careful discrimination; and it is from systematic legislation of this kind that we may expect superior standards of differentiation.

We are so accustomed to identify the term "constitutional" as applied to legislation with "judicially enforceable" that it would be unwise to give the term any other meaning. A system of principles of legislation as above outlined should not therefore aim to receive in its entirety the status of constitutional law. Nor could anyone undertake *a priori* to state which principles are fit to be accepted as mandatory rules. The principle of conserving values, of making criminal offenses specific, of joining essentially correlative rights and obligations, might advantageously be enforced by the courts, while the more remote phases of correlation as well as most of the desiderata covered by the term "standardization" represent ideals rather than imperative essentials of legislation. The injustice which results from their violation is of the kind which we associate with the imperfection of human institutions. An attempt to formulate specific propositions would readily indicate to what extent principle is capable of being raised to rule, but there is no present prospect of so comprehensive an undertaking. If courts could be persuaded of the existence of more specific principles than those with which they operate, their decisions would speedily reflect the effect of those principles which are capable of judicial enforcement.

From a wider, and particularly from a constructive point of view, judicial enforceability is, however, by no means a necessary attribute of principle; on the contrary, many principles would lose much of their force if applied inflexibly. The life of the state cannot well be bound in rigid formulas, and it is in a sense an advantage of extra-constitutional over constitutional principles that they may yield in an emergency. The safeguard of the principle in normal conditions must be found in methods that operate antecedently, and the experience of other nations shows that such methods can on the whole be made reliable and effective. Even the operation of constitutional rules, while sufficiently binding to create at times inconvenience, will yield under the stress of circumstances, and is therefore not as absolute in practice as in theory.

CHAPTER VII

CONSTRUCTIVE FACTORS

The purpose of the preceding chapter has been to indicate the existence of principles of legislation apart from recognized doctrines of constitutional law. If such principles exist—and the attempted analysis claims to be neither final nor exhaustive—it is of importance to inquire by what methods they can be ascertained and made fully available. The factors to be primarily considered are the courts and the legislature, and the examination will involve some estimate of past performance as well as of future promise.

THE COURTS AS CONSTRUCTIVE FACTORS

The function of the courts is to test and judge legislation; not to frame it. We can no more expect that the courts will give us an entire system of principles of legislation than that they will give us a code of private conduct. If then we think of the courts at all as constructive factors, we must bear in mind their limited opportunities. Where the legislative standard is not intolerably defective, they are, generally speaking, powerless to raise it, and in the absence of a corrective jurisdiction a court will feel neither under any duty nor at liberty to volunteer suggestions for improvement. Constitutional limitations enforced by the courts will therefore never produce any but the most rudimentary principles of legislation.

The great opportunity of courts lies in construction, both statutory and constitutional. Construction is essentially supplementary legislation, and it was the recognition of this fact that has made codifiers jealous of the judicial power to interpret, which they sought to supersede by prescribing a recourse to the source of legislative authority in cases of ambiguity or doubt. Statutory construction is, however, inseparable from adjudication, and ultimately the courts are sure to regain and retain it; in Anglo-American jurisprudence no attempt has ever been made to deprive them of it, and in America the power of constitutional construction has been added. The ambiguities of language afford constant opportunity for the exercise of a praetorian power of supplementing the letter of the law, and the spirit of construction will frequently determine the living principle of statute or constitution.

It would be an enormously difficult undertaking to give a critical estimate of the judicial construction of statutes, although there could not be any more valuable contribution to jurisprudence; but the construction of a constitution is a matter of much more limited scope, and some judgment of the manner in which this function has been fulfilled must have been formed in the mind of any student of constitutional law. There has been on the whole a very well defined judicial attitude toward questions of construction, and a few typical cases fairly illustrate the principles upon which courts have proceeded.

The judicial attitude appears in the very first case in which the judicial power over legislation was exercised by the Supreme Court of the United States. The Constitution gives to the Supreme Court original jurisdiction in certain specific cases and appellate jurisdiction with such exceptions as Congress shall make. With reference to such a grant of jurisdiction it is possible to take two opposite views, one non-exclusive and the other exclusive. The non-exclusive view is that the specification of jurisdiction means that the grant in these particulars is not to be impaired, not that it cannot be enlarged. This view leaves the legislative power as far as possible untouched. It reconciles, in other words, constitutional limitations and legislative functions, having due regard for both. It was the view taken by the members of the First Congress, who were fully familiar with the spirit of the Constitution, in framing the Judiciary Act of September 24, 1789, which enumerated among the subjects of the original jurisdiction of the Supreme Court the writ of mandamus, although it had not been included among the cases specified in the Constitution. The exclusive view, arguing from an extreme position, is that affirmation necessarily implies negation, and that, therefore, the specification of the subjects of jurisdiction in the Constitution means that Congress cannot add to them. This was the view taken by Chief Justice Marshall in the case of *Marbury* v. *Madison* (1 Cranch 137), in which he held the Judiciary Act, so far as it allowed original applications to the Supreme Court for the writ of mandamus, to be unconstitutional. That this view was not the only one legally possible is proved by the fact that upon the cognate question whether the grant of original jurisdiction to the Supreme Court is exclusive in the sense that no other court can be given concurrent jurisdiction, the Supreme Court subsequently came to the conclusion that the grant was non-exclusive, so that district courts can be given jurisdiction in cases affecting consuls in which the Constitution gives original jurisdiction to the Supreme Court.[1] It is, however, also true as a matter of legislative or constitutional policy, that the exclusive view is the one less desirable, for the decision of Judge Marshall has had the unfortunate effect that the only court which can exercise jurisdiction in mandamus over federal officers is the purely local court of the District of Columbia, whereas it has become a common practice in the states to vest in the highest courts original jurisdiction in mandamus. Yet such is the authority of judicial decisions that Judge Marshall's construction of the Constitution, ill-advised as it was, has never been seriously criticized.

The decision has struck the keynote for all subsequent constitutional construction. It is perhaps mainly responsible for the doctrine of resulting limitations whereby merely affirmative clauses of the Constitution are by their implications allowed to cripple normal and necessary legislative functions.

It is obviously desirable that powers of appointment and removal should be exercised in accordance with

[1] Willoughby, *Constitutional Law*, sec. 557.

permanent rules. As soon, however, as the Constitution bestows any power of appointment or removal this becomes impossible; for the official vested with the power cannot bind his successor and the constitutional status of his power renders the legislature entirely impotent. The mere fact that an office is created by the Constitution seems to prevent the full application of civil-service rules even to the clerical staff of that office (254 Ill. 1), though as to this position there is some dissent; but no lawyer would contend that the governor's power of appointment given to him by the Constitution can be touched by statute. If we take this universally accepted view as dictated by the spirit of our law, it shows that legal doctrines are likely to run counter to wise principles of legislation; if the Constitution were controlled by a combination of legislative and executive, instead of by judicial, interpretation, a legislative regulation in furtherance and not in impairment of constitutional powers would appear unobjectionable. The judicial view is based upon the spirit of extreme assertion, while the legislative view would represent the spirit of reconciliation.

The entire relation between state and federal powers is controlled by the doctrine that the possession or non-possession of authority must be determined by the possible consequences of its conceivable exercise to the extreme limit. The theory, long disregarded in practice, that abuse and perversion of legislative power, unlike the abuse of administrative discretion, cannot be checked by the courts, leads to the uncompromising negation of governmental attributes which, pushed beyond reason, might jeopardize paramount or co-ordinate interests; whereas upon a theory of an effective judicial control for checking abuses, such as has as a matter of fact been repeatedly exercised, these attributes might be conceded to advantage. The disallowance of a useful function from a fear of its abuse is a legal but not a political attitude.

Upon the plea that the power to tax is a potential power to destroy, the doctrine has been established that the United States may not tax instrumentalities of state government and that, on the other hand, the states may tax neither instrumentalities of federal government nor interstate commerce.

With regard to interstate commerce it has not been possible to carry the doctrine to its logical conclusions, and a complex body of law has arisen, the distinctions of which are a fruitful source of controversy; but with regard to federal property the Supreme Court strictly insists upon exemption from state taxation, although the property is held without reference to any governmental functions, as where lands are forfeited to the United States.

The prevailing opinion supported by the decision of a federal court (64 Fed. 833) is that states cannot tax patents or copyrights because they are granted by the United States. If this view is correct, it would follow that if our private law should be nationalized, as is that of Germany and Switzerland, all property rights, being then derived from federal law, would cease to be taxable by the states—surely a proposition absolutely inadmissible. Such inconveniences are not entirely speculative. When the state of South Carolina monopolized the liquor traffic, it claimed exemption from the federal internal-revenue tax. The United States Supreme Court refused to allow this plea, pointing out that a state by becoming entirely socialistic might cut off all sources of federal revenue within its jurisdiction. This argument, however, works also the other way, for how could the states get their needed revenue if the railroads should be national-ized by the United States? When national banks were organized, Congress found it necessary to subject them to state taxation. If railroads were nationalized, not only would their property have to be made subject to local taxation, but if there were a state income tax it would be impossible to exempt all officials and employees of the nationalized railroads from such income taxation. It may indeed be asked what sense or equity there is in the present exemption of official salaries or of the income from public securities from the taxing power of a para-mount or co-ordinate jurisdiction. Apparently it was the intent of the framers of the income tax amendment to make all exemptions a matter of congressional discre-tion and not of lack of congressional power. This is as it should be and is in accordance with the prevailing German practice. Not only do the officials of the Em-pire pay state and local income taxes, but the state sub-jects its property to local taxation and the Empire claims in each state only those privileges which the state claims for itself; the Imperial Bank is expressly exempt from state income and excise taxes, but pays property taxes, and it is argued that since the statute speaks of exemption from state taxes only, the bank is liable to the local income taxes.[1]

Exemptions may, of course, be wise and proper, and in no event could any jurisdiction tolerate a taxation of its property or of its instrumentalities by another jurisdiction, if such taxation were either confiscatory or discriminating. Upon any theory of co-ordination such taxation would have to be held to be illegitimate and invalid. The legitimate claim of the taxing power can extend only to such things appertaining to a co-ordinate government as are of the same kind and nature as other subjects of taxation, and if it is so limited there is no force in the argument that a taxing power is a power of destruction.

If the doctrine of reciprocal exemption sounds plausible in logic, in practice it works inequitable and sometimes intolerable results. It furnishes another illustration of a judicial doctrine that for constructive legislative purposes ought to be rejected.

Perhaps no better illustration can be found of the difference between constitutional doctrines and principles of legislation than the relation between legislative policy and vested rights. Important phases of the inviolability

[1] Laband, *Staatsrecht*, II, 157, 852; Prussian Act July 11, 1822; July 27, 1885.

of vested rights are expressly recognized in the Constitution, and from the beginning they have stood in the center of the doctrine of inherent limitations. In relatively recent times, however, several qualifying doctrines have gained ground which are based on overriding claims of public interest: that the police power cannot be bargained away, that a legislative policy cannot be forestalled by private contracts that would thwart its enforcement, and that certain forms of private property are inherently and *ab initio* qualified by paramount public rights and powers, the latter doctrine being chiefly applicable to navigable waters. There can be no doubt that the enormous expansion of the sphere of legitimate public interest required a revision of the theory of vested rights. The written constitutions have not undertaken to cope with this task and offer no solution. The solution might have been found in legislative practice; and, failing that, the courts had an opportunity for a constructive development of the Constitution. It is interesting to note that the courts again proceeded upon the theory that where an extreme claim of vested right antagonizes legitimate public interest the claim of vested right must be rejected entirely.

The most striking case is that of *Louisville & Nashville R. Co.* v. *Mottley* (219 U.S. 465). The Interstate Commerce Act forbids free railroad passes. A person, many years before the enactment of the law, had been injured by a railroad accident, and in settlement for his claim for damages had accepted a free pass for life. The court held that this pass was invalidated and rendered illegal by the Interstate Commerce Act on the ground that legislative policy cannot be frustrated or forestalled by private contracts inimical to its objects. The decision seems inequitable; is it sound? Contracts made in fraud of an impending statute have been judicially avoided (*Hendrickson* v. *New York*, 160 N.Y. 144); in England they are dealt with by express statutory provisions. This contract was not of that kind. Bona fide contracts may likewise interfere with a new statutory policy; whether it is constitutional or otherwise legitimate to invalidate such contracts need not be here discussed. The contract before the court was of an infrequent kind, in nowise calculated to disturb the new policy. The integrity of contractual obligation is a constitutional policy of the first order and should be maintained wherever possible. It would have been legitimate for the court to read into the statute an implied exception dictated by the spirit of the Constitution, since Congress obviously had no intent one way or another with regard to so exceptional a case. Surely the saving of such a contract would have been in accordance with the spirit of compromise that should preside over legislation; what the court did, however, was to argue from extreme assumptions and possibilities and sacrifice substantial equities to abstract theories of power.[1]

---

[1] Judicial construction is here considered only in its bearing upon principles of legislation. While I believe that in the cases cited the construction has

It may be said that the spirit of extreme insistence upon abstract power is not a peculiarity of judicial interpretation, but is also the spirit of American legislation. This is partly, though not altogether, true. An uncontrolled popular legislature is indeed likely to be a very jealous guardian of public rights; and private rights that encroach upon the public domain, be it of property or of policy, particularly private rights that savor of privilege or monopoly, are not likely to receive tender consideration. The uncompensated revocation of lottery and even of slaughterhouse charters originated with the legislature, and then the courts laid down the doctrine of the inalienability of the police power. In dealing with structures standing in the way of the improvement of navigable waters, Congress merely failed to make express provision for compensation, undoubtedly meaning to put that question up to the courts. In denying the right to compensation[1] the court may merely mean that the only question left to it was a question of constitutional right, and that the legislature did not exceed the limits of its extreme power; but the extreme of power then tends to become the norm of legislation. For unfortunately the only utterances upon the constitutional justice of legis-

been unsound, the general opinion of the profession indorses, or at least does not question, the prevailing construction of taxing powers and the treatment of vested rights. And I fully realize that in a sense they represent the unyielding spirit of judicial legislation; if so, the main argument is strengthened and not weakened. All I urge is that the judicial spirit, being what it is, is not the most desirable spirit from which to develop principles of legislation, and in so far as the judicial spirit through constitutional construction does control principles of legislation the result is unfortunate.

[1] *Union Bridge Co.* v. *U.S.*, 204 U.S. 365.

lation that carry any authority are those of the courts; from this lawyers are likely to conclude that there are no non-judicial principles applicable to constitutional rights; and legislators (many of whom are lawyers) seem to believe that the principles enforced by the courts are the true and only principles of legislation. How much more then will this be the case where the courts apply inequitable principles to legislation which is capable of bearing a more liberal construction, or where the courts force an illiberal construction of the Constitution upon the legislature. This latter phase is illustrated by the formal or style provisions of the Constitution. Requirements regarding title or amending acts have become stumbling-blocks to legislation. Intended to check certain evils, their operation should have been confined to the narrowest limits, since constitutional impediments of this kind are intrinsically undesirable, and on the whole this has been recognized by the courts; but there has been just enough of purely legalistic construction to create an apprehension that a liberal legislative interpretation of the constitutional requirement may prove fatal to the validity of a statute, with the result that the legislature itself becomes unduly technical and blunders through its very attempt at faithful compliance. Directly or indirectly the courts have become responsible for formal standards of legislation that stand in the way of the simplest and most effective expression of the legislative will.

The spirit of adjudication is after all a very different one from the spirit of legislation. Adjudication decides between contentions for the full measure of abstract rights carried to their logical conclusions, unaffected by the possible expediency of indulgence and concession, for courts deal with human relations in an atmosphere of controversy and extreme self-assertion; they touch life mainly at the point of abnormal disturbance. The function of legislation, on the other hand, is to prevent controversy, and is therefore dominated by the spirit of compromise and adjustment; it is for this reason that legislative rights are likely to be more qualified than common-law rights. The result is that the principle of judicial rule or justice is the minimum, the principle of legislative rule or justice the maximum, of reciprocal concession. If so, judge-made law is ill-suited for guiding legislation, and we should not look to the courts for the development of rules of legislative justice.

It is of course true that legislative justice has often been inferior to judicial justice, and that the lack of confidence in the former accounts for the power of judicial review. Statutes against which the due-process clause has been invoked have generally been defective in some respect, and at times they have been grossly unjust; in these cases the courts were very likely to rise above, and it was hardly possible that they should fall below, the standard of legislative justice, unless indeed there was a broad issue between individualism and social reform. But apart from this, in comparing legislative with judicial justice in America it is necessary to bear in mind that the courts represent our best in government while our legislatures do not; that in any event the courts are, or for a long time have been, the only trained and professional organs that we have in our civil institutions. To estimate fairly the capacity for constructive work, legislation must be studied where its methods are equal to those of the courts, and not exclusively on the basis of American experience.

LEGISLATIVE PRACTICE AS A CONSTRUCTIVE FACTOR

In European countries in which legislation is entirely uncontrolled by the courts, its quality is, generally speaking, higher than it is in America. This is undoubtedly the judgment of all who have had occasion to institute comparisons. Such a comparison should not have primary reference to the social, economic, or political content of laws. There may be ground for believing that our election laws, our married women's acts, our juvenile court laws, and perhaps others are more advanced than those of France or Germany, and if our social legislation may seem backward, that fact is due to reasons which have very little to do with the problems here discussed. Nor should attention be directed merely to matters of style which, even if we give them all the importance they deserve, are after all a secondary consideration. But we should take as a standard of comparison those juristic and technical features of legislation which in France and Germany form the subject-matter of what is called administrative law, taking the term in the wide sense of covering all matters upon which officials have to act in carrying out and enforcing the law. We should, in other words, apply the principles which have been stated in the foregoing chapter, and others of the same nature, to modern statutes abroad and to our own statutes and determine where they are better observed, where there is better correlation or standardization, where there is a more scrupulous regard for vested rights or for procedural protection.

It would not be a difficult matter to demonstrate the superiority in these respects of European legislation to our own, nor would there be much doubt as to the reasons for this superiority. The striking difference between legislation abroad and in this country is that under every system except the American the executive government has a practical monopoly of the legislative initiative. In consequence, the preparation of bills becomes the business of government officials responsible to ministers, these government officials being mainly, if not exclusively, employed in constructive legislative work. In France and Germany the government initiative of legislation has been established for a long time and the right of members to introduce bills is hedged about and practically negligible.

There are two main reasons why executive initiative should lead to a superior legislative product. The one is that it is the inevitable effect of professionalizing a function that its standards are raised. The draftsman will take a pride in his business and in course of time will become an expert in it. He learns from experience, and traditions will be formed. This, of course, presupposes that he is a permanent official. In addition, he will be responsible to his chief, who naturally resents drafting defects that expose him to parliamentary non-partisan criticism. In Germany the best juristic talent that goes into the government service is utilized for the preparation of legislative projects, and these are regularly accompanied by exhaustive statements of reasons which enjoy considerable authority. Drafts of important measures are almost invariably published long before they go to the legislature, in order to receive the widest criticism, and, as the result of criticism, are often revised and sometimes entirely withdrawn. The individual author often remains unknown and the credit of the government stands behind the work.

The second reason is that when the government introduces a bill the parliamentary debate is somewhat in the nature of an adversary procedure, or at least there is, as it were, a petitioner and a judge. The minister or his representative (in Germany and France the experts appear in parliament as commissioners, while in England only parliamentary secretaries may speak—much to the disadvantage of the English debate) has to defend the measure against criticism, and legal imperfections or inequities would be legitimate grounds of attack. The liability to criticism insures proper care in advance. Together with the executive initiative goes a practical limitation of the number of bills introduced, an increased relative importance of each measure, and proportionately greater attention bestowed on it. Where this form of legislative preparation and procedure has been observed, it is not necessary to seek further reasons for a good quality of the product.

The connection between executive initiative and the professionalizing of the work of drafting bills is shown by Sir Courtenay Ilbert in his work on the *Mechanics of Law Making* (ch. 4). Until 1832 even very important measures were private members' acts. From that time on the leading bills originated more and more with the government, the duty of preparation devolving at first in the main on the Home Secretary and later on the Treasury. The responsible ministers found it necessary from the beginning to appoint men to take charge of the work. Thus we find from 1837 on a succession of draftsmen, and it is an interesting fact that the post from that time on has been held by only six men, Sir Courtenay Ilbert himself having served as Parliamentary Counsel of the Treasury (the title of the office) until he became Clerk of the House of Commons. This shows that the work was always treated as non-partisan and was sufficiently attractive to become the lifework of able and distinguished men. The result is primarily apparent in improved form of legislation; but if conclusions may be drawn from a necessarily casual and inexhaustive study of modern English statutes, there has also been an improvement in the standardization of substantive and administrative provisions. If so much has been accomplished through the efforts and the influence of a few individuals, it can be readily imagined how much the cause of scientific legislation must have gained by a century of work carried on in French and German government departments by men highly trained, thoroughly expert in their respective fields, and held to exacting standards by official discipline and tradition. The legislative product under such conditions will be largely of the same high caliber as the judicial product has been under the English system of concentration in the hands of a few high-grade judges.

Increased executive participation in American legislation. —It is not uncommonly urged at the present time that executive officers be given a right to appear on the floor of the houses of the legislature and to participate in debate. It would not be a much more radical step to give the chief executive a right to introduce bills. He has now by all constitutions the right to recommend legislation, and as a matter of power there is no reason why he should not present his recommendations in the form of bills. This would not give the measure recommended the parliamentary status of a bill and as a matter of politics might prejudice it; but to give it such status would not even require a constitutional amendment; a house rule would be sufficient. As a matter of fact, the chief executive can readily find members to bring in bills known to come from him and spoken of as administration bills, and they have been officially recognized as such by house rules;[1] but their status would gain if the executive

[1] *American Political Science Review*, VII, 239.

could formally appear as their sponsor. The constitution of Alabama (art. 4, sec. 70) provides that the governor, auditor, and attorney-general shall, before each regular session of the legislature, prepare a general revenue bill to be submitted to the legislature for its information, to be used or dealt with by the House of Representatives as it may elect. This seems to give the bills submitted a regular parliamentary standing, although not a preferred standing. It would not be for the present practicable or wise to curtail substantially the right of members to introduce bills, and any initiative given to the chief executive would have to be left to work out its own inherent possibilities. Even in Europe the government has no legal monopoly of the initiative, and its practical monopoly is the result of constitutional relations which do not exist in America. It is not impossible that even under our conditions the executive may finally obtain a preponderant share in legislative initiation. But such a development would take a long time, and there can be no thought of forcing it. We should therefore not look in that quarter for a controlling influence upon principles of legislation.

Defects of American legislative procedure.—The characteristic features of American legislative constitution and procedure are unfavorable to a high degree of workmanship. Each member has the right to introduce bills and makes use of it. The number of bills introduced is so great that many receive no consideration whatever, and this inevitably reacts upon the care in preparation. It has become quite common for introducers of bills to admit that "of course the bill is by no means perfect," and that it is simply the framework of something that can be made acceptable. The authorship and sometimes the sponsorship are unknown. Many bills are introduced "by request," the introducing member assuming no responsibility. Indeed, it is only in the minority of cases that responsibility for the form of the bill can be definitely fixed, and even if the draftsman is known he rarely holds himself answerable for defects that mar the bill or that may eventually lead to the judicial nullification of the statute.

Apart from this lack of initial responsibility the course of the bill through the legislature nearly always lacks that element of adversary procedure which is calculated to discover and remedy defects. The debates on the floor of the house can naturally hardly ever go into the discussion of details which must be reserved for committee; in committee there is often keen and valuable criticism, and, leaving aside the absence of executive participation, this stage may be as well handled as a committee discussion in a European parliament. But there is no assurance that an intelligent adverse interest will develop in the committee, and, if not, the measure is likely to be accepted in reliance upon the sponsor's good intentions and sometimes as a matter of courtesy; for all members are both petitioners and granters of petitions, and it would be strange if there were no mutual accommodation. There is no definite allotment of reciprocal responsibility that sharpens both wits and conscience. The multiform organization of the legislature—two bodies with the co-operation of the executive—is not utilized for functional differentiation. The second house of the legislature merely duplicates the work of the first house, and this duplication may, of course, serve to discover and correct defects. In European countries the upper house has not merely a different political complexion—with this we are not concerned, except that a higher degree of conservatism will be more favorable to vested rights—but it is generally composed of men of exceptional legislative or judicial experience or learning or business capacity, so that it is peculiarly well qualified to deal with technical questions. The House of Lords, especially since it has been shorn of political power, has become primarily a revisory body, and its debates show a high degree of expert knowledge and criticism. In the United States the governor has a certain revisory power incidental to the veto power, which might be further developed if adequate time were given to the governor to act on bills after their enactment and after the close of the session. But at best all these revisory functions cannot cure a bill that is badly drafted except by rejecting it. The work of original preparation must, in many respects, remain controlling. For influence in legislation executive initiative without the veto counts for more than the veto without the initiative.

Notwithstanding the disadvantages of unfixed or unconcentrated responsibility, it is still remarkable that the experiences of many years should not have been able to produce in legislative bodies definite and reasonably high standards of workmanship in the business for which they mainly exist. Lack of continuity between legislatures and the frequent changes in membership account for this only in part, for the defects are also found where these handicaps do not exist, and they seem to belong to legislative bodies in general. Perhaps the reasons for the indifference to legislative technique must be found in the predominance of political interests and in the power of traditions which perpetuate low as well as high standards. A large body responds with genuine interest only to appeals of a vital and human nature, and principles of legislation lack that quality. One can, however, easily imagine that if high standards had once established themselves, even a large legislative body might be careful and zealous of their maintenance.

English private-bill legislation.—There is to my knowledge only one instance in which a parliamentary body has by itself produced a method of procedure having primary reference to the observance of principle and the maintenance of right, and that is the English method of private-bill legislation. This is used wherever application is made to Parliament for the grant of powers of local government or for the authorization of public works or undertakings or services that require the use of highways or the exercise of powers of condemnation. The procedure, which resembles a judicial proceeding, leaving only slightly more room for discretion, has been fully described by Mr. Lowell in his work upon the *Government of England* (chapters 19 and 20), and the details are set forth with great fulness in Mr. May's *Treatise on Parliamentary Procedure*. Its main points are: fixed forms of application, notices to adverse parties, precautions against the grant of novel powers, examination of schemes by official experts, and regular hearings—all laid down in an elaborate code of standing orders. Nothing like it has ever been developed in connection with special legislation in the United States. It is to be noted that the system in England originated in the House of Lords, a permanent body, and was apparently due in the main to the efforts of one peer, who for many years was chairman of the committee in charge of private bills; its excellence commended itself to the House of Commons, which adopted substantially the same procedure.

The private-bill procedure in England has elicited the admiration of all foreign students, although its great expense is a serious flaw. When, however, it is considered with reference to its applicability to legislation in general, it appears after all as a very specialized instrument. What is done in England by special acts is done in the United States under general statutes, so that the machinery of legislation in particular cases is entirely dispensed with and the observance of general principles is secured in a much simpler manner. England has preferred not to grant the power required by public-service companies by general provision and was therefore compelled to substitute a scheme of parliamentary administration.

Legislation being used for the purpose of administration, it seeks to attain administrative uniformity, and this the private-bill procedure in the main accomplishes. Prima facie each scheme has to conform to stereotyped standards, and care is taken that deviations are not sanctioned inadvertently; but from time to time new clauses appear which gradually become common and thus pave the way for new norms. Thus a special report on police and sanitary regulation bills made in 1898[1] said that the time had arrived for including in a public bill many of the clauses then frequently introduced in private bills and invariably accepted by Parliament. Private-bill legislation, in other words, is an excellent way of preparing general legislation, but of course not to be thought of as simply a means toward that end. Our general railroad and banking acts have likewise grown upon the basis of special acts, but the abrogation of special acts has nevertheless been desirable and advantageous. When, moreover, we examine the standing orders governing private bills, we find that they cover none of the fundamental principles of legislation which are enforced by our courts as constitutional limitations (non-discrimination, public purpose, compensation, etc.), and the index in Mr. May's *Treatise* does not even contain such words as property, vested rights, injury, or compensation. The standing orders secure procedural

[1] *Commons Papers*, 1898, Vol. 2, No. 291, p. 355.

safeguards, and substantive principles are left to custom, tradition, and the conservative sense of Parliament. Even as respects procedural safeguards the private bill is treated as an issue between petitioners and certain definite and particularly interested contestants; outsiders representing the general public have a *locus standi* only under considerable restrictions; only the public government departments are given ample opportunity for notice and supervision. A report of 1902 calls attention to the desirability of an examination of unopposed bills in the public interest and in the interest of economy, since it may be to the interest of no private individual to oppose a measure.[1] As a means of guarding general public interests the system has therefore not been adequately tried, and it will be observed that in England it has never been applied to general legislation involving matters of public policy, not even to the committee stage of deliberation which is reserved for the technical improvement of measures. Altogether, while the English system of private-bill legislation is valuable for its purposes, its purposes have otherwise been accomplished in America, and the needs of general legislation are not served by it.

Improvement of legislative procedure.—It would probably be a great mistake in any event to try to force a higher quality of legislative work by imposing through the Constitution new procedural requirements. The present rules of procedure have been devised by the legislative bodies themselves in accordance with their

[1] *Commons Papers*, 1902, Vol. 7, No. 378, p. 322.

supposed needs; the placing of a number of them in the Constitution has added little to their effectiveness, but has increased the technical grounds of objection to the validity of statutes, and the most elaborately framed safeguards will prove unavailing if not supported by tradition or by a strong legislative conviction of their wisdom and necessity. If an improvement can be effected by procedure, it should be done through the medium of voluntary and flexible house rules. Appropriate requirements regarding the introduction of bills might lead to greater care in preparation and fix responsibility; but the gain would probably be confined to matters of style and form.

A very noteworthy scheme was presented in 1913 to the legislature of Illinois, but failed to become law. The bill provided for a joint legislative commission composed of the governor, lieutenant-governor, speaker of the House, chairmen of the Committees on Appropriation of the Senate and the House, chairmen of the Committees on Judiciary of the Senate and the House, together with five other senators and five other members of the House. The purpose of this commission would have been to prepare in advance of a legislative session a program of legislation with drafts of bills on subjects investigated by the commission, and the commission was given power to that end to appoint special committees of its own members or others to study particular problems and draft bills. Nothing short of actual experience could determine the value of such a plan or the alterations that might be required in it, but it will be noted that it forces nothing on the legislature and creates no new constitutional problems.

Perhaps the greatest hope for establishing constructive principles of legislation lies in the further development of plans that have already been tried, and of these four deserve particular notice: (1) the preparation of bills by special commissions; (2) the delegation of power to administrative commissions; (3) the organization of drafting bureaus, and (4) the codification of standing clauses.

1. Legislative commissions for the preparation of important measures: Commissions for revising and codifying laws have been familiar in American legislation from an early period, but the practice of creating commissions for particular measures seems to be of recent date, while in England it has been established for many years. It might be interesting to ascertain which of the principal reform statutes of England since 1830 have been originated by royal commission. In America a similar inquiry would probably show very few instances during the nineteenth century; to judge from the Carnegie Institution indexes of economic material, neither in New York nor in Massachusetts were any of the important legislative measures before 1900 (married women, liquor, civil service, ballot reform) preceded by commission study or report.

The most conspicuous instance of the employment of commissions for the preparation of legislation has been in connection with the workmen's compensation acts; less generally the same method has been pursued for mining and factory laws and for land-title registration. The commission generally holds public hearings, gets opinions in writing, informs itself as to similar laws in other jurisdictions, summarizes its conclusions, and submits a bill. The result is generally a measure well thought out and well formulated. Even where the subject is very controversial, the unity of the original draft secures a consistent and co-ordinated statute.

2. The delegation of power to administrative commissions: The grant of rule-making powers to industrial commissions, public-service commissions, boards of health, civil-service commissions, etc., is often advocated mainly for the greater flexibility in enactment or change. From this point of view much may also be said against the practice, since an unstable policy in requirements of any kind is undesirable, and it is doubtful whether powers are likely to be exercised in that spirit. The real advantage, however, of such powers is that the bodies in which they are vested are likely to be better trained and informed and more professional in their attitude than legislative bodies, and that the powers being subordinate in character are more readily controllable by reference to general principles, whether laid down by statute or by the common law. The body will be sufficiently judicial in character to have respect for precedent, and its policy is therefore likely to be less variable than that of the

legislature. These factors will tend to make rule-making more scientific than statute-making. There has been too little experience with the working of rule-making bodies in this country to warrant conclusions of much value; the precise line of demarcation between matter to be determined by statute and matter to be left to regulation has not yet been satisfactorily settled, and procedural safeguards for the making of rules have hardly yet been developed. The method of procedure of the Federal Trade Commission is novel, and is perhaps especially adapted to the delicate and controversial problems with which it is called upon to deal, but its working will be watched with interest, and it may become a valuable precedent for delegating quasi-legislative powers in order that rules may be gradually developed upon the basis of particular cases after the analogy of the common law. If common-law methods can be made applicable to the development of statutory rules, so much the better. There is much reason to believe that many phases of standardization (rates, methods of assessment, safety requirements, classification) can be much more readily secured through the constant thought and ruling of an administrative commission than through the necessarily sporadic acts of a legislative assembly. Legislative power can, in other words, be exercised more effectually and more in accordance with the spirit of the Constitution through delegation than directly. This consideration should weigh against abstract theories regarding the non-delegability of legislative power.

3. The organization of drafting bureaus: This phase of the preparation of statutes is fully described in a report of the Special Committee on Legislative Drafting of the American Bar Association submitted in 1913. It appears that there are now at least fifteen states that have some provision for assistance to legislators in the technical work of drafting, apart from, or in connection with, the supply of reference material. The following is quoted from the report of 1913:

The Legislative Reference Service, now actually carried on in several states, demonstrates that it is entirely practicable to collect, classify, digest, and index, prior to a session of a legislature, all kinds of material bearing on practically all subjects likely to become subjects of actual legislation at the session. This material, where the bureau is well run, includes not only books and pamphlets, such as might be found in an ordinary library, but also copies of bills introduced into the various state legislatures and laws which have been enacted in this and foreign countries, and other printed material relating to the operation of such laws or the conditions creating a need for them. Indeed, on most subjects of possible legislation the difficulty is not to find material, but to arrange the large mass of available material so as to make its efficient use practical. That such service has great possibilities of usefulness is evident, especially where the service is directly contributory to the drafting service, a matter to be presently explained. The increasing complication of our industrial, social, and governmental administrative problems renders it necessary, if the discussion of matters pertaining to legislation is to proceed in a reasonably intelligent manner, that systematic effort be expended on the collection and arrangement of material bearing on current matters of public discussion likely to become the subject of legislative comment.   A central agency to furnish such service does not take the place of special commissions or committees created to investigate particular subjects and recommend legislation.   The object of the central reference service should be to assist such bodies as well as individual members of the legislature and others desiring information pertaining to subjects of legislation.

Existing agencies also demonstrate that it is possible to provide expert drafting service for the more important measures and some assistance in the drafting of all bills introduced.   The number of bills, for which expert drafting assistance can be furnished, would appear to be merely a question of the size of the force and the amount of the appropriation for its support.   Your committee, therefore, believes that it is entirely practicable to establish, in connection with any legislature, a permanent agency capable of giving expert drafting assistance for all bills introduced, and they urge the Association to place itself on record as favoring such an agency as the most practical means of bringing about scientific methods of legislation, that is to say, methods of drafting statutes which will secure: (1) conformity to constitutional requirements; (2) adequacy of the provisions of the law to its purpose; (3) co-ordination with the existing law; and (4) the utmost simplicity of form consistent with certainty.

The organization of the two services, legislative reference and legislative drafting, and their relation to each other are important factors in the usefulness of the results obtained from the establishment of the service.   The agencies now existing, considered from the point of view of organization, fall into two classes: those in which the legislative reference work and the bill drafting are provided for in a single permanent bureau, as in Wisconsin, Indiana, and Pennsylvania, and those in which the legislative work is carried on by the state library or one of its divisions, the drafting work being done by persons appointed by and operating under the direct control of the legislature, as in New York, Connecticut, and Massachusetts. Your committee does not feel that they are as yet in a position to express an opinion on the relative merits of either form of organization. They are, however, of the opinion that the reference service should be so organized and operated as to be directly contributory to the drafting service, and that all questions of organization of the two services, their physical location and the relation of the reference work to other ends than the drafting of bills, as, for instance, supplying to legislators and others material for the discussion of pending or possible legislation, should be decided with this fundamental principle in mind. Where, as in New York, the reference service is not used by the drafting department, comparatively little use of the reference service is made by members of the legislature. Again, if the drafting service makes no use of the reference service, the drafting service is necessarily confined to minor matters of form.

It is, of course, essential that the member, administrative officer, committee, or commission employing the drafting service shall be the final judge of the policy to be expressed in legislative form. Anyone entitled to use the service should be entitled to it without regard to the effect of the bill which he desires to have drawn. It is, however, not only proper but vital, if the drafting service is to do more than correct obvious clerical and formal errors, for those in charge of the work to be able, through their access to the reference material, to indicate, if desired, to the sponsors of the legislation the statutes of other states or countries dealing with the same subject or direct their attention to any other material collected by the reference service. Theoretically the member of a legislature desiring assistance in the preparation of bills, if there is no co-operation between the reference and the drafting service, can go first to the reference service for material and then to the drafting service. Practically, however, in the great majority of cases, the member seeks the aid, not of the reference, but of the drafting service. That service should be in a position to place the member in possession of all pertinent matter in relation to the subject. Furthermore, the draftsman himself should be in a position to ask the person, commission, or committee intelligent questions as to the details of the measure desired. This he cannot do unless he himself has some familiarity with the subject-matter. Where the draftsman is not in a position to refer the person or persons desiring the legislation to material bearing on the subject, and where he is not in a position to ask intelligent questions as to details, his assistance is necessarily confined to minor questions of form, and, consequently, the effectiveness of drafting service is reduced to a minimum. The valuable results obtained in Wisconsin are due to a combination of causes, not the least of which is the personality and ability of Dr. Charles McCarthy, the well-known head of the service. Another contributory cause, however, is the fact that that service has gone beyond mere form, without any attempt to control matters of policy, and this would have been impossible if the reference work had not been organized so as to be contributory to the drafting service.

Clearly an experiment that has so much promise in it deserves every encouragement, and no effort should be spared to direct the movement into scientific lines.

4. Codification of standing clauses: The value of standardizing constantly recurring terms and provisions, which enter into or are subsidiary to the main provisions of statutes, has been discussed before. Such standardization economizes legislative work, helps to avoid duplication and inconsistency, and makes for more perfect equality in the administration of the laws. If effected by separate statutes, it insures a degree of care in the consideration of technical detail which is otherwise hardly

possible. For subsidiary clauses forming part of statutes dealing with contentious policies are often regarded as mere technicalities and escape proper scrutiny. As separate acts their preparation is likely to be committed to lawyers specially familiar with, or interested in, the particular subject, and they will receive the benefit of their knowledge and experience.

We have this standardization in our codes of procedure which control the criminal and civil enforcement of statutes from the point where the aid of the courts is invoked; we have it in the provisions of general city acts which govern the operation of municipal ordinances, since the creation of new administrative powers and remedies is not as a rule within the scope of delegated authority; we have it in interpretation acts, in acts relating to the exercise of eminent domain, in acts relating to public officers and official bonds, in civil-service acts, and perhaps in others. The practice is thus obviously not a new one, but it is capable of much more extensive application.

The report of the American Bar Association Committee, above referred to, submitted a list of topics the standardization of which was thought desirable, if practicable, and suggested the preparation of a drafting manual of instructions and model clauses. The Bar Association authorized the committee to proceed with the work, and the Reports of 1914, 1915, and 1916 brought some instalments of such a manual. There was thus drafted an act providing the procedure for the adoption of statutes or ordinances submitted to popular vote in municipalities. The enactment of such a statute would make it possible to provide very simply in any adoptive act that the act shall not take effect in any city until adopted by popular vote therein. Clearly the existence of such a statute could not be otherwise than beneficial. Desirable legislation has been defeated repeatedly by defective submission clauses.

The result of a series of such "clauses acts" would be the codification of an important section of administrative law. It would give occasion to consider systematically certain phases of legislation upon which neither lawyers nor legislators appear to have settled convictions. The discussion of penalty clauses in the report of 1915 will serve as an illustration of this; no similar discussion of this ever-recurring subject can be found anywhere in our entire legal literature. In our present legislative practice the matter is left to the discretion or whim of the draftsman, and unless he offers some extreme or unusual clause his propositions will arouse only the slightest interest.

Should the Committee of the American Bar Association succeed in completing the outlined manual or a substantial portion thereof, the indorsement of the Association would add considerable weight to whatever intrinsic merit the work might possess. Care would have to be taken, however, not to misrepresent the meaning of such indorsement. For in the nature of things it is impossible that a large body can properly scrutinize such work, and it is compelled to take much of it on faith and credit. No legislative measure, however, can safely dispense with searching and even unfriendly criticism.

There is one body pre-eminently fitted to give this criticism—the National Conference of Commissioners on Uniform State Laws. Its indorsement of an act is nearly always the result of protracted discussion extending over a number of annual sessions, and the value of the indorsement is proportionately high. In such a body the question would of course arise whether uniformity in standing clauses is possible. The impression may exist that local peculiarities enter largely into the subsidiary phases of legislation. Careful examination and still more a practical attempt at unification will probably show this impression to be unfounded.

Clauses acts operate by incorporation into other statutes which tacitly or expressly refer to them. Their mere enactment gives them no mandatory character; that comes only from voluntary acceptance by the legislature in connection with subsequent legislation. The legislature may at any time override them and insert different provisions in a particular act. This may result even from habit, and if possible such abrogation should be avoided by construction. However, in view of this precarious status, a general subsidiary act would have to win favor by its own merits. All the more readily should it be given a chance to prove its merits, and its non-mandatory character should be an argument in favor of its adoption.

JURISPRUDENCE AS A CONSTRUCTIVE FACTOR

There are principles of legislation too varying in their operation to be standardized by codification: that is true of the correlation of provisions, of the conservation of interests, of the protection of vested rights, of adequate differentiation, of the drafting principles that serve to make substantive clauses available with the least friction and ambiguity. These principles can be formulated as rules only to a limited extent, if at all; in the main their application depends upon training and experience, and their statement can be undertaken only in the form of scientific exposition.

What is the outlook for scientific work of this kind? When we consider the amount of trained and systematized thought devoted to legal problems, the proportion of it that goes to constructive principles of legislation is small. I refer to legal, and not to social, economic, or political, principles of legislation, for the latter do not belong to jurisprudence, but to the social sciences, which devote a perfectly adequate proportion of their labors to questions of legislation. Why this difference between the law and the social sciences? Because the former has to satisfy a professional demand while the latter do not, or only to a very slight degree. Practically all legal writing is adapted to the needs of practitioners, and the elaborate apparatus of making legal sources accessible is entirely subservient to that purpose. It is a matter of a market and of supply and demand. The influence extends to the law schools. Being organized for the training of practitioners, they do not concern themselves with problems analogous to those which are dealt with in social-science classrooms. That which is not actually or potentially an appropriate subject for judicial or forensic discussion has no place in legal instruction. The problem of the most effective and frictionless distribution of legislative powers among nation, state, and locality is thus treated as belonging, not to constitutional law, but to political science. The problem being at least as much political as legal, this practical division may be justified. The most equitable method of dealing with vested rights, the practical bases of classification, the subjects most appropriate for delegation of legislative power, however, are not political, but strictly legislative problems and can be adequately handled only by a legally trained mind; yet since they extend beyond the province of judicial cognizance, they are not considered as part of constitutional law, with the result that they are treated nowhere.

This condition is not altogether peculiar to this country. The professional point of view has dominated law teaching since the days when the Roman jurists established their schools, except perhaps during the period when the law of nature had an honored place in the universities; it dominates the teaching of law in Germany today. The situation in Germany is, however, different in two respects.

In the first place, in America law is taught now almost exclusively on the basis of cases, a method superior to

the German system as a training for the future practitioner, but as unfavorable as possible from the legislative
point of view; for the ideals of case law will tend to be
those of the system in which judge-made law had its
highest development, and can hardly be expected to rise
above them; and the case method will foster the common-
law attitude toward legislation, looking upon it as an
inferior product of the non-legal mind to be tolerated
and minimized in its effects. On the other hand, the
entire law of Germany, civil, criminal, and procedural,
has been codified within the last generation or two; in
view of this it is impossible, in teaching it, to ignore the
dynamic or genetic side of the law, and, in comparing
code provisions with the common-law doctrines which
they superseded, the legislative point of view necessarily
asserts itself. As far as public legislation is concerned,
the German law curricula include a course (called administrative law) reviewing the entire body of statutory law—
a field which we ignore.

In the second place, in Germany neglect in the law
school does not mean total neglect, for there is a demand
for constant thought on principles of legislation in the
government departments which are charged with the
working out of legislative projects. The officials to
whom this work is delegated are jurists as thoroughly
trained and of as high standing as the teachers in the
universities; they constituted the majority of the civil-
code commissioners, and the *Motive* of the first draft are
a lasting monument to the high scientific quality of their

work. The preparation of the code afforded the opportunity for a systematic statement of the entire body of principles of private law legislation. Nothing similar exists for public legislation in which legal principles are simply applied and only incidentally discussed when occasion offers. Systematic exposition is the fruit of university teaching, as Blackstone's *Commentaries* demonstrate. But while without such exposition we can perhaps hardly speak of an established science, it is quite possible that a strong and long-sustained official tradition may firmly and quite adequately support certain principles, and this is fully borne out by a study of English, French, and German legislation.

We find such traditions in our judiciary, but not in connection with the preparation of statutes, and this substitute for a science of legislation therefore fails in America. Nor is it likely that the drafting bureaus now being organized will very soon gain sufficient strength to supply the defect, whatever we may expect of them if they are allowed to work under favorable conditions.

In view of these conditions we must necessarily look to American law schools for contributions to the development of the legislative or constructive side of jurisprudence. Effective work in this direction can hardly be expected without the organization of special courses dealing with that aspect of the law, for in teaching the judicial and the legislative point of view cannot be combined to advantage, and the treatment from the latter point of view will inevitably be subordinated, with the result that no systematic work will be produced; the present condition of constitutional law, where the constructive point of view would naturally tend to assert itself with the greatest relative force, proves this incompatibility.

The technical difficulties of courses in legislation from the point of view of instruction must not be underestimated, and this is not the place in which to discuss them fully; but unless they can be overcome the scientific treatment of jurisprudence must remain one-sided and defective, and some of the most important and interesting problems of legislation will continue to be dealt with in slipshod and haphazard ways, because it is no one's business to give them systematic consideration.

SOURCE MATERIAL

The materials for the study of principles of legislation are not as simple as those for the study of the common law.

The statutes, which are the primary source of the history of legislation, are unindexed except for each volume of session laws, which makes the tracing of developments laborious, especially because the phases of legislation which are of particular scientific interest are often merely incidental to the main topics which alone appear in such indexes as exist; no index would thus give a clue whether a prohibition act contained saving clauses with regard to vested rights or compensation provisions. An exhaustive study of such a topic as powers to grant or revoke licenses or of penal clauses would thus be practically impossible. And even if it were possible to collate the entire statutory material, it would hardly be worth the labor expended, for a bare provision without any clue to it is not enlightening. We know how statutes are made today, and the method has not been different at any time in the history of American legislation; an interesting or exceptional provision as likely as not represents nothing but the casual thought of the draftsman, and provisions of common occurrence may rest merely on habit and precedent. The significance of a statutory practice depends upon one of two factors, namely, that it has either been the subject of thought and discussion or that it has been tested by practical application; but in most cases there is no record information on either of these points. The most complete collection of statutory material may therefore be dreary and lifeless and relatively barren of valuable data. For practical purposes, therefore, it must as a rule suffice to pick out some typical state and period in connection with some field of legislation that has stirred public interest, such as liquor, railroads, or elections, although even with this restriction we shall often remain without any clue as to the significance of provisions. For recent periods a good deal has been done by various agencies in bringing together the entire statutory material on certain topics: on railroad legislation by the Interstate Commerce Commission, on electrical legislation by the American Telegraph and Telephone Company, on tax laws by the

Commission on Corporations, on road laws and pure-food laws by the Department of Agriculture, etc.; but the pictures presented by these collections are purely static, and since the dates of statutes are not given, nothing can be learned as to development of laws even by comparison. The most instructive phase of legislation is sometimes its growth by amendments, but nothing is more difficult to trace. Altogether, therefore, the primary source material for a study of principles of legislation is in a singularly inaccessible and unilluminating condition.

The secondary legislative material—debates, reports, documents—is ample for Congress and poor for most of the states. Congressional debates sometimes throw a valuable light on the legal aspects of legislation, although —as should be expected of speeches in open sessions— other aspects greatly predominate. Committee reports likewise concern themselves rarely with technical phases of bills, and discussions of constitutional questions invariably take the form of regular lawyers' briefs digesting court decisions without presenting independent views of constitutional principles—another illustration of the absolute domination of the judicial point of view.

In the states there is practically nothing published in regular series corresponding to congressional debates or documents, but merely scattered papers and reports, which are now being indexed (at least so far as they contain economic material) for the several states by the Carnegie Institution. Committees do not as a rule submit printed reports, and arguments presented to them by interested organizations are not preserved in an accessible form. There is a growing amount of pamphlet literature issued by private and semi-public organizations, such as the National Civic Federation, the Association for Labor Legislation, and others, of which an account is given from time to time by a Public Affairs Information Service, and much of which is available for tracing the history of legislation.

Administrative reports sometimes contain valuable information concerning the working of statutes and needed changes; more commonly they give merely statistics, and comment is perfunctory or tainted by official complacency. Of greater interest are the proceedings of national conferences of various classes of officials (factory inspectors, tax commissioners, etc.) so far as they are published and preserved, which is not always the case. The administration of laws of economic and social interest is also frequently made the subject of comment in the proceedings of scientific associations, in journals and treatises, and particularly the material for the study of the administration and enforcement of labor legislation has become abundant, and much of legal interest can be gleaned from these publications. The report made under the auspices of a Committee of Fifty upon the legislative aspects of the liquor problem[1] is a source of information, of which we have too few examples. On the whole the privately collected material is more valuable than the official reports.

[1] Koren and Wines, Boston, 1898.

In contrast to the United States the secondary legislative material of the European states is of very great value for the study of principles of legislation. Not too much must be expected of parliamentary debates, since speeches in open sessions are mainly political; in Germany, particularly, they are spoken "through the window" and are juristically of hardly any value. Of the English debates those of the House of Lords yield much more than those of the House of Commons, for the House of Lords is full of great experts, and in the House of Commons the real debate on measures of technical difficulty takes place in committee and remains unreported. The French debates seem—at least in the Senate—of a high order and give a better insight into French public law than many a treatise.

The English parliamentary documents known as Blue Books have long been recognized as an invaluable source of economic and social history, and a great deal can also be gathered concerning administration and enforcement of laws. In view of the similarity of common-law foundation, this material is also instructive to American students, although for the study of constitutional and administrative law it has hardly been utilized. Of non-official publications the *Justice of the Peace*, a weekly journal for the use of English magistrates, contains perhaps more of value to the student of legislation than any other, for it is the only publication dealing primarily with public legislation in which the legal point of view distinctly predominates. It does not, however, touch statutes that are not locally administered.

The printed matter published in Germany by or for the various legislative bodies is on the whole similar to that contained in the Blue Books, and the main stress here as there lies on political, social, and economic, and not on legal, questions. Important legislation is usually preceded by preliminary "memorials" (*Denkschriften, Motive*) prepared by officials of the ministries; these are often printed, though not always listed in the book trade, and hence are sometimes not readily accessible. After a statute has been passed, it is likely to be made the subject of an elaborate commentary, in which all preparatory material is digested. Indeed, the official who had the main share in preparing the law often appears as the author of such a commentary. In this way the process by which final results have been reached is often laid bare, and it is possible to trace the underlying principles of legislation. The subsequent operation and enforcement of statutes can then be studied in administrative reports, some of which, like the factory inspectors' reports, enjoy a high authority. Even from the German material we can derive valuable lessons for American legislative problems.

The law reports as legislative material.—If we are poor in sources of information which in European countries are abundant, we surpass them in the volume of reported adjudications. The law reports could probably be made to yield a great deal of valuable information and material bearing on constructive principles of legislation. They are not indexed or digested for that purpose; but revised statutes not uncommonly contain references to the cases in which each particular section is discussed or cited, and on that basis a tolerably complete view of the judicial treatment of statutes may be obtained. This is not merely valuable for purposes of interpretation, but often gives first-hand information concerning the history of a statute and explains subsequent amendments. That a statute becomes the subject-matter of litigation regularly indicates some difficulty encountered in its application and may suggest methods or principles of legislation whereby that difficulty might have been avoided. From this point of view cases could perhaps be selected and worked up to as much advantage as they are now for the study of common-law doctrines.

The legal science of legislation means the knowledge of how to translate a given policy into the terms of a statute. Even if it cannot be carried to the plane of an exact science, it may render possible the delegation to competent hands of the task of statute-making under brief instructions in the confidence that it will be faithfully and impartially performed. The determination of policies might thus be made a purely political function, unincumbered by the confusing bywork of technical detail, and the efficient control of legislation by representative and popular bodies would thus in substance be strengthened and not diminished. The development of this rich and practically unworked field may therefore be urged from the point of view of government as well as from that of jurisprudence. If the foregoing chapters will serve to stimulate interest in the subject and its possibilities, they have not been written in vain.

INDEX

PHOENIX BOOKS

in History

PHOENIX BOOKS
in Political Science and Law